Rock Gardens

Wilhelm Schacht

Rock Gardens

Edited and with an Introduction by Jim Archibald

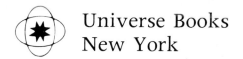

Universe Books
New York

Alphabooks, Sherborne, Dorset, England

First published by Eugen Ulmer GmbH & Co as *Der Steingarten*.

First published in Britain in 1981 by Alphabooks, Sherborne, Dorset, England.
ISBN: 0 906670 19 5

First published in the United States of America in 1981 by Universe Books, 381 Park Avenue South, New York, NY 10016.

Library of Congress Cataloging in Publication Data
Schacht, Wilhelm, 1903–
    Rock Gardens.
    Translation of Der Steingarten.
    Bibliography: p
    Includes indexes.
    1. Rock gardens. 2. Rock plants. I. Title
SB459.S2813   1981   635.9′672   80–54398
ISBN 0–87663–354–8

Typeset by Santype International Ltd, Salisbury, Wiltshire, England, and printed in the Federal Republic of Germany

Contents

Introduction
by Jim Archibald

Twenty years ago, in 1961, Wilhelm Schacht gave a superbly illustrated talk about rare alpine plants to the Third International Rock Garden Plant Conference in Edinburgh. I was then a student at Edinburgh and found it more to my inclination to detach myself from studies in English Literature and attend this and other lectures on rock garden plants—a course which I have adopted ever since. There were only a few overseas delegates at this conference but they included such great names of the past as Raymond Ruffier-Lanche from France, Carl Worth from the United States and Hubert Martin from Austria. Of these, Wilhelm Schacht alone still survives, like a truly indestructible alpine, enjoying his active retirement among the hills of Bavaria.

In 1981, I find myself speaking to the fifth international conference on a similar subject. In the intervening years, I have been able to see many of the world's alpine plants in their homes and have tried to cultivate some of them myself. These years have also seen the interest in these plants grow enormously. In 1981, there will be hundreds of delegates arriving in England from the rest of Europe, North America, Australia, New Zealand and Japan. This increasingly international aspect of rock gardening is singularly appropriate. The true alpine plants make a mockery of man's political boundaries. Their homes, the great mountain ranges of the world, have always created barriers to the movement of mankind and have often become adopted as the frontiers between nations. These mountain plants not only transcend such boundaries but deride man's inability to conquer their stronghold. They are among the few successful colonists of some of the world's last wild places and have been virtually uninfluenced by the crimes, conquests and endeavours of humanity.

Apart from the obvious fact that these little plants are unrivalled in their suitability to the small garden of today, it may be their aura of hardy independence that fascinates so many modern gardeners, engulfed by the technology of mankind. More than any other form of gardening, growing alpines brings us close to plants which have conquered these wild, inhospitable places and, by involving ourselves with them, perhaps we feel that we can make some atavistic association with nature at its most inimical. Whether it is because they appeal to the escapist in us or simply fit in with a practical, present-day attitude, they seem to be plants with a future in gardens. It is surprising, therefore, that, although many excellent specialist monographs have appeared recently, there is almost no sound, up-to-date, general book on the subject.

It is appropriate that the English edition of a book by such a respected alpine gardener as Wilhelm Schacht should appear in the year of an international conference on the subject. When I first read the new German edition, I was impressed both with the comprehensive scope of so small a book and with the effort and good judgement shown in the inclusion of the best new garden varieties and such recent introductions as seem likely to establish themselves in gardens. Above all, great trouble had been taken in putting the names of the plants in line with modern taxonomy. It is, in these ways, a book of the next decade rather than of the past. In helping to prepare this English edition, I have tried to continue this responsible attitude. An enormous amount of recent botanical work has involved rock-garden plants. Even the two years since the publication of the German edition have seen the completion of the *Flora Europaea*, Bean's *Trees and Shrubs* and a revision of *Rhododendron*. As far as it seems relevant, while tempering all decisions with a degree of discretion, these and other significant botanical works have all been taken into account to produce what I believe is the most up-to-date publication available to rock gardeners. This is, in itself, by no means a virtue but, if someone is going to learn a new name, it may as well be the currently acceptable one, which is likely to be adopted for many years to come. This is especially important if the gardener is going to progress to reading the publications and seed-exchange lists of the alpine-gardening societies or the catalogues of informed, specialist nurserymen. I am all too aware, of course, that the use of these Latin names can be a great deterrent to those becoming interested in rock plants. There is no way to avoid this as they constitute the only international language. The use of botanical terms, however, has been avoided almost entirely. For example, ' variety ' has been used not only when referring to a correctly described botanical variety but also where 'cultivar' would be more accurate, and 'race' has been used instead of 'taxon'. Little is lost by this policy and much may be gained by not subjecting the new alpine gardener to what is all too often pretentious, pseudo-scientific jargon.

Wilhelm Schacht originally wrote this book for German-speaking gardeners in the continental climate of central Europe, whereas English-speaking gardeners range throughout the world. His treatment of the broad concepts and methods of rock gardening, in the earlier part of this book, is sufficiently general to stand unqualified. This covers most circumstances that the alpine-grower may garden in, provided that a measure of common-sense is used, such as providing more drainage in wetter climates, more shade in hotter summers and above all avoiding plants which are obviously unsuited to the climate and soil, when selecting material for general planting. His opinions, at the same time, can be individual enough to be stimulating. I read with some pleasure of the good, rich soil he recommends for many alpines. Some British enthusiasts, brought up on the starvation diet of Farrer's artificial moraines and screes, may regard this with horror, but I have always considered my success in cultivating such plants as *Corydalis cashmeriana* and *Calceolaria*

darwinii has been due to giving them a considerable amount of feeding. It is good to find such an authoritative ally as Herr Schacht.

In attempting to internationalize the English edition, I have added a great many plants, which are important to gardeners in such cool, wet climates as the north of Britain and the Pacific coast of North America as well as many for gardeners in more temperate areas, such as western Britain, the milder parts of the USA and much of New Zealand. To try to satisfy everyone is to court disaster. Any compact book claiming to deal with such a wide-ranging subject is inevitably an easy prey to critics, who can seize on its omissions, irrelevancies and unsuitabilities to their own particular gardening circumstances. I hope that most readers will regard it with a more positive attitude and see it not only as a small book, which can stand on its own as sufficiently sound, modern and reasonably comprehensive to be the only book about alpine plants which many gardeners may ever need, but also as a book which opens doors into the more consuming, specialist aspects of this subject. If its fault is that it tries to compress too much into a small space, this is the characteristic of alpine plants themselves, as well as being one of the more infuriating and pleasurable pitfalls of rock gardening as a whole.

Foreword to the fifth edition

It is a satisfactory thing for both publishers and author when a book runs into several editions, since it is an indication that it answers a real need. The first edition of the present book appeared twenty-five years ago under the title *Der Steingarten und seine Welt*. It soon attracted attention in Britain, the true home of rock gardens, and appeared under the title *Rock Gardens and their Plants*.

It is now appearing in its fifth edition, and has been carefully revised. Where necessary, the text has also been expanded with further explanations and with line-drawings.

The chapter on miniature rock gardens has been expanded, as this aspect of rock gardening continues to increase in popularity. It is true that most of the stone troughs and other containers that one sees are filled only with window-box plants and annuals, but there are now firms which regularly exhibit trough gardens planted with alpine plants and dwarf shrubs at flower shows, and so help to excite interest in this type of miniature gardening.

It is not any longer a novelty to see small greenhouses in private gardens, and no doubt many plant-lovers reading the section on the rock garden under glass will want to invest in an alpine house of their own, since it allows a large number of delicate or only half-hardy miniature plants to be successfully cultivated. The lists of plants have been accordingly enlarged, with seventy interesting new species and countless new cultivars. There are now one hundred and eight colour photographs illustrating ideas for garden layout and trough gardens, as well as the most varied selection of plants suitable for dry-stone walls, rock gardens and alpine houses. Some rarer species which are still not very easy to find have been included, along with the more common varieties, to satisfy the growing number of enthusiasts and experts who are not content with the workaday varieties, but are always seeking after something new.

A number of scientific names have also had to be revised in this edition. This circumstance is to be regretted by both gardener and amateur, but can hardly be foregone. However, where the old names are still current among gardeners, they have been included alongside the scientifically correct versions.

Finally, I would like to thank all those whose advice and help have contributed to the success of this book. Thanks are also due to Herr Hans Meyer, garden architect of Villingen, who made the drawings, and to the various photographers who provided the illustrations.

I dedicate this book to all plant and garden-lovers, in the hope that it will continue to be a useful handbook, and give pleasure to many new readers.

Wilhelm Schacht

Introduction to the rock garden

'The world is wide and fair,
 but oh, how I thank Heaven
 that I have a small and lovely
 garden of my own!'

These words of Goethe may serve as an introduction to the rock garden. They might almost have been composed specially for lovers of rock gardens, which enclose the greatest variety in the smallest space and can give the owner the greatest joy.

Rock gardens in our sense were of course unknown in Goethe's time. About the end of the eighteenth century, alpine plants were first illustrated in European botanical and gardening publications, and by the end of the early nineteenth century surprisingly detailed notes on their cultivation appear in English gardening books. In 1864, the Austrian botanist Kerner von Marilaun wrote an entire book devoted to their cultivation. This resulted in 'Alpinums' for these alpine plants then being laid out in botanic gardens. A little later, H. Correvon was cultivating in Switzerland what was, even by today's standards, a remarkable range of species, and writing widely on the subject.

Towards the end of the nineteenth century, William Robinson was bringing his naturalistic philosophy of gardening to bear on the cultivation of these plants in England, where they were all too often being grown on spikey Victorian 'rockeries' consigned to dull corners. His writings, followed later by the florid verbosity of Reginald Farrer, advanced the concept of rock gardening in England to the informal style, which persists today.

This style was not so quickly adopted in continental Europe, where it was the practice, when laying out these Alpinums, to construct real mountains or particular ranges in miniature and plant them. This concept has long since been abandoned. It was in fact a serious mistake, only heightened by the addition of miniature chalets, plaster chamois, and other such figures, distributed in a 'picturesque' and 'natural' fashion. The memory of these mountain gardens has unfortunately persisted, and there are still those who devote much effort to creating gardens of this type. The result has been that some people dismiss anything to do with rockeries and Alpinums from the garden without further ado. This is a case of throwing out the baby with the bathwater. We cannot ignore the existence of a passion, which has thousands of adherents in Britain, New Zealand and the United States, where Alpine Garden and Rock Garden Societies have been formed to organize shows and competitions and publish extremely informative and comprehensive journals. I shall try in the pages that follow to do justice to this consuming hobby, and explain the various ways of using these small and colourful mountain plants to their best advantage in our gardens.

The Alpinums in botanical gardens, which were in a sense the forerunners of the rock garden, were laid out with a definite purpose in mind. They were intended to display the different forms of mountain flora, from cliff, scree and alpine pastures, much as they grow in their natural habitat, to the student and botanically-minded visitor. Sometimes, if space permitted, the mountain flowers of different countries of the world were grouped together according to geographical provenance.

The amateur builds his rock garden from quite different motives. He gains pleasure from the beauty and variety of both wild and cultivated varieties of miniature plants, and he tries to bring out their full glory by planting them among rocks, and by the skilful juxtaposition of plants which bloom at the same season. But more than all this, there is a kind of wild charm in the rock garden which wakens in us memories of the natural beauty of mountain flowers, and it can almost become a point of contact with nature, from which we become ever more cut off as we are forced to live closer and closer together.

Tempting as it may be to bring alpine plants home from holidays in the mountains to plant in our rock gardens, the beginner must be warned against it. People have at last realized that many of the loveliest alpines will not survive long at low altitudes. Either they pine for a short time and then die off completely, or else they flower so poorly that it is not worth the effort of transplanting them. *Potentilla nitida* from the Dolomites and *Silene acaulis* are good examples of this. It is quite impossible to satisfy all the requirements of these mountain plants for them to flourish as they do in their homes. In order to avoid failure and disappointment the beginner should content himself at first with well established varieties, which can be obtained from nurseries. These will be perfectly happy in the garden, as a result of hybridization and selection, and are often more attractive than their ancestors. The experienced amateur or expert will, however, want to bring one or two specimens back home as souvenirs of his expeditions into the mountains. It is best to select small, young plants, since these will survive transplantation and become acclimatized more easily than older plants. Alternatively, and preferably, he may content himself with collecting a few seeds, since raising wild plants from seed is often the most successful way of introducing them into the garden. If plants are taken across international frontiers, it is often necessary to have plant health documentation, and enquiries should be made in advance with departments of agriculture. The movement of seeds presents no problems, as long as these are confined to true alpines. One should be as moderate as possible when collecting wild plants or seed. Rare species, especially those protected by law, should be left untouched. The natural beauty of wild flowers is a heritage and it is our clear duty to preserve it so that future generations will also be able to enjoy it.

Planning and laying out an aesthetically satisfying rock garden is one of the hardest undertakings in all forms of gardening. Rock gardens may either be natural and informal or ordered and formal in design. The basic principles to be observed in creating these two types are explained in the sections which follow.

The informal rock garden

If an informal rock garden is to harmonize with the rest of the garden, it must have suitable surroundings. A rock garden on informal lines is most easily laid out on sloping ground. If the terrain is flat, a screen of trees will create an appropriate backdrop for the natural garden. These trees must, of course, be far enough away for their shade not to fall on plants for too much of the day, since alpines need a bright, airy position if they are to flourish. If there are few or no natural slopes and hollows in the garden, the best and cheapest way to create them is to dig a sunken path through it.

It is rarely possible to construct a sunken garden in areas with a high water-table, but in most such places a rock garden would, in any case, be out of place. If the conditions are right, however, and the soil and subsoil are naturally well drained, then a sunken rock garden can be built without further hesitation. This type of rock garden has the advantage of being the easiest in which to achieve a natural effect, so that with careful arrangement the various groups and layers of rock will appear to be really protruding from the earth. Furthermore, plants do particularly well in these protected 'valleys', especially if there is a pool or stream to increase the humidity of the air.

Now for a few practical hints on laying out a natural-looking rock garden. First of all we must decide on the size of the future garden; then, if the area in question is under lawn, the turves should be lifted and put to compost nearby. It is important to dig up and remove the roots of any weeds in the soil of the future rock garden right from the start. There is no more laborious task than cleaning up a rock garden infested with ground elder (*Aegopodium*), stoloniferous grass or horsetail. From the moment the first sod is turned no effort should be spared in the struggle against these troublesome and fast-growing weeds. Ideally, ground should be left un-cultivated for a full year, while the weeds are treated as necessary with appropriate weedkillers. Older total weedkillers such as sodium chlorate are dangerous, persistent and damaging to the soil. There is a vast range of modern selective herbicides and specialist advice is worth seeking if perennial weeds are a problem. If the garden is to be made on fallow land covered with every variety of annual weeds, two or three applications of a contact herbicide during the first season will reduce them considerably. This again involves waiting a year, but the only alternative for those in a hurry would be not only to remove all the weeds, but to remove the top layer of soil which will be full of seeds. It will be impossible to use herbicides after the rock garden has been planted, so they must be used, if at all, in the very first instance.

When the ground has been prepared, the imagination can be allowed full play before the actual work is begun. The rock garden is envisaged in the mind's eye fully made and planted. Here the ground should rise—so the path must turn aside to give it space, then lead through the hollow, and perhaps fork, one path leading up through a side valley to a little heath-

Particularly attractive stones and
boulders may be used sparingly
in informal gardens, where they
make focal points.

bed, the other climbing slowly across a patch of grass to a nearby seat. The course of the path must be marked out with stakes. When this is done, we can begin to excavate the ground, throwing up the earth and spreading it to right and left into a series of broad rounded knolls. It is always better to make broad, gentle slopes in a garden than steep cuttings. An elevation from the lowest point of between one and three feet ($\frac{1}{2}$ to 1 metre) will usually be ample. When laying out an informal rock garden the best teacher is obviously nature herself. Lessons may be drawn not only from mountains, but from rolling country, hillsides, and rocky wooded valleys with streams and rivers, anywhere in fact where the landscape is not uniformly flat, but broken, with rocks sticking out from the earth. Fresh ideas and suggestions for the layout of a rock garden are constantly to be found in such places.

After we have finished shaping the ground in broad outline, the next part of the work consists of placing the rocks in groups. This, together with the distribution and positioning of the plants, is surely the most fundamental part of the work. The very name of rock garden makes it clear that rocks are the characteristic feature of this kind of garden. A well laid out rock garden will look attractive year in and year out, especially during the winter. Then, on rainy days, when there is no snow, and while the plants are still young, the stones look at their best. It is extremely important not only to obtain good quality stone, but to place it so that it achieves the best possible effect.

A few points may serve as general guidelines.

First, fewer but larger rocks. Too many rocks of the same size will produce a monotonous effect which can only be improved by grouping some of the stones closer together. Later, when the spaces between these stones and the crevices in them have been filled with earth and planted, three or four such rocks will give the appearance of a single large boulder. The different stones must, of course, be of the same type of rock and the whole garden should preferably be built with a single type of material. A mixture of limestone and volcanic rock, or of rounded boulders and sharp rubble, will never look right. When positioning the stones, it is important that they are the right way up—that is, as they would lie in nature. Every stone should lie on the side on which it would come to rest if it had rolled down a slope; this will be the heaviest and broadest side. A mound dotted with a series of uniform, pointed rocks sticking up into the air will look unpleasing and unnatural. Only those who have thoroughly mastered the art of rock garden construction should attempt to stand the odd unusual and attractive boulder on its end here and there, while still respecting its geological formation. A few choice stones like this can make striking features, especially if, later on, they are surrounded by distinctively shaped, dwarf shrubs. The exception proves the rule, however, and that is: lay the stones on their flat side. Always slope them slightly downwards to the back, where they meet the earth. This makes them firmer, looks better, and is more practical, since they carry the rainwater into the earth where it is absorbed and feeds the plants. It is especially important that slabs and pointed blocks of stone should all lie at nearly the same angle. The most natural effect is created by packing and embedding the back edge of the rocks into the earth and leaving the front face uncovered, so as to display the full size of the rock. By levelling the soil in front of each block we shall create a series of stepped terraces. This has the great advantage of preventing the soil from being washed away in heavy rain. Care must, of course, be taken later on, during planting, that the back edges of the stones are not covered by tall herbaceous plants or shrubs.

The best way to proceed is to lay out the largest and most attractive stones first. Some of these may stand alone, so that they produce

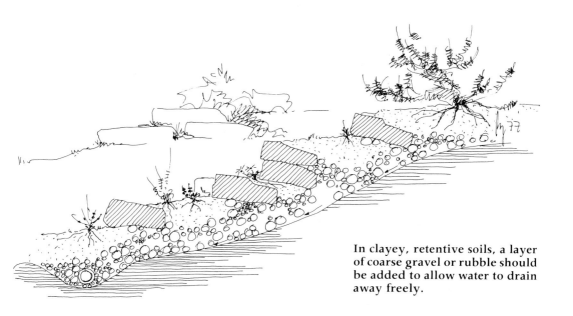

In clayey, retentive soils, a layer of coarse gravel or rubble should be added to allow water to drain away freely.

their full effect as single rocks, and others placed alongside smaller stones of different sizes. Try to break up any regular patterns by making one group project further forward and by pushing another back. This will prevent the layout from beginning to resemble a wall and appearing monotonous. It also means that the areas to be planted will vary in size and position.

Larger stones must be well firmed, especially if they are resting on loose soil, so that they do not in time sink too deep into the earth under their own weight and spoil the effect. The subsoil should first be well rammed, and then covered with a thick layer of builder's rubble, hardcore, or unsightly and unusable stones. The rock is then placed on top of this, preferably slightly raised. Care must be taken that when the stone is in its correct position it is not lying in a hollow. Any depression should be filled with earth or hardcore rammed down with a wooden mallet. Every stone must be secure so that it cannot move—it can be dangerous to step

on stones which are not quite firmly in place, when planting or, later on, when tending the plants.

Working with stones is heavy work. This is especially true of building a fairly large rock garden, using larger stones, which can easily weigh up to a few hundredweight. Much effort can be saved by thoughtful planning, and by then manoeuvering the rocks carefully with crowbars or on iron rollers placed on wooden planks. In this way, impressive-looking boulders can be moved slowly but surely to their places. Medium-sized rocks can easily be moved on a steady sack-trolley which can be pushed or pulled over firm surfaces. The rest can be rolled on to a strong stone-carrier and carried or simply rolled into position. Care must always be taken to avoid accidents and injuries. One should work with stones only in dry, frost-free weather. If the stones are wet and the earth is slippery, the work becomes dangerous and unpleasant.

15

With the stones in place, and approved after critical examination from every possible angle, we can make preparations for planting. This, of course, requires dry weather. First, any earth which has been squashed down in the course of moving the rocks must be loosened with a pick or spade. If the soil is clayey and retentive, sand and gravel should be added to improve the drainage, especially in parts where moisture-hating plants are to be grown. In extreme cases, where the soil is heavy and sticky or the climate wet, the drainage and aeration can be improved by mixing in fairly large amounts of sand or gravel. In such cases, it will be worth the trouble of laying a thick drainage layer of rubble twelve inches (20 cm) deep over the entire area after it has been given broad shape, and then covering it with an equally thick layer of free-draining soil. When deciding how well-drained the rock garden must be, every case must be taken on its own merits, depending not only on the nature of the soil but also on the climate, especially the rainfall, the humidity of the air in the region, and the overall situation—in short, on a whole range of factors. The types of plants which are to be grown are of decisive importance. If these are to consist only of the commonest rock garden flowers, which will flourish on any average soil and even in flat beds, then there is no need to go to excessive trouble concerning drainage.

Matters will naturally be different in specialist rock gardens, where a variety of the more sensitive plants are to be grown. Here great care must be taken over the drainage, since there is a whole range of moisture-hating plants, natives of dry lands, the so-called xerophytes, most of which have grey, felted or hard, needle-sharp leaves, and all of which dislike damp conditions. These include species of *Acantholimon, Artemisia, Asperula, Convolvulus, Edraianthus, Eriogonum, Sedum, Sempervivum, Thymus, Verbascum,* and *Veronica*.

As has already been said, the majority of common rock garden plants do not need special soil. However, although these plants are fairly undemanding, they flourish and bloom more freely if the soil contains plenty of food, and it is therefore advisable to fertilize the ground before planting. If good and weed-free compost or matured and crumbling cow-dung can be had then it can be forked in. If this is not obtainable, a dusting with a balanced artificial fertilizer will be necessary. Do not overdo the process, however; the soil must be quite free-draining and contain a good proportion of humus. The simplest way to achieve this is to mix in some sphagnum peat.

Special attention and care must be given to the larger cracks and crevices between the stones. These are the most important parts of the whole garden and it is here that the more special plants, most of which are natural rock-dwellers, will be planted. Using a hand trowel and a wooden or iron rammer, the bottom of these cracks is firmly packed with sand and fine chippings for drainage and then filled up, preferably just before planting, with a soil mixture suitable for the particular plants.

For some saxatile alpines which grow in tiny cracks and fissures, downward-sloping holes $1\frac{1}{2}$ to 2 inches (4 to 5 cm) in diameter and at least four inches (10 cm) deep may be dug out with a hammer and chisel in blocks of a suitable size and shape, especially limestone rocks. Such crevices occur frequently in Jurassic rock, and here saxifrages of the Euaizoonia and Kabschia

Stones should always slope down towards the back and be well embedded in the earth.

sections, *Asperula arcadiensis*, *Gypsophila aret-ioides* and *G. petraea*, *Potentilla nitida* and all other similar rock-dwellers are mainly to be found. In time these cushion-plants seem to grow into their stones, covering their entire surface. If the plants are to flourish, it is important to take into account the preferences of the individual varieties for sun or shade.

When the ground has been carefully prepared, planting may begin. After the positioning of the rocks, this is the second most important and exciting moment in the creation of a rock garden. Like the placing of the rocks, planting betrays the gardener's skill and know-how to the fullest extent. The usual method of planting a herbaceous border is to draw up a planting plan but with a rock garden this would be a laborious and almost impossible task. The various mounds and hollows, steep crevices and narrow cracks, and the variety of miniature plants could never be represented on a plan; added to which, the garden only begins to take shape when the rocks are laid. Of course, one may decide on the selection of plants to be grown in advance, but the choice of position must be decided on the spot just before planting. The same method should be adopted as with the positioning of the rocks. First take what will be the largest and most striking specimens—the deciduous and coniferous trees. Almost all these trees will have their roots either bound-up or potted, so the proper way to proceed is to place them provisionally about the garden, and check their effect from every significant angle. Remember to take into account not only the effects of mounds and hollows but also of light and shade. A little trouble at this stage will prevent the trees having to be dug up again years later when they have become established. For this reason, the subsequent size of each tree, both in breadth and height, must be considered, so that the fine harmony of the garden is not destroyed by thick or heavy growth.

The common mountain pine, *Pinus mugo* (*P. montana*), for example, can only be used in extremely large rock gardens, or as a background. At low altitudes it will develop within a decade into a broad bush the height of a man and can only be checked by pruning its young shoots in May, after which it will all too quickly grow even faster. For smaller gardens the only suitable variety is the true dwarf-pine, *Pinus mugo pumilio*, of which specially compact-growing forms are available. *Cytisus* × *praecox*, the ivory broom, is usually delivered in pots to ensure good growth, and often the young plants are only about a foot (30 cm) high, with a few thin branches. When released from the confinement of their pots, they will grow within a few years into broad rounded bushes the height of a man. *Juniperus chinensis* 'Pfitzeriana' grows only too quickly into a wide-spreading bush, whilst *J. communis nana*, the dwarf juniper, grows but slowly, and *J. communis* 'Compressa' remains a small columnar dwarf after half a generation. These few examples will illustrate the importance for amateur and expert alike of a proper acquaintance with the characteristics and peculiarities of the different varieties.

Trees should in general be planted in the rock garden as individuals. The delicate leaves and branches of *Acer palmatum* 'Dissectum' are so graceful that a single specimen leaning over a rock will lend atmosphere to an entire area. There are exceptions here too, however. Many dwarf trees, for example *Picea glauca* 'Conica', are more effective when planted in small groups of three, five or seven. It goes without saying that the individual trees in these attractive little clumps should not all be of the same height but as varied as if they were growing wild. They should also be planted at different distances from each other, so as to avoid the appearance of a nursery or a neatly arranged game of skittles.

After the trees have been arranged and planted, it is the turn of the herbaceous plants. In just the same way these must not be planted without proper forethought. The ground should again be surveyed and consideration given as to whether such and such a genus or species would be effective here or there, and whether this or that rare specimen would be suitable for the position selected for it. Is this crevice shady enough for *Ramonda* and *Haberlea*? Will the soil be moist enough for *Primula rosea* even in droughts? Is this position not too sunny for the Kabschia saxifrages? Would *Acantholimon* look well here on the warm stone steps, with the golden flowers of *Onosma* hanging down from over there? The position is a high one and by bending slightly we could see the clusters of golden flowers against the blue sky.

In short, there are a thousand questions to be answered in order to satisfy both the garden-lover and the plantsman. A plant must not only grow and blossom happily in a certain position but must be seen there to its best advantage, blending naturally with other nearby plants, and indeed the whole collection. In order to avoid having to rearrange the herbaceous plants after planting them, one should start by placing their labels instead of the plants themselves about the garden. If, after careful examination, the arrangement seems to be satisfactory, then we may quickly proceed to set them out and plant them. Special care must be taken in planting tiny plants in the cracks and crevices prepared for them. Generally these alpines come potted. If the earth around their roots is matted, it should be teased out with a small stick, and loosened with gentle pressure. If the plant in question is not one that definitely prefers dry conditions (such as *Artemisia*, *Pelargonium endlicherianum*, small *Erodiums*, etc.), the root ball should be wrapped in damp sphagnum moss and pushed firmly into its place in the rock. In any case, roots should never under any circumstances be allowed to dry out. The plant should be carefully wedged into its crevice with suitable stones, hammered in if necessary. Sphagnum moss can be pressed down between the plant and the rock, especially in vertical crevices, to prevent the soil spilling out. This is a useful precaution when planting dry-stone walls also. Adroit gardeners will be able to fill-up parts of large cracks with stones and cement after the plants have been firmed in. The most extreme rock-dwellers such as *Physoplexis comosa* and *Trachelium rumelianum* are happiest when they can tumble out from tiny crannies.

In other parts of the rock garden, attractive pieces of small stone may be placed while planting is in progress, either as ground cover or to form a border or even to support sloping patches of soil. Flat stones placed here and there amongst the plants will also come in very handy as stepping-stones when we have to tend the plants later on.

The best time for planting is of course spring or late summer. Bulbs and corms should be planted in autumn, between cushion-plants or at the base of rocks, where they will give infinite pleasure when they bring the first tidings of spring. It is important to plant these small bulbs and corms quite deeply—at least several times their own depth. The best effect is achieved by planting the different species and varieties in little clumps of at least three to five.

Early spring flowers in the rock garden: (1) *Helleborus niger* (2) *Erica herbacea* (*carnea*) (3) *Galanthus elwesii* (4) *Iris reticulata* 'Blue Veil' (5) *Cyclamen coum*, (6) *Corydalis solida* 'Transsylvanica'.

The formal rock garden

As was pointed out at the beginning of this book, it would be a mistake to lay out an informal garden in the middle of a town. Enclosed and overlooked by houses on every side, a naturalistic garden would seem like an artificially created oasis. In such a setting a formally arranged garden is much more appropriate. There is no basis for the objection that conditions are less varied in this type of garden and so plants will not do so well: in fact, the reverse is rather the case. Free-standing dry-stone walls are full of crannies, facing in every direction, and form an ideal habitat even for the more difficult rock plants. All the different miniature plants can be found positions both in sun and shade on terraced ledges, in walls beside steps and in all the countless cracks and crevices in stone steps themselves and between the flagstones which form the paved walks.

The number of possibilities within a formal garden is enormous. Variety can be introduced, for example, by raising the area of garden between the house and street, so making the path which leads from the garden gate to the front door cut through a series of terraces. There are many houses with flat gardens, where a load of earth can be used to make a paved terrace. The shape and extent of this can vary greatly to fit in with the rest of the garden, and here the plant-lover can assemble his favourite rock-plants right next to the house. The whole can be linked to the rest of the garden without difficulty by skilful planting alongside the flagstones of the paths and steps.

In terraced gardens, dry-stone walls and raised beds make ideal positions for a wide range of rock garden plants.

Small rock-plants make excellent borders for sunken lawns when planted in beds supported by low dry-stone walls. The adventurous spirit with sufficient space at his disposal can include all kinds of architectural devices when laying out a formal sunken garden, with dry-stone walls, rocky slopes, steps, terraced beds, flagged paths, seats and streams. Here all the variety of the plant kingdom can combine to produce a harmonious whole.

In laying out an informal rock garden, the distribution and positioning of the rocks is more an intuitive and instinctive process, but the creation of a formal rock garden along architectural lines is a more intellectual exercise. Raising dry-stone walls, building steps and laying flagstones are, more than any other work in the garden, craftsmen's jobs, requiring much skill and practice. This type of work with stone will only give pleasure in years to come if it is perfect, neat and well-built.

A formal rock garden can stand bright colour combinations in its planting. Every type of garden variety, including variegated Japanese maples and *Berberis*, and large-flowered cultivars of the smaller herbaceous plants, which would be quite out of place in a naturalistic type of garden, can happily be used here. To draw an analogy, an informal garden will only tolerate the delicate tones of string music but, on the more theatrical stage of the formal garden, the powerful tones of brass and drums are extremely effective. Although the framework of the garden will be more or less regular, geometrical repetition should only be employed in planting in quite exceptional cases. Any stiffness in a

formal garden should be removed by variation in planting and by a plentiful supply of miniature trees.

A selection of easy plants for decorative rock gardens

Herbaceous plants
Alyssum saxatile varieties
Arabis caucasica varieties
Armeria maritima varieties
Artemisia 'Silver Queen'
Aster amellus varieties
Aster dumosus varieties
Astilbe chinensis 'Pumila'
Astilbe simplicifolia hybrids
Aubrieta varieties
Campanula carpatica varieties
Campanula portenschlagiana
Cerastium tomentosum columnae
Chrysanthemum low-growing hardy hybrids
Delphinium grandiflorum
Dianthus gratianopolitanus varieties
Dicentra varieties
Doronicum caucasicum varieties
Euphorbia polychroma
Gypsophila 'Rosy Veil'
Heuchera varieties
Iris dwarf, bearded hybrids
Lychnis viscaria 'Plena'
Oenothera tetragona varieties
Papaver nudicaule varieties
Phlox subulata varieties
Polygonum affine
Primula × *pruhoniciana*
Saponaria ocymoides
Saxifraga, mossy varieties
Sedum spurium
Silene schafta varieties
Veronica teucrium varieties

Grasses
Helictotrichon sempervirens
Molinia caerulea varieties
Stipa species

Shrubs
Acer palmatum varieties
Cotoneaster horizontalis
Cytisus × *kewensis*
Helianthemum varieties
Iberis sempervirens varieties
Lavandula varieties
Potentilla fruticosa varieties
Rhododendron dwarf species and varieties

Dwarf conifers
Chamaecyparis obtusa varieties
Chamaecyparis pisifera varieties
Picea abies dwarf varieties
Picea glauca 'Conica'

Many rock plants will thrive in the crevices of dry-stone walls. (1) *Saponaria* **'Olivana' (2)** *Lewisia cotyledon* **on a shady wall (3)** *Campanula portenschlagiana* **flourishes in both sunny and half-shaded positions.**

The dry-stone wall

The dry-stone wall is the most important element of the formal rock garden but it also plays a large part in many modern gardens of every kind. It creates a much warmer, more pleasant and, above all, more natural effect with plants growing out of its crevices, than does a cold, cemented or mortared stone wall.

When building a dry-stone wall, the most important thing to remember is that the sides should not be vertical but should slope back at an angle of one in five or six or, in the case of high walls, as much as one in three. Care must be taken in building to see that the stones are laid so that they slope down towards the back, so as to catch rain-water and carry it to the roots of the plants in the crevices. Low dry-stone walls can be built directly on the ground, and need only be slightly sunk. Higher walls require a foundation 18 inches (40 cm) deep. If the stones are not of suitable shape, they should be roughly hewn with a hammer and then built up. All the cracks and spaces, including those at the back of the wall, should be carefully filled during construction with fertile soil, to make the stones quite firm. The best soil is a mixture of chopped turf, peat and crumbled cow-dung. If possible, long-rooted species of plants (Gypsophila, Alyssum, Acantholimon, etc.) should be planted while the wall is being built. The stones should be laid so that the vertical gaps are not aligned one above another or the earth may be washed out of the crevices. The spaces between the stones should be as narrow as possible, since rock plants are happiest in tiny crannies.

Any type of stone may be used to build a dry-stone wall, including boulders and volcanic rock such as granite and porphyry, though these are hard to work. However, artificial stone and cement blocks should only be used under the most exceptional circumstances and then thickly planted with fast-growing plants (Cerastium, Aubrieta, Arabis, Iberis, etc.), so that the wall is covered with dense, hanging cushions as quickly as possible. Sedimentary or stratified rock is ideal for building dry-stone walls, since it breaks into layers of different thickness and size. The best of these are limestones, which are mostly a clear, more or less yellowish-grey in colour. Sandstones, with red-grey or red-brown tones, are also much favoured for flagstones and for building dry-stone walls.

If a hedge is planted to crown the wall, it should be composed only of compact shrubs, for example Berberis thunbergii or Potentilla fruticosa. Strong growers like Ligustrum (privet) will root down through the stones to the foundations of a six-foot (2 m) wall and draw so much nourishment and moisture from the cushion-plants that they will suffer in consequence. Whenever possible, such hedges should be planted not on top of the wall, but at least a yard (1 m) behind it. The intervening strip can be planted with low and medium-sized herbaceous plants.

A low, dry-stone wall from the front, and a section through the wall to show its structure.

Plants suitable for dry-stone walls

Sunny positions

(* will also grow in semi-shade)

Herbaceous plants

Acantholimon species
Achillea species
Aethionema species
Alyssum species
*Androsace sarmentosa**
Arabis species
Arenaria tetraquetra
Artemisia baumgartenii, nitida
Asarina procumbens
Asperula arcadiensis
Aster alpinus varieties
Astragalus angustifolius
Aubrieta species
Campanula carpatica, cochleariifolia (*pusilla*), *garganica,** *portenschlagiana,** *tommasiniana,** *tridentata, velutina*
Cerastium biebersteinii (rampant), *tomentosum*
Chrysanthemum argenteum
Dianthus gratianopolitanus and *plumarius* varieties, *sylvestris*

Draba aizoides
Edraianthus species
Erinus alpinus
Erodium species (except *manescavii*)
Euphorbia capitulata, myrsinites
*Geranium dalmaticum**
Globularia cordifolia
Gypsophila petraea, repens 'Rosy Veil'
Lewisia species* (mostly lime-haters)
*Linaria cymbalaria,** *pallida* (attractive, but dangerously fast-growing; best used in isolation)
Minuartia species
Oenothera missouriensis
Onosma species
Pelargonium endlicherianum
Phlox douglasii and *subulata* varieties
*Polygonum affine**
Primula auricula forms*
*Saxifraga**—only species of the Euaizoonia section (*S. callosa, hostii, longifolia, paniculata*, etc.) can withstand the noonday sun. The Saxifrages of the Kabschia section (*S. burseriana*, 'Haagii', *marginata*, etc.) do best in an east-facing position.
Scabiosa graminifolia
Sedum album, reflexum, spurium varieties, and other species
Sempervivum species
*Silene schafta,** *saxifraga**
*Trachelium rumelianum**
*Veronica bonarota,** *lutea**
Zauschneria species

25

Shrubs

Ceratostigma plumbaginoides
Clematis species
Cotoneaster adpressus, adpressus 'Little Gem',
    congestus, horizontalis, horizontalis 'Saxat-
    ilis', *microphyllus* 'Cochleatus' (all only
    suitable for walls of at least three feet
    (1 m) in height)
Cytisus ardoini, hirsutus demissus
Daphne arbuscula
Dryas species
Helianthemum species and varieties
Hypericum coris, olympicum
Iberis sempervirens varieties
Jasminum nudiflorum (only as covering for
    large wall surfaces at least six feet (2 m) in
    height)
Lavandula varieties
Moltkia petraea, suffruticosa
Petrophytum caespitosum (*Spiraea caespitosa*),
    hendersonii
Rhamnus pumilus
Santolina species
Spiraea decumbens

Ferns

Asplenium trichomanes, viride
Phyllitis scolopendrium
Polypodium vulgare (lime-hating)

Shrubs

Cotoneaster dammeri, dammeri radicans
    (evergreen cover for walls at least three
    feet (1 m) in height)
Hedera helix 'Conglomerata'
Vinca minor (evergreen cover for very shaded
    walls)
Vinca major (only for large walls, at least six
    feet (2 m) in height)

Shady positions

Herbaceous plants

Aquilegia einseleana
Arabis procurrens
Bergenia species (for large areas of wall)
Chiastophyllum oppositifolium
Corydalis lutea, ochroleuca (can be rampant)
Haberlea rhodopensis
Primula × *pubescens* hybrids, *marginata*
Ramonda
Saxifraga, mossy (*Dactyloides* section)
Waldsteinia ternata

**These exciting hardy relatives of the
tropical Gesneriaceae are relics of the
Tertiary Age. They are saxatile plants
which grow in cracks filled with
humus on shady limestone cliffs in the
Pyrenees and the Balkans. Taking
their natural habitat into account, they
should be planted in north-facing,
dry-stone walls and on groups of
rocks, where they will thrive and
produce lilac and violet flowers in
May–June. Only the rare *Jankaea
heldreichii* from Mt Olympus is truly
difficult to cultivate. Illustrated here is
Ramonda myconi (*R. pyrenaica*);
pale-pink and white varieties of this
also exist.**

Rock garden beds

Almost every type of alpine can be grown successfully on raised beds, and if these are built directly on to a lawn then the great variety of plants which you can grow there can produce a most lovely effect. The beds should be about two yards (2 m) wide at the base, and three feet high (1 m). The walls are generally built of flat stones which slope inwards in such a way that the top of the bed forms a flat area some three to five feet (1 to 1.5 m) across. The bed should run east/west, and ideally be ten or more yards (metres) long. The centre of the bed can be filled with rubble or hardcore, which makes for good drainage, and the narrow crevices between the slabs should be filled with a good and carefully prepared soil mixture.

Nowhere can healthier or more beautiful specimens of the true rock-dwellers be found than on beds like these. The south side can be festooned with strong, thick cushions of *Acantholimon*, *Astragalus*, *Dianthus*, *Moltkia* and many other alpines which love sunny conditions, whilst on the north side *Haberlea*, *Ramonda*, the shade-loving saxifrages, choice primulas and ferns will form dense, strong colonies. The flat top can be planted with all sorts of dwarf bulbs from dry climates, such as dwarf iris and moisture-hating dwarf shrubs, like species of *Penstemon*. In short, the whole can form a microcosm of the alpine plant world, and those true plantsmen for whom plants mean everything and gardens are but a means to an end can indulge their collector's taste here. The raised, dry-stone bed in the alpine section of the

Nymphenburg Botanical Gardens in Munich is over twenty years old—now much larger than when it was first built—and even such an 'impossible' plant as *Rosa persica*, a real moisture-hater from the steppes of Iran and Afghanistan, flourishes there.

Section and front view of a raised bed. Note the sloping walls and narrow crevices.

The best material for building this kind of bank is stone slabs, not too thick, so that there are as many crevices for planting as possible. Where neither flagstones nor other stones are to be had, however, ordinary building bricks, with some artificially made crevices, may be used instead. Warmth- and light-loving plants will flourish in these stone or brick walls, especially in the narrowest crannies or round holes where they will take root and spread, and the colours of the flowers against the red-brown of brick makes a lovely picture. For the best effect, one or two specimens of each species should be planted quite close together, so that in the course of time they grow into dense colonies. The choice and slow-growing plants are recommended for this type of wall.

In a small garden a bed or border will have to suffice as a rock garden. With skilful arrangement low raised beds may be made around the house, beside the entrance path or even on a flat roof, and will look quite charming. These beds should be bordered with low-built stone edging some twelve to eighteen inches (20 to 50 cm) high. Where stone or money is in short supply, effective raised beds with a rustic appearance can be made with rail ties or sleepers. The bed is filled with builder's rubble, gravel or crushed stone topped with a twelve inch-deep (30 cm) layer of soil. When making low beds, the earth should be dug out a spit deep, and left to one side. A layer of drainage material is scattered over the ground and then the soil, enriched with grit and humus, is returned. Finally, add a few inches of stone chips. If the soil is naturally sandy or free-draining, then the drainage material may of course be omitted, since there is little danger of water being retained in a raised bed, even after prolonged rain. Borders for rock plants should not measure more than four feet (1.2 m) across; this makes it easier both to admire the plants and to look after them. If the bed is wider than this, it should be divided along its length by stepping-stones, and the back part should be slightly raised. Well arranged and lovingly placed rocks make all the difference to the general effect. All kinds of dwarf shrubs are suitable for these beds, and may be planted here and there beside the house or along the path. Amongst the deciduous shrubs we could include the small varieties of *Berberis, Caryopteris, Ceratostigma, Cotoneaster,*

Cytisus ardoini, and *C.* × *beanii, Daphne, Erica · herbacea, Helianthemum, Lavandula, Ononsis fruticosa, Potentilla fruticosa,* miniature roses (*Rosa chinensis* 'Minima'), dwarf willows (*Salix*), the dwarf lilac (*Syringa meyeri*), and *Viburnum farreri* 'Nanum'. Small conifers, such as the dwarf varieties of *Chamaecyparis obtusa, Juniperus communis* and *J. chinensis,* and *Picea glauca* 'Conica' are extremely useful in these positions, lending variety to the height and shape of the bed and producing new effects throughout the year, even in winter when they are laden with frost or snow. They provide a charming contrast to the surrounding cushion-plants, small shrubs, and grasses. Bulbs, too, snow-drops, crocus, grape hyacinth, dwarf tulips, autumn crocus and meadow saffron may be freely planted to great effect. Specialists in

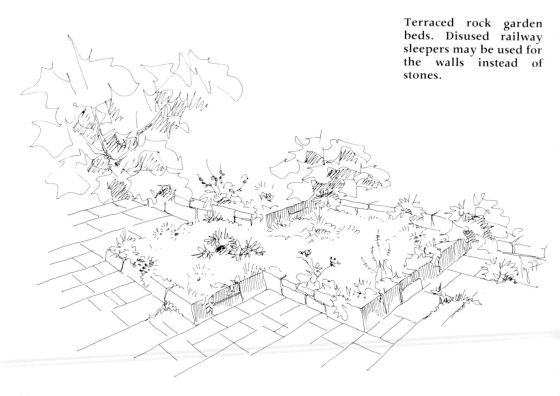

Terraced rock garden beds. Disused railway sleepers may be used for the walls instead of stones.

particular genera of plants can display the full beauty of their collections in beds of this type. *Saxifraga, Sedum, Sempervivum,* dwarf iris, and the different varieties of auricula are also suitable for these beds.

A landscaped garden. Large boulders are scattered here and there and the whole area is covered with plants. A heath garden of this kind makes a good entrance to the rock garden.

Peat beds

These special beds are built with non-calcareous rock or peat blocks and need a favourable sheltered position out of the full strength of the sun. All the different varieties of miniature rhododendrons and heaths and any other lime-hating, humus-loving plants should be planted in them. In laying out the beds it must be borne in mind that all these plants are very sensitive to the soil drying out too much. The beds should, therefore, preferably be at ground level, raised only in odd places. If it is desired to vary the level of the ground, it is better to dig broad, shallow depressions here and there and plant them with *Mazus*, *Mitchella repens* and the small European and Asian gentians (*Gentiana sino-ornata*) and primulas (*Primula farinosa*, *P. frondosa*, *P. vialii*, etc.). Here one can try to grow the flowers of the high snow-valleys, such as *Soldanella pusilla* and *S. minima*, *Ranunculus alpestris*, *Salix herbacea* and other dwarf willows.

It should be noted that many of these high-alpine plants need careful attention. Above all they should not be exposed to the full light of the noonday sun, or feel the effects of drying winds. The peat bed in the rock garden should not be drained with rubble but should have a moist, retentive subsoil. A level, well-rammed base of loam or clay, or even a trough of cement or plastic sheeting with edges eight inches (20 cm) high some eighteen inches (500 cm) below the surface is a good means of preventing rainwater from seeping away. The bed should be filled with peat with a little lime-free loam added. If soft water is not available, the bed should be watered only with rainwater. Only acid rock should be used as an alternative to peat in building a peat-bed, as has already been mentioned. If this is not available, variations in the surface-level can be achieved by using thick branches or roots of hardwood trees, preferably oaks or robinias, or else peat-blocks. A well laid out peat bed should fit harmoniously in with its surroundings. Indeed, wood combines almost more successfully with these plants than does stone. If any attractive boulders are to hand, they may be put to good use here, producing the combination of stone, wood, and plants which is found in the natural habitat of the peat bed plants in woods, on moors, in tundra, in marshes and on pine-covered mountain slopes.

Peat beds should be protected where appropriate with a vertical underground wall of roofing felt or strong plastic to prevent the roots of nearby trees and hedges from penetrating.

The more or less lime-hating plants for the peat bed listed below may of course be used anywhere in the informal rock garden. Few difficulties will be experienced in places where the soil is naturally poor in lime. However, some of these plants, such as the dwarf rhododendrons, are of outstanding beauty and, in lime-rich areas, peat beds can be built so as not to be deprived of them. The beds should be large enough to accommodate a small collection of these lovely plants, which repay all the trouble spent on them. Digging small holes for single specimens and filling them with peat has not proved satisfactory, since the imported acidic soil all too quickly becomes alkaline from the lime which flows in with the water from all around. In such cases lining the holes with plastic sheeting to prevent lime-bearing water from entering has proved useful.

Plants suitable for rock garden peat beds

(l = will tolerate slightly limy soils)

Shrubs
(d = deciduous; the rest are evergreen)
Andromeda polifolia
Arctostaphylos uva-ursi
Betula nana (d)
Bruckenthalia spiculifolia
Calluna vulgaris—garden varieties
Cassiope species and hybrids
Chamaedaphne calyculata 'Nana'
Daboecia
Daphne species (l)
Empetrum nigrum
Erica species and varieites
Gaultheria species
Gaylussacia species
Kalmia angustifolia, polifolia
Ledum groenlandicum
Leiophyllum buxifolium
Leucothoe species
Linnaea borealis
Loiseleuria procumbens
Menziesia ciliicalyx (d)
Mitchella repens
Pachistima species
Pachysandra species
Pernettya species
Phyllodoce species
Pieris (Arcterica) nana
Rhododendron species

Rhodothamnus chamaecistus (l)
Sarcococca species
Vaccinium species

Herbaceous plants
Anemonopsis macrophylla (l)
Aquilegia species
Arnica montana
Astrantia minor
Campanula barbata
Carex fraseri
Codonopsis species
Coptis trifolia
Cornus canadensis, suecica
Cyananthus integer and other species
Cypripedium species
Deinanthe coerulea, bifida
Dicentra cucullaria, eximia, formosa (l)
Epimedium grandiflorum (l)
Fritillaria meleagris (l), pallidiflora (l)
Galax aphylla
Gentiana Asiatic species and hybrids
Haberlea rhodopensis (l)
Hypsella longifolia (l)
Houstonia species
Iris gracilipes
Jeffersonia dubia, diphylla (l)
Lilium species
Mazus species
Meconopsis species
Mitella species
Nomocharis species
Parnassia palustris (l)
Phlox adsurgens
Primula species
Ramonda species (l)
Ranunculus amplexicaulis (l), crenatus
Roscoea species (l)
Rubus arcticus
Sanguinaria canadensis (l)
Saxifraga cotyledon, cortusifolia (l), cuneifolia (l), lilacina, umbrosa (l)
Senecio abrotanifolius, incanus

Shortia species
Soldanella montana (l), *villosa*
Tiarella species
Trillium species
Vancouveria species
Wulfenia species

Ferns

Adiantum pedatum, venustum (l)
Blechnum spicant
Polypodium vulgare
Polystichum setiferum varieties (l)

Rhododendrons in flower are a spectacular sight. Before and after flowering, their neat leaves are very restful to the eye. The evergreen varieties are very pretty in winter, whilst those which lose all or part of their foliage have superb, glowing autumn colours. They make a wonderful sight when planted near dwarf conifers among large stones, against which they can nestle. (1) *Rhodothamnus chamaecistus*, a dainty dwarf rhododendron relative from the limestone Alps, ideal for the rock garden. The evergreen Azalea hybrids have profuse flowers, for example: (2) 'Multiflora', and (3) 'Geisha'.

Miniature rock gardens in containers

The pleasure and enthusiasm felt by the dedicated alpine-gardener can be fully expressed in these miniature rock gardens. Trough gardeners are all passionate lovers of alpines. Many have rock gardens nearby as well, but reserve their favourite specimens for their stone troughs. These small areas may be attractively arranged with plants and small stones, and the choicer alpines do well under these conditions. Anyone who regards this as pretend-gardening has no real understanding or feeling for gardens, and aside from the pleasure and happiness which they provide, trough gardens have the following advantages.

First, they last almost for ever. Stone troughs can be left in the open air throughout the year, without any danger of their being destroyed by frost, or broken, as happens with some cement bowls.

Second, they require little attention. If sterilized weed-free soil is used in planting, they will be protected from the bane of weeds, which remove many people's pleasure in gardening. Windborne weeds are unlikely to invade the trough later on, as the spaces between the plants are covered with stones and a layer of stone chips some three-quarters of an inch (2 cm) deep. The only work necessary is watering the

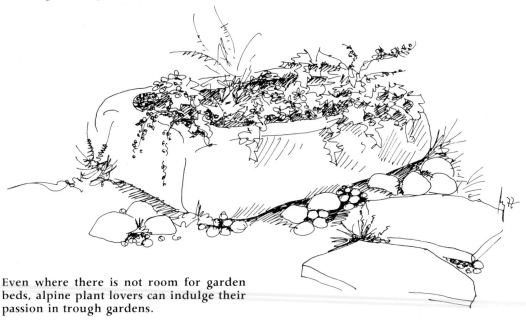

Even where there is not room for garden beds, alpine plant lovers can indulge their passion in trough gardens.

troughs in dry weather, if sprinkling your plants on a summer's evening can be called work.

The third advantage is the ease with which the beds can be admired. On stone supports the trough can be raised to the height of a bench or table and all the wonderful variety of these miniature plants can be appreciated from close at hand.

As for the technical details of trough gardening, the best troughs are made of limestone. They can be of very different sizes, ranging from three feet by eighteen inches by one foot (1 × 0.50 × 0.30 m) to those more than six feet (2 m) in length with other dimensions in proportion. These troughs may be old pig-feeding troughs or watering-troughs for cattle and horses, whilst the larger ones were sometimes smiths' troughs, which were filled with water and in which the smith would dip the hot iron to cool. The walls are usually fairly thick, about four inches (10 cm) or more; they can never be too thick, because the lip can be overgrown with creeping cushion-plants. Old troughs are attractively weathered on the outside due to long exposure to air, sun, and rain, and are often covered with lichens and mosses. New stone or concrete troughs can be painted with a solution of cow-dung and soot or oatmeal and curds to encourage a similar growth of these lichens and mosses.

It is important that the water outlet should be large enough and at the lowest part of the trough, so that water will never stand in the soil. A piece of perforated zinc sheeting should be placed over the inside of the drainage hole and the trough should be filled to about one-fifth of its depth with gravel or polystyrene chips measuring about one inch (2 to 3 cm) across. Above this is laid a layer of coarse peat, then a soil-mixture made up of chopped turf, peat, sharp sand and limestone chips or old masonry mortar.

Receptacles to be planted with lime-hating plants, such as the Ericaceae and alpines which grow on non-calcareous rock, should be made of granite or sandstone, and filled with the mixture of peat, lime-free loam, granite chips and quartz sand.

The newly filled trough should be well watered, to help the soil settle, and left for a few days. Only then can it be planted. Paradoxically enough, the imagination of the experienced gardener will find a wide field in this small space. One man may be a devotee of all the various encrusted saxifrages, with their small or large rosettes of leaves, and will plant them in narrow holes and crevices between stones, until plants and stones seem to grow into one another. Another may be an admirer of small, grey-leaved plants, setting the silver carpets of *Raoulia australis* and *R. lutescens* from New Zealand alongside the charming *Veronica bombycina* from the Lebanon, which dots its snow-white downy mats with sky-blue flowers; or juxtaposing the shining yellow heads of *Andryala aghardii* with the ash-grey cushions of *Vitaliana primuliflora*. There is a limitless number of small, beautiful plants which are ideal for trough gardens, including *Geranium napuligerum* (*farreri*), the delicate species of *Sedum* and *Sempervivum*, small pinks and *Globularia*, dwarf iris, small primulas and gentians, a great variety of dainty bulbs and corms, miniature shrubs such as *Genista pulchella* (*G. villarsii*), bog rosemary (*Andromeda polifolia*), *Cassiope* species, and various dwarf conifers. Rampant growers such as the rock phloxes, *Arabis*, *Cerastium*, and *Saponaria ocymoides* should obviously never be used in small troughs and basins.

Troughs may be placed on terraces in front of the windows of the house, or beside steps, in sunken gardens, or in yards—in fact anywhere where they will be seen frequently and display themselves to full effect. It is better to place them on the cool side of a house than on the west or south side, which can be too hot in some countries. They are especially attractive in front of evergreen hedges.

There is only one disadvantage of these sturdy stone troughs and that is their great weight. This means that they cannot be used quite everywhere—they are hardly suitable for roof gardens. In such places, clay or cement bowls should be used, or even strong containers made of synthetic material which will hold its shape. When planted with alpines any of these will lend variety and beauty to the garden. All these containers must, of course, have drainage holes and a drainage layer of polystyrene or some similar substance, so that excess water can flow easily away. It is very important to grow small shrubs in these gardens as well. These movable rock gardens, measuring some eight inches (20 cm) across, are extremely attractive when they are planted with early-flowering saxifrages, the small iris, hardy succulents, *Sedums*, *Sempervivums*, and so on, but they should be plunged in peat during the winter in deep, covered cold-frames protected from the frost. Do not forget to water the bowls occasionally in winter, especially if the air where they are being stored is dry, but the soil should never be permanently wet, since all alpines prefer to be dry rather than damp during the winter.

Lovers of alpines who do not have a garden can make up for this by growing them in their window-boxes. The direction in which the window faces should be taken into account when planting.

On the sunny side the following plants have proved successful: *Sedum*, *Sempervivum*, *Andryala*, *Acantholimon*, *Armeria*, *Campanula*, *Dianthus*, *Erinus*, *Leontopodium*, encrusted saxifrages, *Tunica saxifraga* 'Plena', and even *Gentiana farreri*.

For the shady side the following are recommended: *Ajuga reptans* 'Multicolor', *Saxifraga umbrosa* 'Clarence Elliott', *S. cotyledon* and the hybrid mossy saxifrages, *Haberlea*, *Ramonda*, *Cyclamen*, and small ferns (*Cystopteris fragilis*, *Asplenium viride* and *A. trichomanes*).

One of the pioneers of the miniature alpine garden was the Austrian Dr Rosenstingl, of Gmunden. He cemented tufa blocks closely together inside wooden boxes measuring not more than seven inches by ten (18 × 25 cm), so that they created the effect of a single block of stone some ten inches (25 cm) high. He planted the narrow crannies and crevices with all kinds of miniature alpines, *Petrocallis pyrenaica*, Kabschia, saxifrages, primulas, small varieties of *Phyteuma* and *Valeriana* and so on. These delicate arrangements naturally need special care, particularly as regards watering. Experienced followers of his have had the greatest success with difficult alpines in boxes of this kind.

Trough garden arrangements: (1) Trough with lush cushions of rock phlox and pinks tumbling over the edge; (2) a trough beautifully planted with miniature plants: silvery-grey foliage of *Raoulia australis*, *Linum iberidifolium*, *Aquilegia* and *Phlox*.

Plants suitable for small troughs and bowls

(* = lime-hating)

Sunny position

Herbaceous plants
Achillea kolbiana, umbellata
Aethionema graecum
Allium flavum 'Minus'
Anacyclus depressus
Androsace sempervivoides, carnea,
  *hedraeantha**
Andryala aghardii
Aquilegia discolor, akitensis
Arenaria tetraquetra var. *granatensis*
Armeria juniperifolia varieties
Artemisia laxa
Campanula cashmiriana, raineri
Centaurium chloodes
Crassula milfordiae, sarcocaulis
Dianthus microlepis, simulans
Draba bryoides imbricata
Erinus alpinus varieties
Eritrichium rupestre
Erysimum kotschyanum
Geranium napuligerum (farreri)
Gentiana verna
Globularia nana
Gypsophila aretioides
Micromeria species
Orostachys spinosa
Petrocallis pyrenaica
Plantago nivalis
Potentilla nitida
Raoulia hookeri, lutescens
Saponaria 'Bressingham', 'Olivana'
Saxifraga cochlearis 'Minor', varieties of Kabschia (shady positions)
Thlaspi stylosum
Veronica bombycina
Vitaliana primuliflora

Grasses
Alopecurus lanatus
Carex firma 'Variegata'
Festuca glacialis

Ferns
Ceterach officinarum
*Asplenium septentrionale**

Shrubs
Genista sagittalis 'Minor', *pulchella*
Hebe buchanii 'Minor', *pimeleoides minor*
Iberis saxatilis

Dwarf conifers
Chamaecyparis obtusa 'Minima'
Juniperus communis 'Compressa'
Picea glauca 'Echiniformis', 'Laurin'

Half-shaded or shaded positions

Herbaceous plants
Astilbe × *crispa* 'Liliput', *glaberrima saxatilis*
Lewisia species and varieties
Omphalodes luciliae
Petrocoptis glaucifolia, pyrenaica
Physoplexis comosa
Primula clarkei, marginata
Saxifraga oppositifolia varieties, *umbrosa*
  'Clarence Elliott'
*Thalictrum kiusianum**
Veronica bonarota

Ferns
Asplenium viride, trichomanes

Dwarf conifers
Microcachrys tetragona
Tsuga canadensis 'Minuta'

Plants suitable for larger troughs—more than three feet (1 m) long

(* = lime-hating)

Sunny positions

Herbaceous plants

Achillea × kellereri
Aethionema grandiflora varieties
Alyssum montanum
Androsace villosa, lactea
Antennaria dioica varieties
Anthyllis montana 'Rubra'
Aquilegia ecalcarata, scopulorum
Arabis ferdinandi-coburgii 'Variegata'
Asperula nitida, lilaciflora var. caespitosa
Aster alpinus varieties
Athamanta haynaldii
Aubrieta varieties
Bellis perennis 'Brillant', 'China Pink'
Campanula aucheri, carpatica, cochleariifolia,
    saxifraga, tridentata, waldsteiniana
Chrysanthemum haradjanii
Convolvulus boissieri (nitidus)
Delosperma cooperi, lineare
Dianthus caesius, slow-growing varieties
Diascia cordata
Draba aizoides, bruniifolia
Erodium cheilanthifolium, macradenum
Gentiana farreri, sino-ornata and hybrids*
Geranium argenteum, dalmaticum
Globularia species
Gypsophila repens varieties
Helichrysum milfordiae
Iris pumila varieties
Linaria alpina
Onosma albo-roseum, stellulatum
Origanum species
Penstemon caespitosa, newberryi, pinifolia,
    rupicola
Phlox subulata, slow-growing varieties
Potentilla aurea
Primula Auriculastrum species and hybrids
Pterocephalus parnassi
Saxifraga callosa varieties, cochlearis, hostii,
    longifolia
Sedum cauticolum, pluricaule, spathulifolium
    'Capa Blanca', sieboldii
Sempervivum species and varieties
Silena schafta
Trachelium rumelianum
Veronica fruticans varieties

Bulbs and corms

Crocus chrysanthus varieties
Eranthis × tubergenii
Iris danfordiae, histrioides 'Major', reticulata
    varieties

Grasses
Poa alpina var. vivipara
Carex dwarf species

Ferns
Pellaea atropurpurea
Cheilanthes, Notholaena marantae*

Shrubs
Andromeda polifolia 'Minima'*
Anthyllis hermanniae
Berberis × stenophylla 'Corallina Compacta'
Cistus dwarf species
Corokia cotoneaster
Cotoneaster microphyllus thymifolius
Cytisus ardoini, hirsutus demissus
Daphne arbuscula, cneorum
Euryops acraeus
Genista tinctoria 'Plena'
Hebe species
Helianthemum alpestre
Iberis sempervirens 'Little Gem'
Moltkia petraea

Petrophytum caespitosum
Salix boydii
Spiraea japonica 'Alpina'
Syringa meyeri

Dwarf conifers
Abies balsamea hudsonia
Chamaecyparis obtusa 'Nana Gracilis'
Picea glauca 'Conica'
Pinus nigra 'Helga'

Shrubs
Betula nana
Cornus hessei
Daphne blagayana (semi-shade)
Linnaea borealis americana*
Rhododendron impeditum,* *keleticum,** and others
Rhodothamnus chamaecistus*
Salix reticulata
Tsuga canadensis dwarf varieties

Plants suitable for half-shady and shady positions

Herbaceous plants
Astilbe × *crispa* varieties
Calceolaria tenella
Campanula fenestrellata
Chiastophyllum oppositifolium
Corydalis cheilanthifolia
Epimedium diphyllum
Haberlea rhodopensis
Moehringia muscosa
Polygonum tenuicaule
Primula auricula hybrids, *hirsuta**
Ramonda myconii, nathaliae
Saxifraga cotyledon, hypnoides
Soldanella montana, villosa
Viola biflora

Bulbs and corms
Cyclamen species (half-shade)
Fritillaria dwarf species
Galanthus species
Narcissus asturiensis, cyclamineus

Ferns
Adiantum venustum
Cystopteris fragilis
Phyllitis scolopendrium varieties

Alpines in bowls and boxes: (1) rosettes of *Sempervivum*, with *Raoulia australis* (2) *Saxifraga callosa (lingulata)*, *Erysimum kotschyanum*, *Iberis saxatilis* (3) *Primula auricula*, *Aquilegia akitensis*, *Phlox douglasii* hybrid (4) *Primula marginata* (5) *Gentiana dinarica* (6) *Saxifraga cochlearis*, *S. burseriana*, *S. burseriana* 'Lutea'.

Water in the rock garden

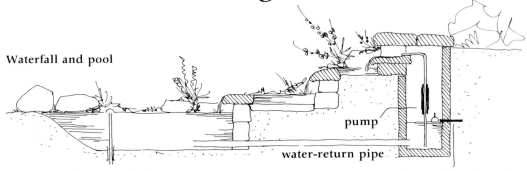

Waterfall and pool

pump

water-return pipe

overflow and drainage

water inlet and floating valve

One would like to lay it down as a general rule that there should be no rock gardens without water. In no other type of gardening does the phrase 'life-giving water' take on more meaning or does the water itself appear more attractive. Whether shimmering, rippling, splashing, running or reflecting the stones, water seems to be the most suitable contrast to the solidity and immobility of the rocks, just as it is in nature. Water will give life to any type of garden, whether formal or landscaped.

Those who have a spring on their land, or a brook running through it, are lucky indeed, and they should try to lead it with all possible variety through their gardens. It may curve around the stones, be dammed here and there and splash down miniature waterfalls before flowing into a pond. But where nature has not blessed us with a spring, we must create one of our own. What else are water pipes for? With these, water may be conducted to a high-lying shady spot, from where the rock garden spring can flow forth from a hidden pipe into a narrow gravelled basin edged with stones of different sizes, thence to pour down from level to level and wind across a flat 'meadow valley' before collecting in a pond at the lowest part of the rock garden. The basin at the spring should of course be cemented, as should the whole course of the

stream, to prevent the water from seeping away. With a little care and imagination, the cement can be so cleverly covered with stones and plants that it will be completely invisible and the uninitiated will take it for a real stream. By placing stones to dam the flow at irregular intervals, it is possible to create the effect of a slow-moving stream with the most economical use of water. A pump can be installed to pump the water back up from the lowest point into the basin at the source.

Planting the banks of the stream and damp places is a pleasant and rewarding task. The dark green of a dwarf conifer or the elegant branches of a Japanese maple may be reflected in the still waters of the source, whilst cushions of mossy saxifrage (*Saxifraga hypnoides* and *S. trifurcata* and a variety of primulas will form flourishing colonies along the damp edges and marshy patches of the stream. The first to bloom is *Primula rosea* in April, which will make a superb show with its glowing pink flowers next to the white blossoms of the Himalayan marsh-marigold (*Caltha palustris alba*). This is closely followed by the purple-blossoming tufty primula (*Primula × pruhoniciana*) which is also a great lover of moisture. Ground-cover is provided by the yellow Creeping Jennie (*Lysimachia nummularia*), whilst in spring the double lilac lady's smock (*Cardamine pratensis* 'Plena') blends with the dull gold of the double marsh-marigolds (*Caltha palustris* 'Flore Pleno'). The basin can be surrounded with globe-flowers, geum, forget-me-not, iris and day-lilies. Water-chestnut (*Trapa natans*) spreads its rhomboid leaves across the surface of the water in floating rosettes, whilst dwarf water-lilies open their lovely buds to the sun. The marsh bogbean (*Menyanthes trifoliata*) spreads its racemes of rosy-white fringed flowers over its creeping palmate leaves as early as April, and in summer mare's tail (*Hippuris vulgaris*) is mirrored in the water, creating a strange, dense, miniature forest.

Care should be taken to plant the fast-growing plants, like arrowhead (*Sagittaria sagittifolia*), *Scirpus tabernaemontani* 'Zebrinus', and the great spearwort (*Ranunculus lingua*) as well as the mare's tail, in long-lasting artificial containers, to prevent them growing too large.

In formal rock gardens the water will run through concreted basins, or through channels and miniature waterfalls, fed by a splashing spring, or gushing out from a fountain set into a wall. If there is not sufficient space for a large pond with water-lilies and goldfish—and this should by no means always be round or square—there should at least be room for a bird bath. Here birds may come down to shallow flagged pools (stone or cement basins sunk in the ground) into which water may trickle through a small hose.

Wherever there is water, small water creatures will quickly follow. Pond-skaters come overnight and can be seen gliding jerkily over the surface of the water, whilst small water-beetles dance hither and thither and dragonflies dart back and forth. Uninvited guests such as midges will of course be given short shrift. The larvae of these pests are eaten by small fish, which should find a place in every pond, both for this reason and for the visual pleasure which they afford.

Plants suitable for stream banks and damp positions

(Not all are included in later sections in the book. * = only suitable for larger gardens)

Herbaceous plants and bulbs
Acorus calamus 'Variegatus'*
Acorus gramineus pusillus
Ajuga reptans varieties
*Alchemilla mollis**
Anemone rivularis
Astilbe chinensis
Bergenia species*
*Brunnera macrophylla**
Caltha palustris varieties
Cardamine pratensis 'Plena'
Dianthus superbus
Fritillaria meleagris
Gentiana pneumonanthe
Geum coccineum, rivale 'Leonard's Variety'
Gladiolus palustris
Hemerocallis minor and low-growing varieties
*Iris bulleyana**, *chrysographes**, *cristata, forrestii, lacustris, sibirica**, *wilsonii*
Leucojum aestivum, vernum
Ligularia varieties*
*Lilium pardalinum**

Lobelia syphilitica*
Lysichiton species
Lysimachia species
Lythrum virgatum varieties*
Mazus pumilio
Mimulus cardinalis, cupreus
Moehringia muscosa
Myosotis caespitosa, scorpioides varieties
Nierembergia repens
Parnassia palustris
Peltiphyllum peltatum*
Polygonum bistorta 'Superbum'*
Primula beesiana*, bulleyana*, burmanica*,
  florindae*, frondosa, helodoxa, japonica*,
  juliae, × pruhoniciana, pulverulenta*, rosea,
  sikkimensis*
Ranunculus aconitifolius*
Trollius species and varieties

Shrubs

Acer palmatum, slow-growing varieties, e.g.
  'Dissectum Viridis' and 'Ornatum'
Betula nana
Kalmia angustifolia, polifolia (need peat)
Ledum groenlandicum 'Compactum' (needs
  humus-rich soil)
Salix hastata 'Wehrhahnii'
Viburnum opulus 'Compactum'

Water-plants

(* = only for larger gardens; the figure is the
approximate depth of water required, first in
inches and then in centimetres in brackets.)
Alisma plantago-aquatica* 2–8 (5–20)Butomus
  umbellatus* 4–16 (10–40)
Calla palustris 0–4 (0–10)
Comarum palustre 0–8 (0–20)
Hippuris vulgaris 8–16 (20–40)
Hottonia palustris 8–24 (20–60)
Hydrocharis morsus-ranae 4–12 (10–30)
Iris pseudacorus* 0–16 (0–40)
Lysimachia thyrsiflora 0–8 (0–20)
Menyanthes trifoliata 4–12 (10–30)
Nuphar pumilum 16–36 (40–100)

Nymphoides peltata 4–12 (10–30)
Orontium aquaticum 2–10 (5–25)
Pontederia cordata* 2–8 (5–20)
Ranunculus aquatilis 12–36 (30–100), lingua
  2–8 (5–20)
Sagittaria sagittifolia 2–8 (5–30) (rampant,
  plant in container)
Scirpus tabernaemontani 'Zebrinus' 2–8 (5–20)
Stratiotes aloides* (floating plant, partly
  under water)
Trapa natans 12–60 (30–150)
Typha gracilis minima 1½–4 (3–10)

Water-lilies (Nymphaea)

Dwarf water-lilies, adequate for small ponds of
up to one square yard in area: 'Tetragona',
'Helvola', 'Rubis' 2–4 (5–10).
Slow-growing water-lilies requiring a surface
area of at least one square yard (metre):
'Aurora', 'Graziella', 'Indiana', 'Laydekeri
Rubra', 'Sioux' 10–16 (25–40).

Water is a charming feature in a rock
garden and can be used in countless
different ways. (1) Rock garden pool
with stepping-stones. On the bank is
yellow striped *Iris pseudacorus*
'Variegata'. (2) Varied treatment of a
stream in the Botanical Gardens at
Genf. (3) Naturalistic arrangement in
the rock garden at Wisley, England.
Ferns and Hostas do particularly well
in the damp, cool air around pools.
Cytisus decumbens blooms in a dryer
position.

Stone for the rock garden

The first to appreciate the beauty of stone and to make use of it in a symbolic way in their gardens were the peoples of East Asia. The Chinese and Japanese have for centuries admired fine pieces of rock in the same way as we admire old and venerable trees. The Japanese are prepared to pay the same, and to us amazing, prices for particularly fine specimens of stone moulded by the action of water, wind, and weather over thousands of years, or with especially attractive veining or stratification, or unusually veined with quartz, as they will for old bonsais or dwarf trees. It seems odd to us that stones are on display and available in all the large department stores in Japan. We may notice in this connexion that not all these stones are used in the garden. Small manageable stones are used as ornaments in houses. Natural pieces like this may be mounted on wooden or bronze stands or set in beds of pure quartz sand or marble chips and put in a place of honour, and they lend a special atmosphere to the stylish simplicity of far-eastern rooms. That the beauty and decorative possibilities of stones are now being appreciated outside Japan can be seen in both flower shows and gardens open to the public, where erratic boulders and striking specimens of rock are now used.

Another clear indication of this is the growing interest in rock gardens. Not only do stones constitute the basic element of these gardens, but whether shaped, hewn or in their natural form, they are the dominant feature influencing the garden's aesthetic value.

There is something wonderful in a beautiful, individually shaped stone. The play of light and shade on its form, the way in which its colour changes in fine and wet weather, the smoothness or roughness of its surface, and the mosaic of lichen and moss which covers it all combine to give pleasure throughout the year.

The appropriate stone for your rock garden will naturally be that which is easiest to procure. Locally available stone will be the best value for money, because the transport costs will be lowest, and local stone looks best in any garden. Stone from other areas usually looks odd and unnatural: red sandstone, for example, looks out of place in a limestone area, and this is especially true of informal gardens. In formal gardens with dry-stone walls and paving sedimentary stone will have to be used even if it is not locally available, because it is easier to work.

At one time, in the Romantic period, tufa was used almost exclusively for building grottoes, as it was later in Alpinums or alpine gardens. The great attraction of this stone is its comparative lightness, allowing it to be easily transported in large blocks, and if necessary sawn or hewn into different shapes without difficulty. This makes tufa the ideal material for many positions, such as roof gardens. The enthusiast for alpine plants prizes tufa for its porous and moisture-retaining qualities and for its many crevices, which can easily be enlarged with a chisel, as rock-dwelling plants do especially well in these crannies. One disadvantage is that self seeding alpines and 'weeds' such as *Linaria cymbalaria* will also colonize the holes in tufa and are almost impossible to root out. Mosses and liverworts especially like damp conditions, and can quickly cover the stone, obscuring its shape. Another disadvantage of this stone is its softness, which often leads to rapid weathering and splitting. For this reason only hard tufa which has been exposed to the air should be worked. Many people also take exception to the bone-grey colour which tufa takes on when it has weathered. It is occasionally possible to find naturally occurring tufa of an ochre or reddish colour, due to the presence of iron compounds. The finest tufa is the hard and long-lasting travertine, the attractive warm ochre tones of which go particularly well with the silver-grey of many cushion-plants, the berry-laden branches of rock-creepers, and the grey-greens of conifers.

Tufa occurs rarely in nature and generally only in places where the slopes of hills have been eroded by man or by natural agents such as running water. Bearing this in mind, use tufa projecting from the earth on shelving ground in the informal rock garden, forming steep bluffs of massed rock. Tufa also looks best when used in conjunction with running water.

Never be tempted into erecting any of those vaguely pyramid-shaped creations made of free-standing blocks of tufa, often embellished with stalagmites, which recall the grottoes so dear to the Romantics, and which can be seen in historic gardens dating from those times. They have an atmosphere of artificial preservation about them today and are out of tune with modern sensibilities and feeling for natural forms.

Tough conglomerate rock can also be used. Skilful workers will be able to make up for the absence of large blocks of stone by using hypertufa or making conglomerate rocks by binding together river pebbles or gravel of different grades with cement. This has a very peculiar appearance, and one would hesitate to recommend it but for the fact that I have seen it used to excellent effect by enthusiasts who have created rock gardens in disused gravel pits using artificial conglomerate walls and boulders. Plants flourish happily in such stones, especially the true rock-dwellers such as the small encrusted cushion saxifrages of the Kabschia section.

When sedimentary rock is used in an informal garden, it should be laid with its strata running more or less horizontally, as in nature.

The various flagstones and blocks should first of all be carefully sorted according to the thickness of their strata, their colour and their degree of weathering, so that in construction the courses will be of the same thickness and look natural. Thick sedimentary layers should be alternated with thinner ones to avoid monotony. Sedimentary rock is especially useful for building steep slopes or banks, each course being set slightly behind the previous one, in the manner of a terrace. It is better to lay the courses on a slight slope than absolutely horizontal. Sandstone may also be laid in courses in the same way, if its warm tones are preferred to the clay colour of sedimentary rock. The softer shapes of the more weathered blocks should be used in the top courses.

Jurassic rock is both useful and attractive, with its edges rounded by weathering, and holes worn into it by the action of water. It may be used in groups or individually.

Volcanic or igneous rock such as granite and basalt is not very suitable for rock gardens, especially informal ones. Those rocks which have had their sharp edges worn and rounded away by nature are usually too large and heavy for comfortable handling. When they are split up the pieces have sharp edges and the shapes they break into are not pleasing. Smooth and worn glacial rocks are even less suitable for the pure rock garden, and should be employed as they are found in nature—preferably scattered as individual boulders lying loosely in a heath garden, next to a juniper or in a shady corner amongst the ferns and woodland plants. They look very well when used in water-courses and along the edges of pools. It is also possible to construct 'dry water-courses' using such rounded boulders and river gravel of different grades. This kind of wadi can be very attractive in the right place, if it is large enough. It should be sparsely planted with a few shrubs and bushes dotted over its stony bed to give the impression of a desert. Curiously shaped trees such as the Siberian *Caragana jubata*, varieties of *Yucca* and all kinds of succulents and shrubs with felty grey leaves will be appropriate here.

There are, of course, other types of stone which can be used in the rock garden, and only the commonest have been mentioned here. The most important thing is to obtain stone of really attractive structure, shape and colour. Wide, flat, more or less squared rock is easier to work than sharp, cubic or even pyramid-shaped blocks. In fact, obtaining really attractive and preferably large rocks is the first and most important prerequisite for a successful and beautiful rock garden.

South America is the home of a large number of species of Oxalis. (1) *Oxalis adenophylla* from Chile sends up clusters of divided leaves and flowers up to four inches high (10 cm) in spring from its fibrous tubers. It likes gravelly, humus-rich soil and a sunny position in the open air. (2) *Oxalis laciniata* from southern Argentina has scaly tubers which spread underground, and delicately veined flowers on short stems an inch (2 cm) high; it is a gem for the alpine-house, as is (3) *Lewisia tweedyi* from north-west USA.

The soil

Rock garden plants come from all countries and regions of the world. A large proportion of them are extremely adaptable and will grow satisfactorily anywhere in the garden, in all sorts of different soils. These workaday rock plants include arabis, aubrieta, alyssum, iberis and rock phlox. Of course, there is an ideal soil even for such adaptable plants as these, in which they will grow best and appear at their finest. The best type is a free-draining, crumbly, well-cultivated soil which is rich in minerals; not too sticky, but well fertilized, preferably with manure or compost. Gardeners who are not blessed with such soil should heap up turves, add manure and peat, and turn it several times a year. The result after two or three years will be a friable, crumbly, rich compost, which will provide the best possible conditions for most alpines. It will also serve as the basis of soil mixtures suitable for more difficult plants, and into which sand, gravel, lime chips or leaf-mould may be added.

There is, however, a whole range of plants which do especially well or badly in particular types of soil. Aside from conditions such as altitude and the humidity of the air, the most important factor is the lime content of the soil. Although the generality of alpine plants may be said to be indifferent, flourishing as well on lime-rich as on lime-free soil, there is a large number of plants and shrubs which are extremely sensitive to lime. For the most delicate of these limy soil spells death. Most of these plants come from mountains formed of primary rock, from heaths and moorlands, where the soil is poor in lime or acidic, with a pH value of between 3.5 and 6.3. Often whole families of plants are lime-hating and will not tolerate limy soil—for example, the Ericaceae—although there may be one or two exceptions: *Erica herbacea* and *Rhododendron hirsutum* spring to mind. In the same way there are lime-loving genera, *Dianthus* for example, of which a few species prefer soil which is poor in lime: *D. microlepis* and *D. superbus*.

For those interested in specializing, a list of lime-hating and lime-loving plants has been appended. No attempt has been made to make it exhaustive (see also the section on peat beds). Lime-loving alpines are in general easier to grow than lime haters. Alpine gardeners and rock gardeners with soil poor in lime are best off, however, since it is always easier to feed the soil with lime than it is to create suitable conditions for lime-haters in lime-rich areas.

Plants which are more or less lime-hating

Achillea moschata, nana
Androsace carnea laggeri, hedraeantha,
    imbricata, obtusifolia
Astrantia minor
Campanula excisa
Chrysanthemum alpinum
Dianthus glacialis, microlepis
Dicentra eximia, cucullaria
Douglasia species
Erigeron aureus
Gentiana frigida, sino-ornata and Asiatic
    hybrids
Helichrysum frigidum
Houstonia species
Lewisia species
Lithodora diffusa
Lychnis alpina
Penstemon davidsonii, menziesii, and others
Potentilla aurea
Pulsatilla alpina apiifolia, vernalis
Saponaria pumilio
Saxifraga cotyledon, cortusifolia, lilacina
Sempervivum montanum, wulfenii
Senecio incanus

Lime-hating plants in limy soil will show their unhappiness by weak growth, and by their leaves yellowing with chlorosis and drying out. Many plants will succumb quickly, and the remedies are to replant them as rapidly as possible in lime-free soil with sphagnum peat and quartz sand, and to water with rainwater. Plants should be watered every week or so with an iron sequestrene. They may also be watered with a weak solution of super-phosphate—1:2000 to 1:1000—which will help to neutralize the effects of the lime. Yellowing foliage can also be remedied sometimes by watering with a solution of Epsom salts (magnesium sulphate): a teaspoonful in two gallons will be about right.

Plants which tolerate or require lime

Achillea ageratifolia, clavenae
Acantholimon species
Acanthus species
Adonis species (except brevistyla and
    pyrenaica)
Aethionema species
Alopecurus lanatus
Androsace lactea, chamaejasme
Aubrieta varieties
Callianthemum anemonoides, kernerianum
Carlina species
Cyclamen species
Cypripedium calceolus
Dianthus (almost all species)
Dryas octopetala
Gentiana clusii, dinarica
Globularia species
Gypsophila species
Haberlea and Ramonda
Helleborus species
Hepatica species
Leontopodium species
Potentilla nitida
Primula auricula, marginata, clusiana
Pulsatilla species (except vernalis)
Saxifraga, especially the Kabschia and Euaizo-
    onia sections, with a few exceptions

The rock garden under glass: the alpine-house

Most owners of rock gardens will be content with the huge number of beautiful plants which can be successfully grown without difficulty. In spring, there are luxuriant aubrietas, phlox, arabis and iberis; in early summer, the scented flowers of pinks and the bright colours of sun roses, asters, and countless other blooms. When flowers are few there is solace in the rich and varied colours and shapes of the sedums, sempervivums, saxifrages and a host of small shrubs and conifers.

Real enthusiasts are quite another matter, however. They will not be satisfied with the gay and heavy blossoms of the rock plants which any gardener can grow. They seek out the special, the rare and the unusual to try their skill, sparing no pains to attain success. Challenging rarities like the gentian-blue, silky cushion-plant *Eritrichium nanum* from the peaks of the Alps, or the felty silver rosettes of *Jankaea heldreichii* from Mount Olympus are the jewels of their collections.

Many of these species are uncommon because they are more difficult to grow than the common rock plants. Even after all their needs have been taken into account, they seldom achieve their full beauty when planted out in the garden, and many of them will ail or die after a short time.

Plants for the alpine-house: (1) *Chrysanthemum hosmariense* from Morocco, **(2)** *Helichrysum frigidum* from Corsica and **(3)** *Briggsia aurantiaca* from south-east Asia.

Too much humidity at the wrong time of year can be fatal. Prolonged periods of rain during the summer are dangerous to many alpines which originate in the mountains of the drier parts of the world. In areas with wet winters, the high-altitude plants often miss their rest beneath a blanket of snow and rapidly rot, no matter how well-drained. Many of the beautiful cliff plants also resent the moist conditions at ground level and can only be grown to perfection when protected. Covering garden plants with glass is only a makeshift measure; too much water will still trickle in, and the plants will rot and die.

Alpine lovers have therefore long made it their practice to shelter their more delicate specimens in an alpine-house. None of the countless lovely Kabschia saxifrages, the Aretian *Androsace* species, the unusual species of *Lewisia* or any of the special plants, only a few of which are listed below, will ever produce such fine blossoms outdoors as they will in an alpine-house. Even small spring bulbs such as *Anemone blanda*, all the species of *Crocus*, the varieties of *Iris reticulata*, fritillaries and dwarf wild tulips grow better indoors, and produce finer flowers if planted in autumn on staged beds or in pots than they will outdoors, where they are often spoilt by inclement spring weather.

The protection of a glass-house, while especially beneficial to all moisture-hating plants, will also provide sufficient protection from icy winds and early and late frosts for the many which are not completely hardy. In the colder parts of the United States, some heat would be needed for non-hardy plants when temperatures fall below 20°F (−7°C). Another attraction of the rock garden under glass is that it is possible to admire favourite specimens in any weather. Furthermore, the plants rest on the staging and are thus closer to the eye.

Especially difficult alpines such as *Androsace alpina*, *Ranunculus glacialis*, *Eritrichum nanum*

and so forth, cannot be kept for long even in an alpine-house. Nevertheless, the attempt to grow these high mountain plants at low altitudes may be crowned with success, perhaps one or two years, under glass, whilst the effort to grow them outdoors is doomed from the start.

There are a number of firms now offering small greenhouses for amateurs. These are either delivered ready-made, or come in easily erected do-it-yourself kits. They may be made of wood, galvanized metal or aluminium, and if the ventilation system is ample and easily managed, and there is provision for creating shade, they may be used for alpines. With all the modern technical apparatus of air humidifiers, air conditioners, ventilators and thermostatically controlled heating systems available, it is becoming possible to create the appropriate conditions for any type of plant in these small greenhouses.

No heating is required in an alpine house if only hardy plants are to be grown there. If, however, half-hardy plants from Mediterranean climates, such as the different species of cyclamen or tuberous orchids are to be grown, then care must be taken that the house is protected from frost. Those who wish to exploit every possibility to the full will be advised to invest in a house with two separate parts, one of which will be kept cold and unheated, and the other frost-free. Inside the alpine-house, the plants may be grown in pots plunged in sand or planted out in beds on the benches or staging. In either case, it is important that the benches are sufficiently provided with drainage holes so that water can run off easily. When constructing such a bed, a drainage layer of gravel or stone chips is first placed on the benches before adding a layer of soil-mixture at least 6 inches (15 cm) deep, topped with stone chips.

An alpine-house should not require too much work, though each plant must of course be individually watered to its own needs. In general, alpine plants require more water between spring and early summer than they do in summer and autumn. In winter they need so little that they should be watered only occasionally in frost-free weather. Alpines such as *Artemisia*, species of *Draba, Lewisia, Pleione*, etc., which are particularly sensitive to winter moisture, should be left quite dry during their winter rest. The best water to use is rainwater. During summer the path and gravel beneath the staging and between the pots on the staging should be well watered to increase the humidity of the air. Not only will alpines feel happier in damp, cool, fresh air, but this will also discourage pests such as woodlice, thrips, and red spider. If pests do appear the plants should immediately be treated with pesticide. The plants must be shaded from the full sun in summer or they will burn, their flowers will quickly fade and the house will become too hot. Roller-blinds made of narrow wooden slats are the best for this purpose, but plastic netting sold for greenhouse shading can be used as a cheaper, if less permanent, alternative. A double layer of this may be needed if many of the choicer cliff plants are to be adequately shaded.

In continental climates it is a good idea to cover the greenhouse with roofing boards from about December to the middle of February, although it is not absolutely essential. The deep shade which this creates will prevent the winter sun from starting the plants off too soon. This practice is quite the opposite to that advocated by enthusiasts gardening in the wet, cloudy climate of Britain. There, all shading is usually removed and the glass is cleaned before winter. It is, in every case, important that adequate ventilation be provided in frost-free weather throughout the year. The air in the greenhouse should never become stuffy, although strong draughts are equally to be avoided.

There is another variant of the alpine-house which has been created by Roy Elliott in England. Beneath a sloping glass roof, rather in the manner of a pergola, he has built up a south-facing garden wall with large blocks of tufa arranged in terraced courses. This 'cliff-garden', as he calls it, is easily entered, being open to the front and one other side, and is both practical and extremely attractive. This well-aired rock garden under glass is ideal for all hardy plants which prefer dry conditions. A raised bed with a similar glass roof, open at the sides, is another variation of this idea, which has proved very successful with other growers.

Special plants for the alpine-house

Shrubs
Cytisus ardoini, hirsutus demissus
Daphne arbuscula, petraea, jasminea
Genista sagittalis minor, pulchella
Hebe species
Hypericum aegypticum, cuneatum
Jasminum parkeri
Teucrium aroanium, subspinosum
Thymus cilicicus, membranaceus
Verbascum 'Letitia'

Herbaceous plants
Acantholimon species
Aethionema (*Eunomia*) *oppositifolium*
Agave megalacantha, parryi
Androsace carnea and varieties, *ciliata, hedraeantha, helvetica, hirtella, vandellii* (*imbricata*), *mathildae, pyrenaica* and many others
Anchusa caespitosa
Andryala aghardii
Artemisia assoana, splendens
Asperula arcadiensis
Campanula allionii (*alpestris*), *cashmiriana, formanekiana, morettiana, raineri, saxifraga, zoysii*

Carduncellus species
Chrysanthemum densum
Convolvulus boissieri (_nitidus_)
Cyclamen, all species
Dionysia species
Douglasia laevigata, montana
Draba mollissima, polytricha
Erodium corsicum, reichardii
Helichrysum frigidum, milfordiae, virgineum
Jankaea heldreichii
Lewisia species
Lithodora oleifolia, rosmarinifolia, zahnii
Omphalodes luciliae
Pelargonium endlicherianum
Phlox bryoides, missoulensis
Primula allionii and its varieties
Primula auricula, marginata varieties

Raoulia species
Saponaria cypria
Saxifraga species and varieties of the Kabschia and Engleria sections
Sedum pilosum, sempervivoides
Sempervivella species
Silene hookeri
Talinum species
Trachelium asperuloides
Verbascum acaule, dumulosum
Veronica bombycina

Ferns
Asplenium fontanum
Ceterach officinarum
Cheilanthes fragrans, marantae
Pellaea atropurpurea

Plants for the alpine-house: (1) _Pleione forrestii_ from south-west China (Yunnan), a lovely species with striking yellow blooms; it must be kept dry and frost-free during its resting-period in winter. (2) _Verbascum_ 'Letitia', a hybrid between _V. spinosum_ and _V. dumulosum_, raised in Wisley Gardens. Although both parents of this semi-shrubby plant come from the Near East (Crete and Turkey), it has proved hardy. In an alpine-house, it develops its beauty to the full, forming round bushes up to a foot (30 cm) high, covered with flowers in June.

Lewisias too can come under glass, where they find protection from winter rain. All like a very free-draining soil, poor in lime, and should not be allowed to dry out when they are in growth, when they appreciate weak liquid feeding. As well as the pure species there are many beautiful hybrids: (3) 'George Henley' and (4) 'Sunset Strain'. (5) _Sedum pilosum_ from the Caucasus and Turkey is a charming biennial which is easily propagated from seed. In its first year it forms large rosettes of grey-green leaves, one or two inches (3–4 cm) high, with thickly clustered, hairy foliage; in the following year it produces short-stemmed pink flowers in June–July. (6) _Dionysia aretioides_ from northern Iran. These cliff-plants from the mountains of south-west and central Asia are extraordinarily sensitive to moisture and need careful cultivation by experienced growers.

59

Animal life in the rock garden

The living creatures which we find in our gardens probably bring us pleasure and annoyance in equal measure. Just as we welcome harmless creatures, especially useful ones, so we wage war against the other unwanted infiltrators and pests with every available means.

The same is true of the rock garden. The lovely flowers of rock phloxes and aubrieta are crowned in the spring sunlight by the first of the butterflies, and bees feast on the pollen and nectar of the earliest flowers: winter heaths, *Adonis*, and crocus. Next comes *Cotoneaster horizontalis*, which provides a rich banquet, whilst the carpet sedums (*Sedum spurium*) and winter savory (*Satureja montana*) bloom in early summer.

If the garden is not in the middle of a town, but close to fields, woods, and streams, black-snakes or grass-snakes may occasionally be found there. They are not venomous and are quite harmless, and live by rock garden pools and in planted marshy hollows. They are extremely good swimmers, and lie in ambush for all sorts of small animals. Although they catch small fish and frogs, which is less to our liking, they will also catch and eat mice, in recompense for the other damage they cause. There is no need to be afraid of these elegant creatures; they should be left in peace, and observed in action.

Finches, goldfinches, and linnets are occasional visitors to the rock garden, where they steal young artemisia shoots for their nests. There is no need to worry about these depre-dations. If the cushions of artemisia are too heavily damaged, they can be easily protected by covering them with fine-meshed netting. Much worse damage is caused by blackbirds. They spend the whole year in the rock garden, plucking off crocus and primula flowers in spring, plundering the lovely cotoneaster berries in autumn, and pulling up and tearing to pieces whole cushion-plants in their search for food, causing a great deal of damage. The beautiful songs which they sing in spring can be small compensation for the destruction which they wreak.

Do not forget when building large dry-stone walls to put small pieces of drain pipe here and there in the angles of crevices, leading into small hollows, the entrances disguised with stones. Birds which nest in holes, especially the useful and sprightly chickadees or tits, will nest here, and the nestlings are usually safer from cats here than they would be in hanging nesting-boxes.

Hedgehogs and moles are excellent allies when it comes to destroying mole-crickets and other insect pests, and are in themselves useful animals. In the rock garden, however, the burrowing of moles undermines and throws up the plants, causing much damage. They can be fumigated out by putting rags soaked in petrol or creosote in their runs, but it is safer to trap them. Mice are even more destructive. Not only do they eat crocus and all sorts of other bulbs, but in winter they hide under the snow and feast off *Campanula*, *Dianthus*, *Geranium*, and other herbaceous plants. Voles are very destructive and should be trapped or destroyed with one of the proprietary brands of poison which are also useful against field-voles and field-mice. Take care when laying poison that the bait is placed as far as possible into the holes so as not to endanger birds. Drain pipes are useful for laying bait, and they should be concealed beneath bushy plants or covered with twigs.

We have already mentioned the mole-cricket, which occurs in some regions, and is a dreaded garden pest. Of all plants it eats dwarf iris with most relish, and nests only too happily in rock gardens. It can be eliminated with proprietary brands of poison. Small red ants sometimes invade the rock garden in wet weather, and give gardeners much trouble as they tend to build their underground nests beneath thick cushion-plants, but effective ant poisons are available. In dry spring weather, destructive flea-beetles invade the garden in huge numbers, and will quickly destroy the flowers of crucifers such as alyssum, arabis, aubrieta, etc., if they are not attacked with appropriate insecticides.

There should be no respite in the battle against all slugs, which have a particular fondness for fine varieties of campanula, and can only be eliminated by slug-poisons. Common toads and frogs are natural enemies of slugs and woodlice, so that they are welcome guests in the garden, and should be protected. Rock garden pools provide them with the best mating conditions.

Any rock garden basin of a sufficient size will contain fish. Not only do they give extra attraction to the water, they are also avid devourers of gnat and midge larvae. Goldfish are the most popular fish because of their vivid colouring, but they are rather sluggish and not very keen hunters of larvae.

The year in the rock garden

There can be no one who longs for the end of winter more than the rock gardener. This does not mean that the rock garden does not have its charms in winter: on frosty days hoar-frost outlines cushions and rosettes, stems and branches in delicate filigree; or a soft blanket of snow lies everywhere, smoothing out sharp edges, and strange effects are created above this peaceful white carpet by the crabbed shapes of dwarf shrubs, by the stark lines formed by the stems of isolated grasses and the dark bowed forms of dwarf conifers, recalling the chiaroscuro of Japanese ink drawings.

Nevertheless, as winter progresses, so the longing for life and colour, for flowers and foliage increases. As soon as a patch of milder weather comes, and the ground is free of frost and snow for several days, we hurry out to our favourite plants. A few degrees of warmth suffice for the yellow flowers of the witch-hazel (*Hamamelis mollis*) to burst out from their buds on spindly branches. The flowers look almost like living creatures and create a magical effect on the bare branches.

Lifting the winter coverings of pine branches from places where early-flowering plants are growing, you may discover that the greenish-brown shoots of *Adonis amurensis* are already pushing through; *Cyclamen coum* is lifting its buds with their delicate pointed crimson tips, and the earliest dwarf irises (*Iris bakeriana, I. danfordiae, I. reticulata* and *I. histroides*) have already broken through the wintry ground. It is not a good idea to remove the covering completely as yet. Its shade will prevent the soil warming too quickly in the winter sun and stop the plants growing too rapidly. It is still very early in the year and winter can return overnight with snow and ice. Winter coverings should not be removed before the month of March in Europe and, even then, a few boughs should be kept ready to cover early-flowering plants, which will now be appearing in their multitudes, from heavy night-frosts. Snowdrops, crocus, early irises and Christmas roses can bear quite a few degrees of frost without suffering any damage, and although they lie limp on the ground after a frosty night, as soon as the air warms up and the hoar-frost melts, they raise their heads again as if nothing had happened.

As soon as the winter coverings have been removed, we should set about spring-cleaning the garden. In an informal garden, where everything should look natural and as if self-sown, the cleaning-up operation should not be too radical. It does no harm to leave a brown ring of dead leaves around the new shoots of the Pasque Flower, so that its grey tufts can spring up undisturbed from the midst of it. After all, it is contrast that produces half the charm. With ferns, too, last year's fronds should be left on the stem, and not removed—if removed they must be—until the young fronds have fully unfurled. Have no scruples, however, in removing ugly, blackened leaves of such plants as *Bergenia* or *Brunnera macrophylla*.

Old clumps of *Epimedium* stalks and leaves which looked so fine in their bronze autumn colours and winter green must now be cut down close to the ground. The young leaf and flower shoots will soon appear and will only unfold their full beauty if they are not hidden by last year's growth. Brooms, rock-roses and any other plants with dead and frosted branches should be cut back to the green wood, and any damage caused by a hard winter must be removed. Most plants will shoot again after being cut down to the ground, so caution should be exercised in pulling out ones which look dead. Many herbaceous plants are naturally slow in shooting, so that we should not start worrying too soon if they do not appear. *Primula vialii* is one which only sends up its pointed, hairy young leaves in May and *Roscoea* appears even later but then develops very quickly.

Rock garden plants grow in very different ways, not only as regards time, but also shape and colour. The young steel-blue leaves of *Mertensia virginica* protrude strangely from the earth, whilst the young rosettes of *Meconopsis* resemble soft nests. *Sedum heterodontum* signals its growth with mysterious red buttons and all the various bulbs send up differently shaped shoots. The leopard's bane (*Doronicum*) greets us with fresh green, heart-shaped leaves, and the red, brown, or pale green palmate leaves of the Japanese maple (*Acer palmatum*) hang limply, like freshly hatched butterflies from their thin branches. The unfurling fronds of the different ferns are especially lovely and many of them recall rearing cobras. Such is the hart's-tongue (*Phyllitis scolopendrium*) for shady nooks and crevices, where it quickly becomes established and scatters its spores to grow in other similar corners. *Dryopteris atrata* from China is a very strange specimen, for the young plants hang limply from the ends of its rolled-up, black, scaly fronds, looking like diminutive elephants' trunks.

The fresh-green, mossy fronds of *Polystichum setiferum* 'Plumosum Densum' unroll from reddish-brown coils and look quite magical when the dew-drops sparkle on them in the morning sun. Other ferns, such as *Adiantum pedatum* and *Gymnocarpum robertianum*, grow into diminutive thickets with flimsy fronds, like bishops' crooks, on brownish or sea-green stems.

Early spring is one of the high points of the year in the rock garden, and a book could be filled with the pleasures and surprises afforded by the varied forms and growth patterns of the plants at this season.

We must examine what needs doing at this time, when plants are beginning to grow. Here and there, where mice and moles have burrowed under the ground and turned it up, it needs pressing down again, so that no plants are uncovered and left to dry out. Herbaceous plants which have been planted too late in the autumn may have been lifted by the frost and must be firmed back into place. Gaps, where plants have died, been eaten by mice or rotted away, must be filled up with new specimens. In these cases, if you can, remove some of the old soil and replace it with fresh. This should be the procedure also when plants which have been a long time in one place are divided to rejuvenate them, or when leggy, old clumps of *Primula auricula*, *P. marginata*, *Aster alpinus*, and others are replanted deeper down. The plants will be very grateful for a yearly application of good, old compost in the spring, spread carefully by hand between the clumps. Soil should be replaced at the same time, wherever it has been washed out or sunk into hollows. Add a fresh layer of stone chips.

It is almost impossible to conceive how full of flowers the rock garden is in spring. After the first flush of phlox, iberis, aubrieta and alyssum is passed, there is a second riot of colour with the pinks, whose small, thick bushes, grassy green mats, blue-grey cushions and spiny, hedgehog-like clumps are now decorated with filmy, scented flowers, spraying up like fireworks. Next, the rock roses (*Helianthemum*) explode into a profusion of yellows, oranges, pinks and reds. The summer is made gay by sky-blue and yellow flax, evening primroses, blue-grey catmint, lavender, thyme and potentillas. Last but not least, the glistening flowers of the water-lilies appear in the ponds.

With autumn come the carline thistle, mountain asters, mints, the thick carpets of flowers belonging to the various sedums, the lovely cups of the meadow saffron and autumn crocus, the fire-coloured berries of cotoneaster and berberis, the last white-flowering saxifrage (*Saxifraga fortunei*) and, as a precious parting gift, the shining blue trumpets of the autumn gentians (*Gentiana farreri*, *G. sino-ornata* and *G. scabra* and their hybrids). In early winter the first Christmas roses flower (*Helleborus niger* 'Praecox'), often emerging at Christmas-tide from sudden snow-storms, just as its larger-flowered relative from the southern Alps, *H. niger macranthus*, does later on, at Shrove-tide.

Rock gardens do not require a great deal of attention during the summer. Weeds and pests must be continuously combatted. Thorough watering, in the evening, is only necessary during particularly severe droughts. Otherwise, the plants may be refreshed and the humidity of the air increased, by spraying lightly over them in the evening. Plants which grow too fast and encroach on their neighbours should be controlled by pulling up part of them, or cutting them back, and dead flowers should be removed immediately they have faded, unless the seed is wanted. This is especially important with plants which can become a nuisance by self-seeding, such as alyssum, *Papaver nudicaule* and *Primula denticulata*.

Unsuccessful combinations of plants can be rearranged in the late summer. Experience shows that not even a rock gardener can remember everything, so it is a good idea to note down any necessary alterations or additions in advance. Since almost all small shrubs and alpines are raised in pots or containers, one can be sure that they will establish at practically any time of year.

Most bulbs, however, should be planted only in the autumn. New strains and varieties are constantly being produced, whether of crocus (*Crocus chrysanthus*), dwarf tulips (hybrids of *Tulipa kaufmanniana* and *Tulipa greigii*), *Iris reticulata*, or the hybrids of the much-loved, dwarf narcissi (*Narcissus cyclamineus* and *N. triandrus*). All these must be planted in autumn if they are to give pleasure in the spring, as well as *Scilla* and *Chionodoxa*, grape-hyacinths (*Muscari*), fritillaries, *Erythronium* and so on. Whenever it is possible, snowdrops (*Galanthus*) should be planted immediately after flowering, whilst meadow saffron and autumn crocus should be planted in early autumn.

The last work to be undertaken in late autumn is providing protective covering for some rock plants. Most of them are hardy but one never knows in advance whether the winter will be snowy (in which case the snow will provide the best possible natural, light cover for the plants) or not, so that it is best to take precautions. Evergreen herbaceous plants and shrubs, especially those growing on south-facing slopes and dry-stone walls, can be covered with conifer branches, preferably of pine, to protect them from the winter sun, which can be very damaging in severe climates.

(1) *Erythronium dens-canis* (enlarged), a striking woodlander with greenish-brown dappled leaves and lily-like flowers. (2) *Pulsatilla slavica*, one of the prettiest of these flowers. (3) *Ranunculus calandrinioides*, a large-flowered buttercup from the Atlas Mountains.

Evergreen shrubs should be thoroughly watered, if the autumn has been dry, and then covered around the base with compost, peat and leaves or pine-needles. This layer should not be removed in the spring, and all types of shrub, especially rhododendrons, will be grateful for it, since it prevents the ground drying out later. Smaller plants, such as cyclamen, respond well to a looser covering of pine-needles or salt hay, but these must be removed early in the year. Plants which are especially sensitive to winter damp, such as *Meconopsis regia* and others with overwintering rosettes of leaves are best covered with rigid, translucent plastic sheets of an appropriate size. A loose layer of brushwood should be spread first to allow air to circulate freely, the sheeting is laid over this, with a further layer of conifer twigs on top. A similar arrangement can be used to protect the choicer alpines in rock garden beds, where the sheeting can rest on rocks and be weighted down with a few heavy stones.

The plants

The number of plants which can be grown in the rock garden is almost incalculable. It would be as impossible to list them all here as it would be to assemble them all in one garden. I shall try to mention at least all those which I feel are especially worthy of notice by both beginner and expert.

Herbaceous plants

Acaena (Rosaceae)
These undemanding plants from South America, Australia and New Zealand like sun and light soil. Their fast-growing shoots form large, flat, grey or brownish carpets of pinnate leaves with decorative, round, thorny fruits in summer. They are useful for paving and ground-cover and look splendid with bulbs planted amongst them. They also look well in combination with contorted dwarf shrubs. The best species is *A. microphylla*, of which the excellent variety 'Copper Carpet' is a striking reddish-brown. *A. buchananii*, *A. glaucophylla* and *A. novae-zealandiae* can also be recommended. 'Blue Haze' has particularly fine bronze-tinged, blue-grey foliage.

Acantholimon, Prickly Thrift (Plumbaginaceae)
These evergreen plants from Turkey and Iran make spiny cushions and enjoy a dry position in full sun. They do best in crevices in tufa, in crannies in dry-stone walls and in steep, well-drained, south-facing sites. All like limestone chips mixed into the soil. Only pot-grown specimens can be established; old plants do not move well. One of the most attractive species is *A. olivieri* (*A. venustum*), with grey, spiny cushions and clear pink flowers. *A. glumaceum*, with its dark-green foliage, and *A. androsaceum* with its thick, short, grey foliage, are also well worth growing.

Acanthus, Bear's foot (Acanthaceae)
While *A. balcanicus* and *A. spinosus* are decorative foliage plants for larger gardens, there is a dwarf variety suitable for the rock garden. *A. dioscoridis perringii*, from Turkey and Iran, has beautiful spikes of pink-lipped flowers one foot (30–40 cm) high, if given a really hot, dry position or grown in a raised bulb-bed.

Achillea, Milfoil, Yarrow (Compositae)
The best species are *A. ageratifolia*, *A. serbica*, *A. clavennae*, *A. umbellata* and the hybrids × *kellereri*, × *jaborneggi*, and × *kolbiana*, with their silver foliage and white blossoms. They look very well with thymes, campanulas and veronicas. *A. rupestris* is also worthwhile, with its abundant white flowers over cut, green leaves. All these grow only six to eight inches (15–20 cm) high and flower from May to July.

Of the yellow-flowering species, *A. chrysocoma* and *A. tomentosa* with golden-yellow heads over mats of woolly leaves can be recommended. All are extremely easy in any well-drained soil with plenty of sun.

Aconitum, Monkshood (Ranunculaceae)

While there are truly dwarf, high-alpine monkshoods from North America and Asia, such as Himalayan *A. hookeri* and *A. kashmiricum*, none has yet settled down and proved a good, reliable garden plant. We are left with the more stalwart meadow plants and woodlanders which, while far too large for the rock garden, are splendid wild-garden plants. European *A. anthora* is dwarfer than most, not much more than two feet (60 cm), with dense spikes of yellowish flowers. It is at home in sunnier positions planted between blocks of limestone. The hybrid 'Ivorine' grows three feet (90 cm) tall with ivory-white flowers. Among the large rich, violet blue hybrids of European *A. napellus* and Asian *A. carmichaelii*, 'Sparks Variety', 'Arendsii' and 'Barker's Variety' are notable but about five feet (150 cm) high.

Acorus, Sweet Flag (Araceae)

A. calamus 'Variegatus' with its rush-like clumps of cream-and-green sword-shaped leaves should only be planted on the banks of large ponds. *A. gramineus pusillus* is a dwarf with dark-green, grassy tufts of leaves and can be used in the smallest areas. It is extraordinarily adaptable and will grow in and under water, as well as on dry ground. There is a pretty white-striped form, *A. gramineus* 'Variegatus'.

Actinella (Compositae)

These small herbaceous plants from the drier ranges of western North America have rosettes of downy, grey leaves, and yellow, daisy-like flowers resembling small gaillardias. They are happiest in dry, narrow crevices in full sun. *A. acaulis*, *A. scaposa* and *A. grandiflora*, with disproportionately large flowers, can be worth searching lists for, and are sometimes included under *Hymenoxys* or *Rydbergia*.

Adenophora (Campanulaceae)

These pretty, campanula-like flowers from north-east Asia resemble each other closely and like a good soil in sun or half-shade. Most species have blue flowers, like tall *A. bulleyana*, *A. forrestii* and *A. polymorpha tashiroi*, but the rare *A. liliifolia infundibuliformis* has beautiful hanging white bells. These are rather tall for the rock garden though there are dwarfer, alpine species, such as the Japanese *A. howozana*.

Adonis (Ranunculaceae) p. 69

These are beautiful, anemone-like spring flowers with finely cut, feathery foliage. Golden *A. amurensis*, of which there are many Japanese garden varieties, is the earliest species to flower. Two weeks later comes its double form, opening its full yellow blossoms with greenish hearts. These should not be put in too dry a position but *A. vernalis* from the Steppes is happiest in a sunny position, with lime-rubble mixed into the soil. *A. brevistyla* from Tibet likes humus, and plenty of moisture during the growing season. Its white cups open later in spring from bluish, silky buds. *A. pyrenaica* is also later flowering. It has yellow flowers like *A. vernalis* but is a much rarer, more demanding species.

(1) *Adonis amurensis* often flowers in February. (2) *Euryops acraeus*, a small, bushy shrub from South Africa, which loves sun. (3) *Oenothera missouriensis*, a lush and easy plant.

69

Aethionema (Cruciferae)

A. saxatile (*A. graecum*) is only a biennial but it sows itself without becoming a nuisance. In spring, pale-pink flowers cover its small bushes. *A.* (*Eunomia*) *oppositifolium* also blooms in spring, with pale-lilac flowers above its blue-grey, creeping, fleshy rosettes. *A. iberideum* can be extremely rewarding when in early spring it covers its wide, thick bushes with white flowers. The most attractive species, one of the loveliest of all rock garden plants, is *A. grandiflorum* (*A. pulchellum*), a sub-shrub from Turkey and Iran, which has cylindrical clusters of sweet-scented pink flowers in summer. The dwarfer hybrids, 'Warley Rose' and 'Warley Ruber', have deeper pink flowers. All species are lovers of sun and warmth and are indispensable for dry-stone walls.

Agave (Agavaceae)

A. megalacantha and *A. parryi* are but two of the cold-climate representatives of this large American genus. Both of these are fairly hardy, if protected from moisture in winter. Their unusual appearance means that they are only suitable for specialized, succulent-gardens, where they strike an exotic note, especially when protected from excessive damp under glass. The South African *Aloe aristata* has similar qualities and is equally hardy if kept dry in winter.

Ajuga, Bugle (Labiatae)

A. reptans forms thick spreading mats of rosettes, which are adorned in early summer with blue whorls of flowers. The bright-pink 'Rosea', 'Multicolor', with its mottled brownish-green, yellow, and reddish leaves and the white-variegated 'Variegata' are all attractive. However, the most striking is *A. reptans* 'Atropurpurea', with reddish-brown carpets of leaves contrasting with deep-blue flowers. All are useful ground-cover where the soil is not too dry, looking delightful between

pink *Primula rosea* and gold marsh marigolds, but are too invasive for small rock gardens.

A. pyramidalis does not produce runners but forms beautiful, regular pagodas of blue flowers among reddish bracts. It can stand a drier position but needs a rich soil. The strange *A.p.* 'Crispa' is very dwarf with tightly crinkled foliage.

The annual or biennial *A. chamaepitys* is a real drought-lover. It has pure yellow, long-lasting, lipped flowers in summer.

Alchemilla, Lady's Mantle (Rosaceae)

One of the best-known and effective species is *A. mollis*. It forms mounds of downy, grey-green leaves up to a foot (30 cm) in height, covered in early summer with greenish-yellow veils of flower. It is a great joy when its large leaves glisten with drops of dew or rain. It is a very easy plant, growing equally well in sun or shade, but seeds itself so freely that it can be a nuisance in small gardens. *A. hoppeana*, *A. alpina* and others with silky, silver hairs lining the backs of their lobed leaves, are also attractive and will flourish in most places.

Alyssum (Cruciferae)   p. 153

The golden-yellow *A. saxatile* and its various forms, the dwarf 'Compactum', the bright sulphur-yellow 'Citrinum', pale biscuit-yellow 'Dudley Neville' and the double golden-yellow 'Plenum' are so well-known and loved as plants for dry-stone walls that nothing more need be said in their favour. *A. murale* (*A. argenteum*) is an extremely undemanding summer-flowering plant, growing a foot (30 cm) high, but can become a nuisance through self-seeding. *A. moellendorfianum* and *A. montanum* are early-flowering creeping species which look very attractive on sunny slopes between aubrietas. The more distinctly shrubby alyssums will be found under *Ptilotrichum*.

Amaracus see **Origanum**

Anacyclus (Compositae)
These North African sun-lovers form rosettes of much-divided leaves with daisy-like flowers which hug the ground. At night, and in wet weather, they shut and show the bright red backs of their petals, but they open in sunshine to pure white. All require a very well-drained soil and resent dampness in winter. *A. depressus* is the best-known and most reliable species but there are several others on a similar pattern.

Anagallis, Pimpernel (Primulaceae)
The forms of the giant Scarlet Pimpernel from Spain *A. monelli* (*A. collina, A. linifolia*) flower all summer in rose-red, soft brick-orange or deep gentian-blue. While true perennials, they tend to flower themselves to death, though they can sow themselves in sunny, well-drained places. The Bog Pimpernel has precisely opposite needs of cool soil which is evenly moist and never dries out. When suited, *A. tenella* 'Studland', though collected on the coast of southern England, shows all the qualities of the finest high-alpines, forming wide cushions of tiny, rounded leaves, smothered in summer with small stemless, pink, starry bells. It makes a superb specimen in a pot.

Anaphalis (Compositae)
Grey-leaved herbaceous plants are always useful as an effective contrast to other colours. Among such plants we must include the silvery everlasting flowers and downy, white leaves of *A. triplinervis, A. nubigena* and the hybrid 'Summer Snow', which grow to about twelve inches (30 cm) high. These are easy, fast-growing plants with yellowish-white, papery flowers in summer, and look well beside such plants as *Berberis thunbergii* and red-berried cotoneasters.

Anchusa (Boraginaceae)
A. angustissima loves the sun and dry positions, where it makes bristly, green rosettes covered, throughout summer, with gentian-blue flowers on branched stems about eighteen inches (30–50 cm) in height. *A. caespitosa* is an outstanding plant for the alpine house. A native of the Crete mountains, its neat tufts grow tight to the ground and its pure, deep-blue flowers are almost stemless. In a pot, it requires frequent re-potting as it dislikes starvation.

Androsace (Primulaceae)
The species of this delightful genus which grow best in the garden are those from furthest off, namely the stoloniferous species from the Himalayas: *A. primuloides, A. sarmentosa,* and the charming *A. sempervivoides*. In early summer they produce lovely pink, primula-like flowers but they are also attractive during the rest of the year, with their neat rosettes and, in some cases, autumn colours. Lilac-pink *A. lanuginosa* which dies back in winter, and its garden form 'Leichtlinii' are also natives of the Himalayas flowering late, from midsummer. *A. strigillosa* has loose umbels of flowers, red-backed but white above, on long stems about nine inches (20 cm) high.

Of the Europeans, the most worthwhile and reliable is *A. carnea* and its subspecies: *laggeri* from the Pyrenees with its mossy cushions and pure pink flowers, *brigantiaca* with white flowers and *rosea* (*halleri*) with pink flowers. The tiny, bright-pink *A. hedraeantha* from the Balkans is similar. They thrive best in gritty, lime-free, humus-rich soil, in slightly shaded positions. White *A. villosa* and its ruby-pink Himalayan variety *jacquemontii*, with mats of silver, downy leaves, are lovers of sun and lime, as is *A. lactea*, with spreading, white flower-heads.

For the experienced specialist, there is the Aretia section—the tight-cushioned species from high altitudes: *A. ciliata* with deep-pink flowers, and *A. mathildae*, *A. vandellii* (*imbricata*), *A. pubescens*, *A. hirtella*, *A. cylindrica* and *A. pyrenaica* with white flowers. These and the rounded, grey-green *A. helvetica* will grow best in deep pots in a very well-drained, gritty soil in the alpine-house.

Pink or white *A. alpina* (*A. glacialis*) and its bright pink relatives *A. brevis* and *A. wulfeniana* are difficult plants to cultivate, growing best in raised scree beds, covered in winter, or in pots, plunged outside in summer. The recently introduced Himalayan species enjoy similar cool, summer conditions. Of these, pink or white *A. globifera*, *A. delavayi* and *A. muscoidea* grow without too much trouble but seldom cover their woolly cushions with flower, so continue to test the skill of the enthusiast, who considers the cultivation of these high alpines one of the greatest and most rewarding challenges.

Andryala (Compositae)

A. aghardii is a four-inch high (10 cm) cliff plant from southern Spain, which must have full sun in a dry position and bears lemon-yellow, hawkweed-like flowers over its silver-grey rosettes of felted leaves, in the summer. It is a first-class, neat foliage plant for the alpine-house.

Anemone, Wind Flower (Ranunculaceae)

The garden varieties of the Wood Anemone *A. nemorosa* are most lovely early spring flowers: 'Allenii', the largest, lavender-blue; 'Blue Bonnet', azure-blue and silver on the outside, with bronze-green leaves; 'Robinsoniana', pale lavender-blue; 'Leeds Variety', a very large, pure white; 'Rosea', white with pink tones outside. *A. ranunculoides* is similar with deep-golden flowers and brownish-green foliage, whilst *A. trifolia* is the last of these to flower in May, with pure white blossoms over its tripartite leaves. All of these are for woodland conditions, with light shade and leaf-covered soil. The elongated rhizomes should be planted in groups in early autumn to mingle with lungwort, primulas, woodsorrel and ferns.

A. apennina and *A. blanda* from southern Europe require more sun and open their violet-blue flowers in March, along with *Adonis amurensis*. There are many garden varieties of *A. blanda*, of which the prettiest is 'Atrocoerulea', with dark violet-blue flowers. Both naturalize well in grass.

A. sylvestris is a lime-lover, which thrives in both sun and half-shade, and produces white flowers on one foot (30 cm) stems in great abundance in May, but it can become a nuisance in light soil by spreading too far.

In the early summer come the lovely upright branching heads of *A. narcissiflora* and *A. multifida*, with white or pinkish flowers, and *A. × lesseri* with crimson flowers. They look well planted between dwarf junipers but do not like to be too dry.

Of the attractive Japanese autumn anemones, few are dwarf enough even for large rock gardens. The neater hybrids of *A. hupehensis* are 'September Charm', pink; 'Praecox', reddish-pink; 'Splendens', dark-pink. All are about eighteen inches (50 cm) high, flower from August to October and look very effective alongside *Anaphalis*, *Cotoneaster* and *Berberis*. After flowering they have attractive, woolly, grey seed-heads.

Among the Himalayan species for cool, rich, moist soil are *A. rivularis* with two foot (30 cm) branching heads of blue-backed, pearly white

(1) *Aster alpinus* often grows near (3) the downy Hawkweed (*Hieracium villosum*) on stony alpine meadows or rocky outcrops in the limestone Alps. (2) *Cyananthus lobatus* is a member of the Campanulaceae family from the Himalayas, which likes acid, sandy, humus-rich soil.

cups and prostrate *A. obtusiloba* with its form *patula*. The latter is known as the Blue Butter-cup and is precisely this, both in its foliage and its radiating stems of rich, lavender-blue butter-cups, which only achieve their full depth of colour in acid, peaty conditions in cool gardens. Hot, dry gardens, however, can enjoy the tuberous-rooted Anemones from the Mediter-ranean, such as the brilliant scarlet forms of *A. pavonina* and dainty, mauve or pink *A. hor-tensis*. The charming, shell-pink *A. tschernajewii* from Kashmir is usually offered as *A. biflora*, which is a very different tuberous species, from Iran, usually with striking red flowers and a challenge to grow.

Anemonopsis (Ranunculaceae)
A. macrophylla from Japan grows up to about two feet (60 cm) high, and has nodding, lilac, waxen columbine-flowers in August. It requires humus-rich soil and looks at its best with ferns, among shady rocks or in the peat bed.

Antennaria (Compositae)
A. dioica has pretty, pink, 'everlasting' flowers on grey carpets. It is a plant of poor heathland and grows best in sandy, lime-free soil in the garden. *A. dioica* 'Rubra' is a dark rose-red; *A. dioica borealis* (*A. tomentosa*) has white blossoms on attractive thick grey mats. *A. plantaginifolia* from North America has broad, plantain-shaped leaves and greenish-white heads.

Anthemis, Chamomile (Compositae)
One of the prettiest species is *A. biebersteiniana*, with its shimmering green, dissected leaves and golden-yellow daisies in summer on stiff eight-inch (20 cm) stalks. The selection 'Tetra' has larger heads. White-flowering *A. carpatica* is small and attractive and the Bulgarian *A. sancti-johannis* grows to one foot in height (30 cm). It is a handsome plant with fiery orange-yellow daisies in summer, lovely in combination with blue *Linum narbonense*. The wide-spreading,

silver carpets and profuse white daisies of *A. cupaniana* look well in sun beside stone-steps or paving.

Anthericum (Liliaceae)
A. liliago and *A. ramosum* are pretty, unde-manding, mountain plants, suitable for the informal garden and looking well planted among brooms and grasses. In early summer their one foot (30 cm) sprays of white stars can contrast with pink heaths and blue globularia.

Anthyllis, Kidney Vetch (Leguminosae)
A. montana 'Rubra' should find a place in every rock garden. It delights in sunny positions, spreading its grey-green mats over the rocks, and bearing an abundance of clover-like, wine-red flowers in summer. It is a slow grower at first but, when it has become established, its beauty and robustness will repay your patience.

Antirrhinum asarina see Asarina

Aphyllanthes (Liliaceae)
A. monspeliensis is a delightful and unusual plant for a really sunny, well-drained position, where it will form clumps of rush-like foliage about eight inches (20 cm) high. Blue starry flowers appear at the tips of these stems in summer. It looks like blue flax, when massed along a Spanish roadside. It dislikes disturbance and should be left alone when established.

Aquilegia, (Ranunculaceae)   pp. 39, 43, 77
A. alpina, the true Alpine columbine, is a lovely mountain plant, but unfortunately it will not grow well in the garden. Its hybrid strain with *A. vulgaris*, 'Hensol Harebell', will prove a satisfactory substitute. *A. bertolonii*, *A. einseleana* and *A. pyrenaica*, with violet-blue flowers, and *A. discolor*, with bright-blue and white flowers, grow only four to twelve inches (10–30 cm) high and are dwarf species from the mountains of Europe. From Japan we have the

four-inch (10 cm) *A. akitensis*, with blue-grey broad-lobed leaves and chubby, blue and white flowers. The similar but taller *A. flabellata* bears lilac-blue or milk-white flowers ('Nana Alba') above thick tufted foliage.

A. (Semiaquilegia) ecalcarata is another lovely Japanese species with small, spurless, dull wine-red flowers, and Siberian *A. viridiflora* has fascinating sombre greenish-chocolate blooms.

The American species of aquilegia are quite different, mostly having long spurs. *A. canadensis*, *A. formosa*, and *A. shockleyi*, have elegantly-shaped orange-red and yellow flowers. *A. scopulorum* is only four to six inches (10–15 cm) high, and with its long-spurred, upright blossoms looks like a dwarf version of *A. caerulea*. In its dwarfest forms it is very similar to *A. jonesii*, which differs in having only short, stubby spurs. Its blue and white flowers sit on tiny tufts of exquisite blue-grey foliage only two inches (5 cm) high. Sadly it is shy-flowering and none too easy to grow, even in the alpine-house. Even tinier, but with proportionately smaller flowers, is *A. laramiensis* with minute, white columbines and dark leaves. Only a little larger is *A. saximontana*, again in blue and white. Apart from these Rocky Mountain species, the enthusiast can find a challenge in *A. nivalis* from the Kashmir Himalaya, with dusky purple flowers with black stamens.

The State flower of Colorado, *A. caerulea* itself, along with many other species, is rather large for the rock garden, but a delight in shady beds. The small species prefer a position, shaded from the full strength of the midday sun, in gritty, humus-rich soil. Their attractive, divided leaves and graceful flowers give them a distinctive charm, best appreciated when they are planted in solitary groups, in rocky nooks or beside dwarf shrubs.

Arabis, Rock Cress (Cruciferae)   **p. 153**
The double *A. caucasica* (*albida*) 'Plena', with its showers of white flowers, the variegated 'Variegata', the lovely pinks of 'Rosea' and 'Rosabella', the deep rose 'Monte Rosa', and the large-flowered, single 'Snowcap' all produce spectacular cushions of flowers in spring. These are perhaps too strong-growing for the small rock garden, but are without rivals wherever there is space. Turkish *A. aubretioides* bears its purplish-pink flowers a little later on, as does the bright carmine-pink *A. blepharophylla* from California, though this is sadly not very long-lived.

A. procurrens and its selection 'New Snow' is a strong grower, with mats of small, bright-green leaves, scattered with white blossoms, which thrives in half-shade. Similar, but more compact and with larger blooms, is *A. ferdinandi-coburgi*, a lovely and rather daintier mountain-plant from Bulgaria. Both of these species are useful evergreen ground-cover. *A. ferdinandi-coburgi* 'Variegata' has striking, variegated white leaves in summer, tinged with red in winter. *A. androsacea* and *A. bryoides* are hairy, white-flowering, cushion-forming plants from the limestones of Turkey and the Balkans for a sunny position in a trough or the alpine-house.

Arenaria (Caryophyllaceae)
All species of *Arenaria* are mat or cushion-forming plants which flower in early summer. *A. montana* from southern Europe is one of the prettiest. In May and June its flat carpets of leaves are covered with its large flowers and it is very effective with thymes, erinus, and small campanulas. *A. balearica* is much more delicate. It grows like moss over moist, shaded rocks and covers itself with tiny, white stars all summer. It is sometimes not completely hardy but survives by self-sowing. *A. gracilis* from Jugoslavia is also attractive. All have white flowers.

A. tetraquetra from the Pyrenees and the even smaller *A. tetraquetra granatensis* (*A. nevadensis*) from the mountains of south-east Spain are real sun-lovers. They do best when planted in scree or in tufa, when their tight cushions of grey-green, starry rosettes flow over the stone, decked with white flowers.

Armeria, Thrift (Plumbaginaceae)
There are many forms of *A. maritima*, the hardy sea-thrift of northern shores: 'Alba', white; 'Düsseldorf Pride', rich red-purple; 'Bloodstone', rosy crimson, eight inches (20 cm) high; 'Vindictive', six inches (15 cm) high, rich rose-pink. *A.* 'Bees' Ruby' has grey-green leaves and pinkish-red flowers on stems twelve inches (30 cm) high. All these are good border-plants but they are also attractive in the rock garden, where their flat carpets can be planted with the stronger-growing bulbs.

A. juniperifolia (*A. caespitosa*) is much more compact and choicer. It is a pretty alpine from Spain which covers its tight cushions in May with bright-pink flowers. 'Roger Bevan' and 'Rubra' are deeper pink selections. The hybrid *A.* × *suendermannii* is easier and only slightly more spreading. It has fresh-pink flowers in May. These should be planted between stones in a sunny, dry position and reveal their full glory in troughs or raised beds.

Arnebia echioides see **Echioides**

Arnica (Compositae)
A. montana is a most lovely golden-yellow daisy of the Alpine meadows, but a very difficult plant to grow well. It will only thrive in acid, humus-rich soil and seldom survives in the garden more than two or three years, though it can be propagated from seed. *A. sachalinensis* and many other species are, on the contrary, rampant and are best avoided.

Artemisia (Compositae)
The small, bushy, silver-leaved species such as *A. nitida*, *A. splendens brachyphylla*, and *A. umbelliformis* (*A. mutellina*) are most attractive. They all need a sunny, airy position in free-draining soil, since they are extremely sensitive to damp. *A. schmidtiana* 'Nana' from Japan is easier and forms soft, silver mats of deeply cut leaves. Two stronger growers are *A. pontica* and the scented *A. vallesiaca* which form small bushes up to eighteen inches (50 cm) in height. The latter is one of the most useful silver-grey plants and looks most attractive with blue *Linum perenne* and *Helictotrichon sempervivens*. *A. stellerana* is also very useful with its low, snow-white, downy shoots and broad-lobed leaves. A very compact form of this collected in Japan is known as 'Boughton Silver'. *A. assoana*, a small Spanish race of the fine but large *A. pedemontana*, is choice and tiny enough for a trough or the alpine-house.

Asarina (Scrophulariaceae)
A. procumbens (*Antirrhinum asarina*) is a crevice-plant, especially suitable for sunny and half-shaded positions in dry-stone walls. Its shoots with their soft yellow snapdragons can hang down to three feet (one metre). It will occasionally fail to survive over winter but usually seeds itself.

Asarum (Aristolochiaceae)
A. europaeum is a small running, European woodland plant and has its uses in the rock garden. It will cover the bare ground with its dark, evergreen leaves, in difficult shaded positions where very little else will grow—beneath pine trees for instance. The

(1) *Helichrysum milfordiae*, from South Africa. (2) *Onosma stellulatum*, from the Balkans. (3) *Viola × florairensis*, a vigorous pansy. (4) *Aquilegia akitensis*, a bicolor dwarf columbine from Japan. (5) *Hypericum olympicum*, a rewarding summer flower. (6) The two foot (60 cm) alpine thistle, *Eryngium alpinum*.

American *A. caudatum* and *A. shuttle-worthii* are similar with more intriguing flowers, if you are prepared to search for them beneath the leaves.

Asperula (Rubiaceae)

The Sweet Woodruff (formerly *A. odorata*, now *Galium odoratum*) can become a nuisance by growing too rampantly, and is only suitable for rough, wild places, where it should be planted in shady corners amongst columbines, Turk's-cap lilies and ferns. *A. tinctoria* is a wiry-stemmed plant some twelve to twenty inches (30–50 cm) high, which has white clusters in June, and should be planted on sunny slopes in the rock garden, next to violet-blue *Aster amellus*, for instance. Its beauty does not compare, however, with that of its relatives from the mountains of Greece and Turkey, the rock-dwelling *A. nitida*, with its crisp, grey-green cushions and tiny pink flowers, or of *A. arcadiensis* (*A. suberosa* of gardens) with slender stems clothed in downy leaves and salmon-pink, long-tubed flowers in May. A well established cushion of this last species is one of the most beautiful sights the rock garden can offer. All that this needs is a sunny, dry niche in the rocks or a crevice in a dry-stone wall. Unfortunately the scented flowers can be spoilt by a May downpour, but if the plant is grown in an alpine-house it will remain in its full glory for at least two weeks. *A. hirta* from the Pyrenees can fill whole rock crevices with its loose, green cushions, covered with pinkish-white flowers in May. *A. lilaciflora caespitosa* from Turkey prefers a flat or only slightly sloping position, where its cushions of dark-green needles are crowded in early summer with long-lasting pink flowers.

Asphodelus and Asphodeline, Asphodel (Liliaceae)

A. ramosus and *A. albus* are characteristic plants of poor mountain pastures in southern Europe. Their three-foot (one metre) high white flower-spikes and narrow grey-green, foliage appear in summer. They are effective with dwarf pines, grasses and yuccas in large informal gardens, as are the similar but bright yellow *Asphodeline lutea* and *A. liburnica*. The only really dwarf species, however, is *A. acaulis* from the Moroccan Atlas Mountains. Its clusters of soft-pink stars are almost stemless and appear in early spring from the tufts of narrow, grassy foliage. It lies dormant in summer and repays dry treatment, covered in a raised bed or a deep pot in the alpine-house.

Aster (Compositae)

A. bellidiastrum (*Bellidiastrum michelii*) is the first to bloom. Its large daisy-like flowers on slender stems, while not of exceptional beauty, are attractive in a damp and shady position.

A. alpinus is the outstanding mountain aster and a joy to behold in May and June, both in the mountains and in the garden. Attractive garden varieties are 'Albus', white; 'Susanne', double white; 'Abendschein', pinkish-red; 'Frühlicht', and 'Dunkle Schöne', deep violet. They make a lovely contrast with white edelweiss and pink *Dianthus sylvestris*.

Its clear-lilac hybrid *A. × alpellus*, which is the next to flower, is also attractive. In spring and early summer come the eighteen-inch (50 cm) Himalayan asters, *A. tongolensis* (*A. yunnanensis*, *A. subcaeruleus*) violet-blue 'Leuchtenburg', 'Wartburgstern' and 'Sternschnuppe'; lilac-blue 'Berggarten' and 'Napsbury', all of which look well both in the garden and as cut flowers, with their many-petalled, dark-lilac daisies with orange-yellow centres.

Colour in late summer comes with *A. amellus*, when its different tones of violet are very welcome. It is followed by the profuse flowers of the dwarf Michaelmas Daisies, hybrids of *A. dumosus*, with mounds of white, pink and violet-blue, beloved of bees and butterflies. They should be used in formal rock gardens, and make good edging-plants in borders as well.

Aster sedifolius (*A. acris*) 'Nanus' is equally bushy and grows one foot high (30 cm), retaining more of the character of a wild flower, with its lavender-blue or pink (*A. sedifolius* 'Nanus Roseus') stars.

Astilbe (Saxifragaceae)

While the many, tall *A.* × *arendsii* hybrids look misplaced in the rock garden, the hybrids between these and *A. simplicifolia* in white and various shades of pink are suitable for formal surroundings, growing only about eighteen inches (30–50 cm) high. They should be planted with *Epimedium* and ferns in slightly shaded positions. Most of these are of German origin and are well worth searching for. 'Dunkellachs' and 'Bronze Elegance' add the attraction of bronze-tinted foliage to their pink sprays, as does the English hybrid 'Sprite', a vigorous plant with shell-pink flowers, and the excellent Scottish hybrid 'William Buchanan', which is even neater, and creamy white. The wild plant from Japan, *A. simplicifolia* itself, is rather rare but quite exquisite with its six-inch (15 cm) white sprays from slowly spreading clumps of distinctive, toothed but undissected, foliage. This and the following are excellent in a peat bed or other cool, rich shady situation.

A. × *crispa* 'Lilliput' and 'Perkeo', with crinkly leaves and pink spikes, also grow only six inches (15 cm) high, but they are more curious than attractive.

A. chinensis 'Pumila' from China is about twelve inches (30 cm) high and forms dense colonies. Its spires of lilac-pink flowers look somewhat stiff but it provides useful late flowers in August and September. The tiny, four-inch (10 cm) Japanese plant grown in gardens as *A. glaberrima saxatilis* is much daintier with its dark-green, curiously-shaped, pinnate leaves forming close mats and upright, pink sprays of flowers in July.

Astragalus and Oxytropis (Leguminosae)

These large genera, which are such a feature of the dry steppes of south-west Asia, North America and the Andes, seem very reluctant to settle down in gardens. *A. angustifolius*, with its thick spiky cushions, revels in full sun and stony soil. It can never be too hot or dry and only produces white blossoms from its six-inch (15 cm) cushions of needles in such conditions. *A. alopecuroides*, also a great lover of warmth, grows to two feet six inches (80 cm) tall, with thick shoots and woolly, yellow balls of flowers from the axils of its divided leaves.

The four-inch (10 cm) *O. halleri* (*O. sericea*) from the central Alps is worthy of note. It has silken-haired, pinnate leaves, violet-purple blossoms and likes gravelly soil.

Astrantia (Umbelliferae)

While pink *A. maxima* and variable, green-tinged *A. major* are indispensable in the wild garden, *A. pauciflora* and *A. minor* are dwarf species growing only eight inches (20 cm) high. They are plants for the connoisseur, who will take pleasure in their finely divided leaves and dainty, parchment-white flowers. All are woodland plants, enjoying some shade and a humus-rich soil.

Athamanta (Umbelliferae)

A. haynaldii looks like filigree-work in summer when its white flower heads rise over its eight-inch tall (20 cm), bright green bushes of finely divided thread-like leaves. This sun-loving plant should be planted in a deep, vertical hole in a block of tufa, or in a dry-stone wall, where it will give pleasure for decades.

Aubrieta, Rock Cress (Cruciferae)   p. 153

There is no need to waste words in describing the beauty and advantages of this well known cushion-forming plant, which is indispensable for dry-stone walls and terraces. Of the many different varieties, the following are some of the best. Blue-violet shades: 'Schloss Eckberg', 'Triumphant', 'Neuling', 'Dr Mules'; pink and purple: 'Bressingham Pink', 'Red Carpet', 'Maurice Prichard', 'Rosengarten', 'Firebird', 'Vesuvius' and the double 'Bob Saunders'. Aubrieta will create an explosion of colour in April and May if planted along with *Arabis caucasica, Iberis, Phlox* and *Alyssum*.

Azorella (Umbelliferae)

A. trifurcata is a curious dwarf from the southern tip of South America, forming dense, evergreen mounds of stiff, spiky rosettes. The small, yellowish flowers are of no interest but its large, shining, dark-green cushions provide a contrast to the strong colours of the rock garden. It looks especially striking when covered with hoar-frost in winter.

Bellis, Daisy (Compositae)

The tiniest of the double daisies, *B. perennis*, are pink 'Dresden China', crimson 'Rob Roy' and dark red 'Brilliant'. These dainty flowers last well in spring but they must be divided and replanted frequently. The pale lavender-blue *B. rotundifolia coerulescens*, which likes a rather sheltered moist position, is the pretty, North African race.

Bergenia (Saxifragaceae)

Bergenias are among the hardiest of garden plants and will grow in any soil, in sun or shade. They have a very distinctive appearance, with their large, round, leathery leaves and dense heads of flowers in early spring, and are not to everyone's taste. Most are best suited to spacious rock work near large blocks of stone or in the vicinity of water (though not in wet soil), or they may be planted in generous numbers near paving and on dry-stone walls. Among the most attractive species are *B. cordifolia, B. purpurascens* and its hybrids. 'Abendglut', with its crimson flowers and

excellent, low foliage, is one of the dwarfest of these but the only one truly suited to the small rock garden is the Himalayan *B. stracheyi* in white or pink and only nine inches (20 cm) high.

Biscutella (Cruciferae)

The variable, short-lived *B. laevigata* is an undemanding plant which blooms in May and June and is reminiscent of *Alyssum*. Its bright-yellow heads standing eight inches (20 cm) high look pretty amongst dwarf alpine asters in a dry place. The disc-shaped seed pods are also attractive.

Bletilla see Orchids

Boykinia (Saxifragaceae)

B. jamesii, from humus-filled crevices in the Colorado Rockies, presents a challenge if it is to flower well. It grows happily in a cool position outside in summer, forming slowly spreading mats of rounded leaves, but really needs confining in very rich gritty compost to produce its six-inch (15 cm) spikes of brilliant cherry-red flowers in late spring, which it will do when it becomes pot-bound. This may also be found under the generic name *Telesonix*.

Briggsia and other Asian Gesneriaceae p. 55

Like the European Gesneriaceae (see under *Haberlea*), *B. aurantiaca* is a rosette-forming plant with glossy, wrinkled, slightly bristly leaves. Its light-yellow, tubular flowers with their insides dotted with red and their three-pointed lips appear in May to June, and look

---

(1) *Geranium cinereum subcaulescens* 'Splendens' from the mountains of Macedonia. (2) *Dianthus pavonius* (*neglectus*), a lovely pink from the western Alps which forms thick mats. (3) *Pleione limprichtii*, a hardy orchid from China.

somewhat like yellow foxgloves. This is a charming plant for the skilled grower, best cultivated in the alpine-house. Its requirements are the same as those of *Ramonda*, though it likes more moisture in the summer.

B. muscicola has leaves like apple-green velvet and tubular pale-yellow flowers. Both species are sometimes grown as *B. penlopii*. There is an interesting hybrid of *B. aurantiaca*, raised in East Germany and called × *Brigandra* (*Gomiocharis*) *calliantha*, which has beautifully marked flowers of a soft orange-pink. The other parent is the pale lilac-flowered, Japanese *Opithandra* (*Chirita*) *primuloides*. Also from Japan is the tuberous-rooted *Conandron ramondioides* with pale purple or white, starry, *Ramonda*-like flowers. Its rosettes of wrinkled, glossy green leaves disappear in winter, when it should be kept dry. *Petrocosmea kerrii* with pure white flowers and lilac *P. parryorum* and *P. nervosa*, like all the above, can be grown in the cool shade beneath the staging of the (preferably frost-free) alpine-house.

Brunnera (Boraginaceae)

B. macrophylla is a spring-flowering plant with large, heart-shaped leaves, and it likes a slightly shaded position in cool soil. Its scented blue flowers look best beside orange *Geum coccineum* and yellow *Epimedium* in the more spacious, wild garden, as it is rather large and coarse for the small rock garden.

Bulbinella (Liliaceae)

B. hookeri is a foot high (30 cm) native of New Zealand, and resembles a miniature red-hot poker. It forms loose rosettes of grooved leaves, from which golden-yellow pyramidal spikes rise in summer. It likes lime-free, peaty soil, and needs protecting in winter, in severe climates. *B. rossii* is not seen so often in gardens but is equally good, with broader heads of slightly larger flowers.

Calamintha see Satureja

Calandrinia (Portulacaceae)

These small, fleshy alpines are centered on the South American Andes. Several white-flowered species, rather like unexciting white Lewisias, have been introduced. *C. umbellata* has narrow leaves, and shining reddish-violet flowers from July to September. The variety 'Amaranth' is also an attractive colour. These sun-loving, long-flowering plants look best when planted with *Sedums*, *Sempervivums* and other succulents. Protect from winter damp or grow in the alpine-house.

Calceolaria (Scrophulariaceae)   p. 89

This is an extraordinary and exclusively South American genus. *C. biflora* with its flat rosettes, *C. acutifolia* (*C. polyrrhiza*), which forms spreading mats, and their large-flowered hybrid 'John Innes' are irresistible in summer with their red-speckled, yellow pouches. They go well with *Mazus* and *Mimulus cupreus*, which share their need of a position which stays cool and moist, with plenty of peat and grit, and shaded from the midday sun. Several other interesting species can be grown in the alpine house, such as *C. arachnoidea*, covered entirely with white down and with clusters of dull-purple flowers. *C. cana* is similar but tawny-yellow. *C. darwinii* from southern Argentina has low-growing rosettes of leaves from which its flowers rise on two-inch (5 cm) stems, like fat brownish-yellow dwarfs with white belts. Hairy-leaved *C. fothergillii* from the Falkland Islands is similar but lacks the white band. There are hybrids between them. Both need a rich, gritty soil and detest drought. They grow best with cool, moist summers and cold, dry winters. *C. tenella* is easier and creeps over cool rocks or peaty soil with mats of tiny bright-green leaves which are adorned with abundant lemon-yellow pouches on thread-like stalks.

Callianthemum (Ranunculaceae)

C. anemonoides (*C. rutifolium*), *C. kernerianum*,

and *C. coriandrifolium* are alpines for the skilled connoisseur. Their anemone-like flowers, white or tinged with pale-pink, appear in spring and the plants die back after flowering. They like deep, gravelly soil which is cool and moist, and seldom flower freely in gardens but their finely cut, grey-green foliage is always a pleasure.

Caltha, Marsh Marigold (Ranunculaceae)
C. palustris 'Flore Pleno' is a long-flowering, double marsh marigold with deep-gold flowers and *C. palustris alba* from the Himalayas has white flowers. They look pretty beside pink *Primula rosea*, where their colours make an effective contrast. They should be planted on the damp banks of a stream or pool. The Australian alpine, *C. introloba*, has strange, pinkish-white flowers but enjoys the same sort of site or peat-bed conditions.

Campanula, (Campanulaceae) pp. 23, 85
Campanulas are among the loveliest of rock garden flowers and there is a wide diversity in their qualities, from those which dance high in the air on thin stalks to those which hug the ground with giant bells; their flowers vary from long, thin funnels to wide, flat bowls and cups, and even spreading stars, almost invariably in some shade of blue or white. Their worst enemies are slugs and snails, which prefer the finest, daintiest and rarest species and will consume them overnight, and mice, which even eat the hardier species, like *C. carpatica*, during the winter when they are covered with a carpet of snow.

The preferences of campanulas in the garden are as wide as their variety. The majority are small and grow happily in sun and half-shade in all types of rock gardens, on dry-stone terraces or in the crevices between paving. The following species grow only four to eight inches high (10–20 cm): *C. cochlearifolia* (*C. pusilla*), *C. carpatica*, and its lovely varieties: 'Blue Clips', sky-blue; 'Blue Moonlight', silvery-blue, and

'White Clips', white; *C. fenestrellata*, *C. garganica*, the unparalleled *C. portenschlagiana* (one of the most useful of all rock garden plants) and *C. tommasiniana* with its narrow lavender-blue bells. The dark-blue 'G. F. Wilson' is very free-flowering and is a hybrid of the delicate deep purple *C. pulla*. *C. poscharskyana* produces long prostrate shoots with star-shaped flowers. There are several useful varieties of this strong-growing species, such as the bright-blue 'Stella'. All these are extremely easy plants for larger areas, where they can spread without making a nuisance of themselves. For small rock gardens and troughs one can recommend the charming, neat *C. waldsteiniana*, *C. pilosa*, the hybrid *C. × wockei*, as well as the group of species from the Caucasus: *C. tridentata*, the earliest campanula, with lilac-blue flowers in April/May, and the very similar, violet *C. aucheri* and *C. saxifraga*. Nor should lavender-blue *C. barbata*, a short-lived, lime-hating alpine-meadow plant, be forgotten. It looks very well with orange *Arnica* and can be planted with it in the peat bed. There are many more demanding species to test the skill of those prepared to cosset them in troughs, raised beds or in the alpine-house: *C. arvatica*, *C. allionii* (*C. alpestris*), *C. cashmiriana*, *C. cenisia*, *C. excisa* (lime-hating), *C. mirabilis*, *C. morettiana*, *C. piperi*, *C. raineri* and *C. zoysii*.

Cardamine, Lady's Smock (Cruciferae)
C. pratensis 'Flore Pleno' is the double variety of lady's smock. It is a pretty plant with pale-lilac flowers, reminiscent of double stocks, which go well with the golden-yellow of the double marsh-marigold. *C. waldsteinii* (*Dentaria trifolia*) is a lime-loving woodlander, which grows about a foot (30 cm) tall. In damp, shady places, its white flowers appear in spring. Creamy *C. enneaphyllos*, purple *C. bulbifera* and several more of these Dentarias have similar good qualities in such shady spots.

Carduncellus (Compositae)

These are interesting dwarf plants from the stony soils of southern Europe and North Africa. *C. mitissimus* is a native of southern France and Spain. Its deeply cut leaves form cupped rosettes and, in May, small, pale-lilac, thistle heads appear. *C. rhaponticoides* comes from the Atlas Mountains in Morocco. It has crimson-veined, leathery, dark-green leaves in flat rosettes up to twelve inches (30 cm) across, in the centre of which a two-inch wide (5 cm), lilac-blue cornflower appears in May. *C. pinnatus acaulis* from the High Atlas is similar but neater, with deeply cut foliage which looks like silver-filigree when glistening with frost in winter. These curious plants are hardy but need a sunny position and a free-draining soil.

Carlina, Carline Thistle (Compositae)

The pretty silver stemless thistle of the Alps, *C. acaulis*, and the golden *C. acanthifolia* from the Balkans are excellent lime-loving plants for associating with *Thymus*, *Dianthus deltoides*, *Gentiana cruciata*, and so on. They flower late, in summer and autumn, and last long in bloom, which makes them very worthwhile and deserving of more popularity.

Celmisia (Compositae)

This is a large genus, almost confined to New Zealand, and of importance to rock gardeners in climates where the summers are cool and moist. They all have white, daisy-like heads, which makes them sound uninteresting. This is far from the truth as they have an incredible variety of foliage forms and colours, often being clothed in silvery hairs. Among the larger, tufted species, *C. lyallii* and *C. coriacea* are splendid. One of the more obviously shrubby ones is dark, glossy-green *C. ramulosa*. More compact is silver-plated *C. hectori*, but the tightest-growing of all are *C. sessiliflora* and *C. argentea*, which build up mossy cushions of silvery needles only a few inches (5 cm) high. All the Celmisias like a

peaty soil which does not dry out in summer. Those who can grow them will want to find out about the many additional species which can be grown from seed, which must be sown fresh after collection and is distributed by enthusiasts in New Zealand.

Celsia see **Verbascum**

Centaurea (Compositae)

While there are many species in this genus, the following are among the most suitable for the rock garden. White *C. cana* and its pink form 'Rosea' have flower-heads on short stalks over mats of silver foliage; they like a sunny position and gravelly soil. *C. pulcherrima* is attractive, with grey-green, pinnate leaves and scented, pink flowers. Both this and the bushier *C. bella* and *C. simplicicaulis*, also pink-flowered and silvery-leaved, can be planted on sunny slopes, where they will flower generously.

Centaurium (Gentianaceae)

C. chloodes is a pretty biennial, only two inches (5 cm) high. It comes from the coastal cliffs and sandy beaches of western Europe and has an endless succession of large, pink flowers. It is attractive in trough gardens and raised beds where it can be easily admired. *C. scilloides* is more perennial but taller (20 cm). All are on a similar pattern to and reminiscent of pink *Gentiana verna*.

A selection of alpine campanulas: (1) *Campanula speciosa* from the Pyrenees, only biennial. (2) *C. tridentata* is the first to flower at the beginning of May; it comes, like (3) *C. aucheri*, from the Caucasus. (4) *C. pulla* from the eastern Alps likes a fairly moist, stony soil. (5) *C. raineri*, a plant from the limestones of the Italian Alps. (6) *Edraianthus pumilio*.

85

Centranthus, Red Valerian
(Valerianaceae)

C. ruber is useful on large, sunny dry-stone walls and banks. It grows two feet (60 cm) tall with scented, flesh-pink heads from June to September. There are white forms and deep red ones, 'Atrococcineus'. They often naturalize on old, crumbling walls.

Cerastium, Snow-in-Summer
(Caryophyllaceae)

There are few rock garden plants which one must be so carefully warned against as *C. biebersteinii*. It will soon take over if planted in small gardens, smothering everything else. If not constantly checked, it will cover many square yards (metres) of ground. Its rampant grey carpets, thickly covered with white flowers in May–June, are, however, indispensible for covering dry concrete-block walling and retaining banks.

C. tomentosum columnae is less luxuriant and its silver carpets are more striking and more useful. It is pretty throughout the year and is beautiful with saponaria, veronica, campanula, dwarf berberis and cotoneaster.

C. arvense 'Compactum' is not rampant and has attractive, dull-green cushions with white flowers in early summer. *C. alpinum* var. *lanatum* is much choicer and needs more attention. With its downy leaves it may be planted to intermingle with other tiny alpines in troughs, as may the lime-hating *C. uniflorum*.

Chaenorrhinum (Scrophulariaceae)

The small Spanish toadflaxes, *C. crassifolium* with its thick, smooth leaves, and *C. villosum* covered in fine down, are modest but useful small rock plants. They seed themselves but never become a nuisance, growing only three inches (5–10 cm) high and flowering tirelessly throughout summer with dull-pink or lilac blossoms.

Chamaenerion see **Epilobium**

Chiastophyllum (Crassulaceae)

C. oppositifolium (*Cotyledon oppositifolia*) is a pretty plant for dry-stone walls. It is only four to six inches (10–15 cm) high, and comes from the Caucasus. In shady crevices it produces hanging yellow panicles, in June, from its neat rosettes of shining, bright-green leaves.

Chrysanthemum (Compositae)   p. 55

This genus has been greatly mutilated by botanists and at present only includes a few annuals. The species of interest to the alpine enthusiast have been split among *Dendranthema*, *Tanacetum*, *Leucanthemopsis*, *Leucanthemum* and others. These are all retained together here, as they are most familiar to gardeners under the name chrysanthemum.

C. (*Leucanthemopsis*) *alpinum*, the alpine marguerite, will not grow well in the garden. *C.* (*Matricaria*) *oreades* from Turkey may be grown in its place. It quickly forms grassy, green mats which, in spring, look like tiny fields of daisies. *Galanthus* and *Iris reticulata* bulbs may be planted amongst it and the blue flowers of *Muscari armeniacum* look particularly well amongst its white flowers.

C. (*Tanacetum*) *cinerariifolium* looks striking with its stiff heads of daisy-like flowers above rounded cushions, as does the bushy, grey-leaved *C. argenteum*, *C. densum*, and the silver-grey, finely cut foliage of *C. haradjanii* (*Tanacetum praeteritum massicyticum*) from Turkey, which can be recommended for dry-stone walls and sunny slopes. *C. hosmariense* from Morocco is a lovely late-flowering species, especially suitable for sunny raised beds. It has silver-grey foliage and aristocratic white daisies. *C. gayanum*, also from Morocco, is a much branched plant twelve inches high (30 cm), with small but abundant rose-pink flowers. *C. weyrichii* flowers in summer with pretty, pink daisies three inches (7 cm) wide, on four-inch (10 cm) stems. C. (*Dendranthema*) *zawadskii* comes later on, with whitish flowers on branching stems in August–September. Later still is C. (*Dendranthema*) *arcticum*. The typical, compact species grows twelve inches (30 cm) high, and bears white flowers in September–October, whilst 'Rosea' has pale pink flowers and 'Schwefelglanz' bright yellow flowers. All of these look very well in combination with *Aster dumosus*.

C. (*Leucanthemopsis*) *pallidum spathulifolium* and C. (L.) *radicans* are exquisite, soft-yellow daisies from south-east Spain and by no means easy to grow. They are worth every effort in the alpine-house or a sunny trough. Also best grown in the alpine-house, as it is slightly tender, is C. (*Leucanthemum*) *catananche* with cut, grey leaves and heads in an unusual pale, biscuit-orange shade.

The low, hardy varieties of the florists' chrysanthemums (hybrids of C. *indicum*) are only suitable for formal beds near the house.

Chrysobactron see Bulbinella

Claytonia (Portulacaceae)
Most of these are rather uninteresting, fleshy-leaved plants but the compact, high-altitude race of North American C. *megarrhiza*, grown as C. *nivalis*, is a superlative plant with a succession of bright sugar-pink flowers from rosettes of dark, spoon-shaped leaves. Strangely, for such a succulent species, it grows best in areas with a cooler summer climate and prefers some shade in gritty, peaty soil.

Clematis see page 154 for both herbaceous species and climbers.

Codonopsis (Campanulaceae)
There are many extremely attractive species among these bell-flowers from north-east Asia. Upright forms are pale-blue C. *clematidea*, the rarer C. *ovata* with milk-blue hanging bells, and

C. *meleagris*, which grows only four to eight inches (10–20 cm) high and has pendant brown-chequered, bluish bells.

The twining species, C. *vinciflora* and C. *convolvulacea*, are particularly attractive with their flat, lilac-blue flowers, and they can be planted to climb through the branches of dwarf rhododendrons. The leaves of most species have a strong, foxy scent when disturbed. C. *clematidea* is the easiest to grow. All like a good depth of gritty, humus-rich soil and a cool, slightly shady position.

Coluteocarpus (Cruciferae)
C. *vesicaria* (C. *reticulatus*) is a dwarf crucifer from Turkey. It needs a hot, dry site and has unremarkable white flowers in spring. The large, inflated seed-capsules, however, are very striking. The North American genus *Physaria* has similar extraordinary capsules and needs the same treatment.

Convolvulus (Convolvulaceae)
All species of *Convolvulus* are attractive, but for the rock gardener the finest of all is C. *boissieri* (C. *nitidus*) from Spain and its subspecies C. *b. compactus* from Turkey and the Balkans. Its mats of glistening, silver leaves hug the ground and when they are covered in June with white, pink-backed flowers the effect is magnificent. It grows best in poor, very well-drained, stony and limy soil in the full sun and should be protected from winter wetness. Small C. *lineatus* spreads underground, and does best in almost pure grit. C. *calvertii* and C. *cantabrica* grow eight to twelve inches (20–30 cm) high, with pink flowers on upright stalks; they like a slightly loamier soil, and make a fine show with *Linum austriacum*. C. *althaeoides* is a low trailing plant with silver-grey, lobed leaves and large pink blossoms. It is so pretty that it is easy to forgive the nuisance it causes by growing over everything.

The soft mauve-blue C. *sabatius* (C. *mauretan-*

icus) has similar wide-spreading habits and is equally forgiveable. A good idea is to plant them together, so that they can compete and intermingle their pink and blue flowers and silver and green leaves. They both need a sunny, well-drained place and are both better if protected with a sheet of glass or plastic in winter.

Coreopsis (Compositae)
The dwarf *C. verticillata* 'Zagreb' has bushes of bright-green needle-like leaves and golden-yellow starry flowers. It is only ten inches (25 cm) tall, and can be recommended for more formal rock garden beds. *C. rosea* is about the same height but has pink, yellow-centred daisies on branching stems in summer.

Cornus see page 155.

Coronilla (Leguminosae)
Of the herbaceous species of *Coronilla*, *C. cappadocica* from Turkey is perhaps the most beautiful. It grows up to twelve inches high (30 cm), and has bluish-green pinnate leaves. In early summer it bears shining yellow flower heads, and is an asset on any sunny slope.

Cortusa (Primulaceae)
The rich purple-pink bells of *C. matthioli* from the moist mountain woodlands of Europe and northern Asia are small, dainty and appealing. There are many variants, of which *C. matthioli pekinensis* is by far the best. It needs to be protected from wind and strong sun, and does best in humus-rich soil among rhododendrons and other *Ericaceae* in the peat bed.

Corydalis (Papaveraceae)   p. 19
C. nobilis is one of the finest of this genus, growing about one foot (30 cm) high, with striking foliage and flowers. Planted amongst the blue-flowered *Brunnera macrophylla*, its yellow racemes dotted with black make an effective contrast.

With its delicate green filigree foliage *C. lutea* can replace *Adiantum* on shady walls. In a sunny position its mounds of leaves will be covered all through the summer with yellow flowers. *C. ochroleuca* is very similar but has yellow-and-cream flowers. Both can become pests through self-seeding and are more suitable for larger wilder areas.

C. cheilanthifolia has fern-like, pinnate leaves and narrow racemes of yellow flowers. It also thrives in shady positions, and sows itself in any suitable corner, but seldom becomes a nuisance.

C. cashmiriana is delightful but temperamental and rare. It is a precious Himalayan plant with brilliant azure-blue flowers and delicately cut leaves. It grows only four inches (10 cm) high and likes rich, gritty soil and a cool position. *C. ambigua yedoensis* from Japan grows about twice as tall but is the same penetrating blue. *C. bracteata* from the Altai can also be recommended; its pale-yellow flowers resemble those of *Orchis pallens*. *C. bulbosa* and *C. solida* have deep purple racemes, but are not very prepossessing. The white form is more outstanding, and pink forms grown as *C. solida* 'Transsylvanica' are even prettier. Most have flowers of a fresh salmon-pink and look lovely with *Chionodoxa luciliae* beneath *Salix* × *wehrhahnii*. A particularly deep brick-red form is grown in England as 'G. P. Baker'. All the last-named species are tuberous, prefer a loose, woodland soil and die back soon after flowering. In favourable positions they will propagate themselves by self-seeding. *C. wilsonii* is a true rock plant from China with six-inch (15 cm) spikes of bright-yellow flowers over blue-grey

(1) *Calceolaria darwinii* (enlarged), a dwarf plant from Tierra del Fuego, only suitable for experienced gardeners, as is (2) The Horned Rampion (*Physoplexis comosa*) from the Dolomites.

leaves. It is an easy alpine-house plant in sun or shade but usually finds outdoor conditions too wet.

Cotula (Compositae)

The flat carpets of *Cotula squalida*, *C. dioica* or *C. potentillina* make good backgrounds, with their neutral tones, for striking colours, e.g. *Mimulus cupreus*, or curious dwarf shrubs such as *Corokia cotoneaster*. *C. potentillina* is green in summer and brown in winter. All these have uninteresting flower-heads and are undemanding so far as soil is concerned.

On the whole these are unexciting plants and also rather aggressive in the garden. *C. atrata* from the shingle-slips of the New Zealand mountains is as difficult to grow as the others are easy, and seldom produces its black button-heads in cultivation. It has a very local race, *C. atrata luteola* from the Kaikoura Mountains, which is an excellent easier plant for troughs or scree-beds, where it will form mats of brownish leaves and produce wine-red and cream flower-heads unlike anything else in the garden.

Crassula (Crassulaceae)

C. milfordiae comes from the Drakensberg Mountains in Lesotho in southern Africa. Its little succulent rosettes form dense, even mats with white star-like flowers in summer, and turn bronze-red in autumn. It appeals to those who collect unusual, small plants and will do well in the alpine-house, trough garden or in a dry, sunny position in the rock garden. *C. sarcocaulis* enjoys similar treatment and is perhaps hardier. It is a shrubby succulent about eight inches (20 cm) high with pale-pink flowers from red buds. There is a hybrid between them. All look well with species of sempervivum.

Crepis (Compositae)

C. aurea is like a tiny coppery-orange dandelion and can be tried planted next to gentians, as it

grows in the Alps. *C. pygmaea* and *C. terglouensis* are other small, yellow, high alpine plants which grow in limestone. These are all difficult to keep in character in the garden, but *C. incana* from Greece is both reliable and outstanding in poor, well drained soil in full sun. Its long succession of pink dandelions appear on nine inch (20 cm) stems in summer from grey-leaved clumps and look lovely with soft-blue *Geranium wallichianum*.

Crucianella see Phuopsis

Cyananthus (Campanulaceae)   p. 73

This genus of fine, low-growing plants belongs to the campanula family and comes from the high pastures of the Himalayas. It prefers lime-free soil made up of grit, peat and humus and likes to be cool and damp in the summer but is sensitive to wetness in the winter. It does best in a light position but not in the heat of the full sun. All have thin, prostrate shoots covered with dense foliage and with shining, blue gentian-like flowers in summer. *C. microphyllus* (*C. integer* of gardens) and *C. lobatus*, of which there is a rare pure-white variant, have proved the most satisfactory species for the garden. *C. sherriffii*, with hairy, grey leaves and pale-blue flowers, is safest in the alpine-house.

Cymbalaria see Linaria

Cynoglossum (Boraginaceae)

The Himalayan *C. nervosum* grows about two feet (60 cm) tall, with fresh-green, lanceolate leaves and azure-blue flowers. It is sadly not well known but its flowering-season lasts from June to September and it can look splendid in moist, wild places with the yellow bells of *Primula sikkimensis* and the golden grass *Milium effusum* 'Aureum'.

Cypripedium see Orchids

Deinanthe (Saxifragaceae)
D. caerulea is a distinguished, shade-loving plant for the enthusiast. It grows twelve inches (30 cm) high and should be planted in the peat bed between rhododendrons or other dwarf shrubs, which will protect the attractive, bronze new growth from late frosts or the cold, dry winds which it detests. Nodding, crystal-line, lilac, cup-shaped flowers appear in summer over the bristly, hydrangea-like leaves. *D. bifida* has cream flowers and curiously notched foliage and needs the same conditions.

Delosperma (Aizoaceae)
This is a large South African genus, of which only the following species have proved com-paratively hardy in central Europe. They form loose bushes some four inches high (10 cm), and have round, fleshy leaves and shining disc-shaped flower heads. *D. cooperi* has bright purple heads with whitish centres, whilst *D. lineare* is lemon-yellow. The blossoms appear in summer and open only in strong sunlight. Both of them are somewhat exotic in appearance and look best planted with other succulents, like the hardy cacti, sedums and sempervivums.

Delphinium, Larkspur (Ranunculaceae)
The tall alpine Larkspur, *D. elatum*, can only be used in large gardens. The smaller species from China, only one foot or so (30–50 cm) high are more useful. These are *D. cashmerianum*, *D. grandiflorum*, and *D. tatsienense* with violet and gentian-blue flowers. The soft yellows and oranges of *Potentilla fruticosa* look well beside them. There is a species with shining, orange-red flowers, which grows only about one foot (30 cm) high; this is *D. nudicaule* from California, which likes a very warm position in sandy soil, and must be protected in winter in severe climates. The small, tuberous root-stocks may be kept in the cellar in sand over winter.

There are a few other dwarf, tuberous-rooted North American species with purple-blue flowers, around *D. menziesii* and *D. glareosum*. These die away in summer, when they like to be dry, so are in place on a raised bed or in the bulb-frame. These are worth searching seed-lists for, as are the dwarf Himalayan *D. muscosum* and *D. brunonianum*. Neither of these two is an easy plant and they grow best where summers are cool and moist and they are protected from wetness in winter.

Dentaria see **Cardamine**

Dianthus (Caryophyllaceae)   p. 81
These are among the most important of rock garden plants, and when their profuse, scented flowers appear in June, it is surely one of the high points in the rock garden year. There is a vast number of worthwhile dwarf hybrid pinks but somehow the wild species seem more fitting in the alpine garden. The small cushion-forming species are very dainty. Such are *D. microlepis* (lime-free soil), *D. musalae*, *D. simulans*, *D. freynii* and *D. haematocalyx*, all carrying their flowers on short stems above tight, grey cushions. Slightly taller species are *D. gratiano-politanus* (*D. caesius*), *D. campestris*, *D. nardifor-mis*, *D. pavonius* (*D. neglectus*), *D. nitidus*, *D. sylvestris* and *D. subacaulis*.

The richly blooming mats of *D. deltoides* are especially striking. The loveliest of these are the shining crimson 'Brilliant', and the scarlet 'Flashing Light'. They seed themselves only too well, and can become a nuisance.

The long-stemmed, cushion-forming pinks are quite lovely, and are excellent for dry-stone walls. Such is *D. petraeus noeanus*, with late, heavily scented, white flowers. *D. plumarius* has both double and single varieties and *D. petraeus* 'Suendermannii' produces its pure white blooms at the end of June. The pink *D. erinaceus* from Turkey is more prized for its firm, prickly cushions than for its sparse flowers. The long-stemmed species, usually with red flowers and dense, bushy foliage—*D.*

carthusianorum, *D. giganteus*, *D. cruentus* and the sulphur-yellow *D. knappii*—are particularly charming.

One of the prettiest of the wild pinks, *D. callizonus* from the Carpathian Mountains has lovely, spotted flowers, and can be temperamental, as can *D. alpinus*, one of the glories of the eastern Alps. It needs a cool position which is not too dry. As well as the fresh-pink wild form, there is a pure-white one and a crimson one with a dark centre, 'Joan's Blood'.

All pinks like plenty of sun and well-drained soil, except *D. superbus*. This should be planted in a damp place, on the edge of a pool or stream, where its delicately cut, pale lilac, sweet-scented flowers will billow out in summer.

Diascia (Scrophulariaceae)
Of this South African genus, there is a dwarf, hardy perennial species, *D. cordata*, which is a dainty, four-inch (10 cm) high plant with prostrate spreading shoots, bearing sprays of comparatively large, salmon-pink, spurred flowers in summer. The hybrid between this and the more tender, showier *D. barberae* is called 'Ruby Field' and is slightly more strongly coloured. Both enjoy a sunny, well-drained place and should be divided and transplanted every few years to keep them vigorous.

Dicentra (Papaveraceae)
The loveliest and stateliest of these is, of course, the tall, pink Bleeding Heart, *D. spectabilis*, from China. It is a fine sight in combination with *Doronicum* and *Brunnera macrophylla* on terraced beds near the house. There are many fine garden varieties derived from *D. formosa* and possibly the other American species *D. oregona* and *D. eximia*. These all have delicately cut foliage and graceful pendant flowers which look well against the solidity of rock and stonework. Crimson and deep pink varieties are 'Baccharal', 'Paramount', 'Adrian Bloom' and 'Bountiful'. Creamy pinks and whites include 'Langtrees',

'Silver Smith' and 'Stuart Boothman', which is outstanding in its finely cut, bluish foliage. These grow about eighteen inches high (40 cm) and flower in late spring. Dwarfer and earlier is the white yellow-tipped *D. cucullaria*. *D. canadensis* is similar but will not settle down so well in gardens. All these enjoy rich, moist but well-drained conditions in some shade. A true alpine and one of the most exquisite of all is *D. peregrina* from Siberia and Japan. Sadly it is not easy, requiring cool, moist summers and cold, dry winters, potting in a very gritty but rich mixture and copious watering in the early part of the growing season. Its crystalline pink lockets on three-inch (7 cm) stems over cut, silver-blue tufts of foliage are ample reward for any trouble.

Digitalis, Foxglove (Scrophulariaceae)
D. dubia from the Balearic Islands is the dwarfest species but can still reach eighteen inches (50 cm). It is a lime-loving perennial with grey-felted rosettes and purple-pink flowers. The taller foxgloves look at their best among shrubs in the wild garden.

Dimorphotheca see Osteospermum

Dionysia (Primulaceae) p. 59
These extraordinary cushion-forming plants are more or less Primulas which have tried to adapt to the dry climate of Iran and Afghanistan. There they grow on cool, shady cliffs, usually of limestone, so must be kept shaded in cultivation, where they demand the protection of an

---

(1) *Vitaliana primuliflora*, a lovely plant from the southern Alps. (2) *Moltkia* × *intermedia*, a pretty, easily cultivated summer flower. (3) *Roscoea humeana*, a member of the ginger family from West China.

alpine-house at all times to keep off overhead water. They are intolerant of excess moisture around them so must be kept well-ventilated and grown in a very gritty but not poor mixture. While they are very demanding, they can be very beautiful and the challenge they offer has attracted many specialist growers. *D. aretioides*, with its selected, free-flowering varieties 'Paul Furse' and 'Gravetye', is the easiest species, forming soft, rounded cushions covered with yellow flowers. Pink *D. curviflora* and yellow *D. tapetodes* are the best of the tight-cushioned species to start with. More demanding but occasionally available are pale violet *D. archibaldii* and yellow *D. michauxii*, which likes a little more sun and even drier conditions than the others.

Dodecatheon (Primulaceae)

D. meadia, *D. pulchellum* and other similar species are welcome spring flowers with low clumps of leaves and clusters of cyclamen-like flowers, pale pink to red-purple in colour, and standing on long stalks. They like a rich soil and plenty of moisture in the spring, when they will tolerate the full sun (they die back in summer). They look attractive beside lilac-blue *Phlox divaricata* and yellow *Epimedium*.

Apart from these taller, woodland plants, there are several choicer or dwarfer species from western North America. The very dwarf race from Vancouver Island, known as *D. hendersonii* 'Sooke Variety' is a tiny version of the larger ones already mentioned, only an inch or so (2–5 cm) high with red flowers. *D. dentatum* likes quite a lot of shade and is white-flowered, as is *D. ellisiae* from New Mexico.

Doronicum, Leopard's Bane (Compositae)

D. orientale (*D. caucasicum*) is a pretty April flower. It has fresh-green, heart-shaped leaves and yellow daisy-like blossoms. The bright-yellow 'Goldzwerg' and *D. cordatum* of gardens are especially lovely dwarfer varieties, both of which grow no more than ten inches (25 cm) high. *D. plantagineum* flowers later and grows almost three feet (80 cm) tall. Doronicums like cool, damp earth and look well planted alongside blue *Brunnera macrophylla*, or *Omphalodes verna* in the case of the dwarfer ones.

Douglasia (Primulaceae)

The European *D. vitaliana* will be found under *Vitaliana primuliflora*. The American species are dwarf, mat or cushion-forming plants with pink and red flowers. They grow best in lime-free, gritty, humus-rich soil, with cool, moist summer conditions. The most usually grown is *D. laevigata*, of which the variety *D. l. ciliolata* is the largest-flowered. *D. montana* is a dwarfer plant, and *D. nivalis*, while sometimes rather loose-growing, is an unusual wine-red shade. These closely resemble Androsaces and are included with them by most botanists today.

Draba (Cruciferae)

The earliest species is *D. aizoides*, with spiny rosettes, but more attractive is *D. bruniifolia* (*D. olympica*) which covers its diminutive cushions of foliage with golden-yellow flowers in April. *D. rigida bryoides* produces thick, mossy, mats with tiny yellow flowers on wiry stems. *D. dedeana* has grey-green cushions and white blossoms; *D. sibirica* (*D. repens*) forms a loose ground-cover with yellow flowers. All of these are quick growing plants when planted in gritty soil in full sun.

D. mollissima is very sensitive to moisture and is best grown in the alpine-house. This is a cliff plant from the Caucasus, which forms round, symmetrical cushions of tiny grey, felted rosettes, and bears yellow blossoms on thready stalks. *D. polytricha* from Armenia also needs protection from the damp. In the alpine-house it will produce shining-yellow flowers over its cushions of hairy, grey rosettes in early spring. *D. rosularis*, with felted rosettes and soft-yellow flowers completes this trio of superlative alpine-house plants.

Dracocephalum, Dragon's Head (Labiatae)

Dwarf *D. botryoides* has hairy, grey leaves and dull-pink flowers in April. It repays careful cultivation in gritty soil. *D. grandiflorum* and *D. purdomii* have pretty, violet-blue flowers and bloom in summer. These will flourish in full sun in any well-drained soil and grow about one foot (30 cm) high. There are other worthwhile species but they are seldom available.

Echioides, Prophet Flower (Boraginaceae)

E. longiflorum (*Arnebia echioides*) grows a foot (30 cm) high and comes from the Caucasus. Its wide, funnel-shaped flowers appear in late spring, and are yellow with a prominent black spot on each petal. These gradually fade and disappear. It needs a warm corner in free-draining soil. In spring it needs to be damp and repays a mulch of compost. It dies back in summer and should then be kept dry.

Edraianthus (Campanulaceae)   p. 85

These are true rock- and scree-dwellers, and must be planted in narrow crevices if they are to last long. *E. pumilio* and *E. serpyllifolius* form dense cushions of narrow foliage covered with violet bells and are the best species. However, all the others are pleasant, especially the *E. graminifolius* group with violet-blue flowers on long, prostrate stems.

Epilobium, Willowherb (Onagraceae)

E. fleischeri is an alpine scree-plant. It forms large clumps about eight inches (20 cm) high of linear leaves with deep rose-pink flowers which look superb in the informal rock garden alongside *Dryas* and *Gypsophila*, in stony scree. *E. dodonaei* is its rather taller, lower altitude counterpart.

Epimedium, Barrenwort (Berberidaceae)

All species of this genus are worthwhile all through the year. The delicate leaves look attractive in spring as they unfold, in pale shades of green and brown, and the flowers are delightful, although they last all too short a time. Their bright-green clumps look refreshing in summer, whilst their bronze autumn colours are quite lovely. *E. grandiflorum* (*E. macranthum*) is an elegant, slow-growing species which has a fine pink variant, 'Rose Queen'. *E. × rubrum* has red flowers, *E. × warleyense* coppery-brown ones, *E. × youngianum* 'Niveum' white ones and *E. × versicolor* 'Sulphureum' sulphur-yellow blossoms. The similar yellow-flowering *E. pinnatum* and *E. perralderianum* are two of the loveliest of evergreen herbaceous plants. *E. diphyllum* is a small Japanese species (formerly *Aceranthus diphyllus*), with bright-green, heart-shaped leaves and pearly-white flowers in April. In America, the similar genus *Vancouveria* takes over. *V. hexandra*, with white flowers, grows easily but pale yellow *V. chrysantha* and lilac-white *V. planipetala* from the Californian Redwood forests are more temperamental.

It is impossible to tire of these delicate and long-lived plants, which will thrive in any half-shaded position in loose, humus-rich soil.

Erigeron (Compositae)

The compact, English hybrid of *E. glaucus*, 'Four Winds', looks well with formal rock-work and the many larger German hybrids such as 'Adria', 'Foersters Liebling', 'Darkest of All', 'Rotes Meer', 'Schwarzes Meer' and others, with their profuse daisies in shades of lilac, blue, and rose-pink, as well as the orange-yellow *E. aurantiacus*, are good, long-flowering summer flowers for terraced gardens. For the enthusiast there are also the small species, golden *E. aureus*, mauve *E. trifidus*, *E. compositus* and other North Americans.

Erinus (Scrophulariaceae)
E. alpinus grows only four inches (10 cm) high, forms small tufts of foliage and has long-lasting pink flowers. It is one of the easiest rock-dwellers and it will seed itself, when it has become established in crevices. The best varieties are 'Dr Hähnle', with crimson flowers, clear pink 'Mrs Charles Boyle', and 'Albus' with white flowers. They flower from May right through the summer and are excellent in sunny dry-stone walls.

Eriogonum see page 158

Eriophyllum (Compositae)
E. lanatum (*E. caespitosum*) comes from western North America and flowers tirelessly through the summer. It forms grey-green bushes eight to twelve inches (20–30 cm) high, covered with yellow, daisy-like flowers. This is a pretty and extremely easy plant for poor soil in a dry, sunny position.

Eritrichium (Boraginaceae)
E. nanum, with its silver velvet cushions covered with gentian-blue forget-me-nots, is one of those plants which everyone dreams of growing but which seldom survives for long at low altitudes. This and its similar cousins from North America, *E. howardii* and *E. argenteum*, taunt even the most expert grower. *E. rupestre* (*E. strictum*) is not so fine as these high-alpine species and its leaves grow in rosettes, not cushions, but it is still a choice plant and is much easier to grow. It comes from Kashmir and has small, sky-blue flowers on grey-green, six-inch (15 cm) stems. It will bloom throughout the summer in a sunny position and it is a special delight in a trough or on a raised bed.

Erodium, Heron's-bill (Geraniaceae)
Those who do not like startling effects but prefer a more modest beauty should plant the small species in crevices in sunny dry-stone walls. There, their clusters of finely cut leaves and delicately marked flowers will give much pleasure. The prettiest are white *E. absinthoides amanum*, pink *E. reichardii* (*chamaedryoides*) 'Roseum', yellow *E. chrysanthum*, violet-pink *E. petraeum glandulosum* (*macradenum*) and pink *E. rupestre* (*supracanum*). Pink *E. corsicum* is a species with small grey felted rosettes suitable for the alpine-house.

Eryngium, Sea Holly (Umbelliferae)   p. 77
E. alpinum and its varieties, 'Superbum' and 'Opal' are among the stateliest and prettiest sea hollies. *E.* × *zabelii* (*E. alpinum* × *bourgatii*), especially the dark-violet 'Violetta', is not to be disdained, however. The silvery *E. giganteum*, which is a biennial, the spiky *E. tricuspidatum*, and *E. planum* 'Blue Dwarf' are also attractive. All these need deep, stony soil, on a sunny slope, and grow one foot to two feet (30–70 cm) tall. Dwarfer than all these and one of the loveliest rock-garden plants is the true sea holly *E. maritimum* of European coasts. It needs full sun in a very gravelly soil when it will produce its spiny, thick foliage in an incredible blue-grey shade and prostrate stems of the same colour bearing blue heads.

Erysimum, Wallflower (Cruciferae)   p. 43
Used in moderation, the Siberian Wallflower, *E.* (*Cheiranthus*) × *allionii* with its fiery orange-gold flowers can be contrasted with *Arabis* and *Phlox divaricata* in the context of more formal stone-work. Although it is biennial, the small trouble

---

The stemless gentians comprise several closely related species which stretch from the Pyrenees across the Alps to the Balkans. They vary in the types of soil they require and in their ease of cultivation. (1) *G. kochiana* is a difficult lime-hater. (2) *G. clusii* likes lime. The best species are (3) *G. dinarica* and *G. angustifolia*, seen here with *Anthemis carpatica*.

needed to sow it every year in June is repayed by its glorious colour. The four-inch (10 cm) clear yellow, Alpine *E. pumilum* is longer-lived, as is the dwarf bright yellow Turkish *E. kotschyanum*. These like to grow in warm, sunny positions between rocks. Sulphur *E. alpinum* and primrose *E. a.* 'Moonlight' are another pair of delightful miniature wallflowers. The perennial Spanish *E. linifolium* also has dwarf, lilac variants.

Euphorbia, Spurge (Euphorbiaceae)

E. polychroma (*E. epithymoides*) is a well known and much loved early-flowering plant, which forms rounded bushes of long-lasting, yellow flower heads. It looks well near Japanese maples. *E. myrsinites* and *E. rigida* (*E. biglandulosa*) from the Balkans have sculptured whorls of pointed, grey leaves, which look as if they were cut out of metal. Planted amongst succulents, like *Sedum* and *Sempervivum*, in a sunny, dry-stone wall, their great architectural value can be fully appreciated. The prettiest dwarf species is *E. capitulata*, which forms low mats of blue-grey leaves nestling amongst the rocks, where it will produce yellow flowers and reddish fruits.

Felicia (Compositae)

While these blue South African daisies are quite important for gardeners where winters are mild, such as parts of New Zealand and California, they are too tender for most North European gardeners. However, cuttings can easily be rooted in autumn and overwintered under glass. *F. amelloides* and *F. pappei* are those most usually seen. Both have pure-blue daisies all summer on their 12 inch (30 cm) bushes. They are sometimes listed under *Aster* or *Agathea*.

Filipendula (Rosaceae)

The dwarf form of *Filipendula palmata* grown as 'Digitata Nana' has feathery, divided leaves, and heads of deep-pink flowers on stalks about one foot (30 cm) high. It enjoys a rich, moist soil, like most other species, which are all taller plants, superlative in the wild garden.

Galax (Diapensiaceae)

G. aphylla is a beautiful shade-lover from North America suitable for the peat bed. It has slender, white flower spikes in early summer and rounded, shiny evergreen leaves which turn bronze-brown in autumn.

Galium see Asperula

Gentiana, (Gentianaceae)   pp. 43, 97, 101

Gentians are among the loveliest plants which can be grown. For those who want the large-blossomed, stemless gentians of the *G. acaulis* group, pot-grown plants of *G. dinarica* or *G. angustifolia* should be planted in good loamy, well-drained soil, fairly close together in a sunny position, and these will bloom profusely and gloriously. The stemless, trumpet gentians which flower in spring and are known to most gardeners as *G. acaulis* comprise a group of several species with distinct tastes in soil in nature. *G. acaulis* (*kochiana*) and *G. alpina* are lime-haters. *G. clusii*, *G. dinarica*, *G. angustifolia* and the others grow on limestone.

The group of species around *G. verna* is even more widespread and diverse. These are the incredibly blue spring gentians of the Alps, ranging from Britain and Morocco, where they are violet, to the Caucasus, where there is a yellow one, on into Central Asia. Most are difficult to grow well. The garden strain grown in Britain as *G. v. angulosa* is by far the most reliable. It comes nearest to *G. v. tergestina*, from south-east Europe, and is best established by sowing fresh seed.

The finest autumn gentians are *G. farreri*, *G. sino-ornata* and their hybrid, *G.* 'Macaulayi'. The hybrids *G.* 'Farorna' (*G. farreri* × *ornata*) and *G.* 'Inverleith' (*farreri* × *veitchiorum*) along with many others are quite superb. *G. farreri* does not mind limy soil but the others are definitely lime-haters. They are suitable for planting with small rhododendrons, but should not be too shaded, and like to be kept moist in summer. Their prostrate shoots form fresh-green, turfy mats which look attractive all the year round and only turn yellow in winter. Two late flowering one foot (30 cm) high species from north-east Asia are G. *makinoi*, which is slate-blue with red autumn foliage, and deep blue G. *scabra*. The latter provides a good substitute for the Himalayan autumn gentians in climates with hotter summers, as in the eastern USA. The North American species are little known in gardens but are also well worth the attention of gardeners unable to grow the species from the Alps and Himalayas. G. *sceptrum* and G. *puberulenta* are two of the finest.

G. *lagodechiana* and G. *septemfida* do not produce such pure, deep-blue flowers as the better-known species, but they grow easily and may be recommended for their long flowering in summer. G. *asclepiadea* is an elegant species suitable for shady places between dwarf shrubs, whilst G. *lutea*, the stately yellow gentian, which grows up to three feet (one metre) high, may be used in larger areas. The last two species are best planted as young, pot-grown plants.

The New Zealand gentians look very different from the Asiatic and European species. The most frequently grown are G. *bellidifolia* and the dwarfer G. *saxosa*, which both have pure white flowers, somewhat recalling snowdrops. They like gritty, peaty soil and cool conditions.

Geranium, Crane's-bill (Geraniaceae) **p. 81**
G. *dalmaticum* is one of the finest of this genus for rock gardens and dry-stone walls. It grows only four inches (10 cm) high, and has glossy, round leaves and silky, pink or white flowers. Its autumn colours are lovely. The even smaller G. *napuligerum* (G. *farreri*) with its disproportionately large, pale-pink flowers is quite delightful, but slower growing. G. *cinereum sub-*caulescens 'Splendens' has striking crimson flowers with black eyes, whilst the choice low-growing G. *argenteum* has silvery-grey foliage and pale-pink flowers. G. *argenteum* 'Lissadell' ('Purpureum') has beautifully veined wine-purple flowers and may be a hybrid with G. *subcaulescens*. G. 'Gypsy' certainly is, and is closer to the latter in flower but has a very compact habit. G. 'Ballerina' and possibly 'Appleblossom' and 'Laurence Flatman' are hybrids between the two subspecies of G. *cinereum*. All are lovely, long-flowering plants with pale pink flowers with darker veining. On well-drained slopes, G. *sanguineum prostratum* (*lancastriense*), a four-inch (10 cm), bright-pink flowering plant, and its excellent selected seedling 'Jubilee Gem' are useful.

All plants with clear violet-blue flowers are welcome in the garden, and G. *wallichianum* 'Buxtons Blue' is no exception. It grows eight inches (20 cm) high, and looks most striking with its white-centred flowers and its deeply cut, five-lobed leaves. It starts flowering in July and continues till stopped by the autumn frosts, by which time it will have spread to 3 feet (1 m) across. This quality makes it suitable for planting with spring bulbs or even with pinkish G. *tuberosum* and rich lilac G. *malviflorum*, which are tuberous and die away in summer.

Geum, Avens (Rosaceae)
Few other flowers possess the lucent orange-red colour of the G. *coccineum* hybrids 'Borisii' or semi-double 'Feuermeer'. In its native Balkans, G. *coccineum* grows in damp mountain pastures and forest clearings alongside forget-me-nots and marsh-marigolds. *Brunnera macrophylla* looks well with it in the garden. In wet places, G. *rivale* 'Leonard's Variety', a sadly neglected plant, makes a good effect with its pretty copper bells, as does the soft yellow hybrid 'Lionel Cox'. Golden G. *montanum* and its hybrid G. × *rhaeticum* (G. *montanum* × G. *reptans*) are splendid plants but G. *reptans* is seldom a

success in the garden. The American G. *triflorum* is unusual and can carry up to three nodding dull-red bells on its eight-inch (20 cm) stems above silken, hairy leaves.

Glaucidium (Glaucidiaceae)

This is a precious woodland plant from Japan about eighteen inches (50 cm) high, with maple-like leaves and large, poppy-like flowers of frosted lavender or, in G. *p. leucanthum*, pure white. There are few lovelier plants in spring for the peat bed or any other sheltered shady place in moist, rich woodland soil.

Globularia (Globulariaceae)

These are semi-shrubby plants with dark-green, leathery leaves and globular flower-heads. The most worthwhile species are undoubtedly the blue-flowering G. *cordifolia* from the Alps and G. *meridionalis* from the Balkans, which is similar but has steel-blue blossoms. Together with *Dryas* it will form natural alpine carpets. G. *repens* (G. *nana*) is a dainty and quite remarkably undemanding plant which covers the rocks with a fine lattice of branches. G. *nudicaulis* and G. *trichosantha* will form effective, bushy, dark green mats if quite closely planted, making an attractive setting for wild tulips, while Spanish G. *spinosa* strikes a different note with its blue-grey, holly-like leaves.

Gypsophila (Caryophyllaceae)

G. *repens* from the mountains of Europe is a natural lime-lover and does well in the rock garden. Its dark-green spreading foliage is covered from May to July with white flowers. The pale-pink 'Dorothy Teacher' and the more strongly coloured 'Pink Beauty' are pretty varieties of this. The strong-growing, late-flowering double 'Rosy Veil' and 'Pink Star' are especially suitable for dry-stone walls or cascading down beside stone steps.

Enthusiasts may grow white G. *petraea* from Romania in crevices, where it will form small floriferous bushes. G. *aretioides* from the Caucasus and Iran is also a rock-dweller. Although it will not flower well, its dense, hard, grey-green cushions which thrive in dry crevices in full sun make up for this. G. *cerastioides* from the Himalayas is a mat-forming plant with grey, hairy leaves and pink-veined, white flowers on short stems.

Haberlea, Ramonda (p. 27) and Jankaea (Gesneriaceae)

These genera of limestone cliff-plants are described together since they belong to the same family and need the same treatment. They like a shady position in a dry-stone wall or rock crevice, and humus-rich but limy soil. *Haberlea rhodopensis* has pale lilac, bell-shaped flowers, and its beautiful variety 'Virginalis' is white. *Ramonda nathaliae* and R. *myconi* (R. *pyrenaica*) have flat, violet blossoms. They should always be planted in colonies, as they grow in their natural habitat, and if small ferns such as *Asplenium trichomanes* and A. *viride* are planted beside them, one will never weary of admiring their exquisite beauty. R. *serbica* from the Balkans has more bell-shaped flowers and distinct dark violet-blue anthers. It is not so vigorous in the garden and is best grown in the alpine-house, as is the beautiful *Jankaea heldreichii* from Mt Olympus in Greece. It has pale

Autumn gentians. The west-Chinese gentians were brought by British collectors: (5) *Gentiana sino-ornata* was introduced by George Forrest in 1911 and (4) G. *farreri* by Reginald Farrer in 1916. The hybrid varieties range from azure to white and the flowering season of these magically beautiful flowers (1, 2, 3) is from August to November. (6) G. *clusii* 'Coelestina' is a sky-blue variety in the alpine stemless gentian.

violet, tubular bells from hairy, silver-leaved rosettes, which are very sensitive to excess water while needing a cool humid atmosphere in the shade.

Haplophyllum (Rutaceae)

Haplophyllum patavinum (*Ruta. patavina*) from the Balkans is one of the most rewarding long-flowering, summer plants. Its yellow flowers stand on branched umbels on stems six to twelve inches (15–30 cm) high. It likes a limy soil and plenty of sun, and once established it will spread about without becoming a menace.

Haquetia (Umbelliferae)

H. epipactis enjoys shaded, woodland conditions in the same places as Christmas Roses, *Hepatica* and *Pulmonaria*. It lends colour and gaiety to the early spring with its heads of tiny, yellow flowers, surrounded by brilliant yellow-green bracts on four-inch (10 cm) stems.

Hedysarum (Leguminosae)

H. hedysaroides (*H. obscurum*) grows into bushes about eighteen inches (40–50 cm) high, and bears reddish-purple racemes in summer. This is a plant for the full sun between prostrate junipers and mountain pines. The shrubby *H. multijugum* from Central Asia is gaudier and more worthwhile. It is a looser-growing plant, about three feet (one metre) in height, with pinnate, grey-green leaves and slender crimson-purple flower spikes from June to August. It is a glorious plant for sunny slopes between yuccas, *Helictotrichon sempervirens* or other grey-leaved ornamental grasses.

Helichrysum (Compositae)   p. 55

Those who know only the annual 'Everlastings' will be astonished to discover that there are many perennial and shrubby species in this genus. *H. plicatum*, *H. thianshanicum* and the hybrid 'Sulphur Light' are white-felted, strong-growing, mat-forming plants with yellow clusters twelve inches (20–30 cm) high, suitable for dry sunny slopes, where they look well from summer to autumn.

The four-inch (10 cm) *H. bellidioides* from New Zealand with white flowers is a mat-forming plant, and *H. sibthorpii* (*virgineum*) from Mount Athos with pinkish-white everlasting flowers and woolly, white leaves is neat and suitable for sheltered, sunny positions.

H. milfordiae, from Lesotho, is even more compact. It forms tight, thick, woolly, grey cushions and bears strikingly large, white flowers on very short stalks from fat, pointed, pink buds. This is a gem, which thrives on east-facing crevices in the rocks and is completely hardy; it is one of the loveliest of rock garden plants.

The dainty, fine-stemmed Corsican *H. frigidum*, as well as the more robust, grey-leaved *H. orientale* with most attractive yellow flowers, from the eastern Mediterranean, are more suited to alpine-house cultivation. In severe climates, the dwarf, shrubby New Zealand species are also better grown there. *H. selago*, *H. coralloides* and *H. plumeum* are all striking foliage plants with their stems tightly packed with small, scale-like leaves set in white felt.

Heliosperma see Silene

Helleborus, Christmas and Lenten Roses (Ranunculaceae)   p. 19

H. niger, the glorious winter-flowering plant from the Alps, is one of the most treasured garden plants. Along with its variety 'Praecox', which blooms in November, and the large-flowered subspecies *macranthus* from the southern Alps, it should be planted with mountain pines, pink daphne and winter-flowering erica, with the sulphur-yellow wild primrose, blue hepatica and *Omphalodes*.

The *Helleborus* hybrids which have been produced from *H. orientalis* and related species are also attractive, varying from creamy-yellow through pink to dark red, and flowering in early spring, from large leafy clumps. The green-flowering *H. foetidus* and *H. corsicus* are useful evergreen foliage plants.

All these species are happiest in limy, rather heavy soil, in a fairly shaded position. They are permanent, long-lived plants, resenting disturbance and repaying an annual mulch with compost. *H. lividus*, a rather tender plant from Mallorca, is dwarf enough to make a fine alpine-house plant, enjoying the same conditions as the more tender cyclamen and flowering with them in early spring. Its little mushroom-grey cups are beautiful, as is its grey-green foliage, veined and marbled with white.

Hepatica (Ranunculaceae)

H. nobilis (*H. triloba, Anemone hepatica*) is a blue woodland plant and one of the prettiest of spring flowers. Along with its white and pink forms, it should be planted beside Christmas and Lenten Roses, daphnes, and primulas. The double varieties are rarely seen but they are charming and much sought-after. *H. transsilvanica* (*angulosa*) from Romania is a much stronger grower and flowers two weeks earlier. Both like lime and should be left undisturbed for many years. There are hybrids between them, *H. × media*, of which the form 'Ballardii' has extremely fine, large lavender-blue flowers.

Heuchera (Saxifragaceae)

These are useful plants from North America which form mounds of dark-green leaves and bear dainty bells in summer on spikes around eighteen inches (50 cm) high. The varieties of *H. × brizoides*, like the dwarf 'Shere Variety' and 'Red Spangles', which have shining red flowers, are especially valuable. The pink 'Gracillima' and 'Scintillation' are also pretty. They do well in any ordinary soil in sunny or half-shaded positions and look well with blue veronicas and campanulas.

× *Heucherella tiarelloides* and × *H. alba* 'Bridget Bloom', crosses between *Heuchera* and *Tiarella*, produce runners, attractively marked leaves and pink flowers. They are long-flowering plants, attractive from May onwards, which like half-shade and humus-rich soil. They look well with ferns and *Saxifraga rotundifolia*.

Hieracium, Hawkweed (Compositae) p. 73

Although there is a large number of species in this genus only a few are suitable for gardens. Alpine enthusiasts will appreciate the silky hair on the loose rosettes of *H. villosum*, which shimmers like silver in the dew of the morning. It has handsome, dull-yellow flowers in summer. This looks well alongside *Dryas* and alpine asters. *H. × rubrum* grows eight inches high (20 cm) and bears orange-red flowers in summer; it is not a very rapid grower and is sterile, so that it will not become a nuisance by seeding itself. This is not the case with *H. aurantiacum*, against which a warning must be given.

Horminum (Labiatae)

H. pyrenaicum, a native of both Pyrenees and Alps, is not especially exciting but it is modestly attractive with its puckered rosettes of leaves and violet-blue, lipped flowers from May to July.

Houstonia, Bluets (Rubiaceae)

H. caerulea 'Millard's Variety' and *H. serpyllifolia*, both from North America, are among the daintiest rock garden plants. They will thrive only in semi-shaded positions in lime-free soil, where they will cover their diminutive cushions of leaves with tiny sky-blue, star-shaped flowers in spring.

Hutchinsia (Cruciferae)

H. alpina and its subspecies *H. a. brevicaulis* and *H. a. auerswaldii* are tiny plants from the

European mountains with white flowers in spring over dark green leaves. They enjoy damp cracks between stones in both sun and shade.

Hylomecon (Papaveraceae)

H. japonicum is one of several delightful woodland plants from Japan for cool moist soil in some shade. Its clear, bright yellow poppy-like flowers appear in spring on twelve-inch (30 cm) stems. It has slowly spreading tuberous roots to which it dies down in autumn.

Hymenoxys see Actinella

Hypsela (Campanulaceae)

H. reniformis is a creeping plant from Chile with fresh-green, rounded leaves and pale pink flowers, striped with red, on short stems. These somewhat resemble lobelia flowers and appear in summer. It likes a cool position in peaty soil and needs protecting in winter.

Incarvillea (Bignoniaceae)

Chinese *I. compacta* and *I. mairei* (*I. grandiflora*), with its brilliant stemless form 'Frank Ludlow', have large, yellow-throated, rich-pink flowers on short stems, whilst the taller, eighteen inch (50 cm) *I. delavayi* has reddish-pink, or in 'Bees Pink', bright pink trumpets. They flower in June and are strikingly unusual plants meriting careful positioning on raised ground to achieve their full effect. Their exotic flowers need carefully chosen companions—Bergenias, maples and Chinese junipers look well alongside them. Their fleshy root-stocks resemble parsnips and should be planted in good, deep well-drained soil, in sun or light shade. They die back in late summer and vanish underground in winter.

Inula (Compositae)

I. ensifolia 'Compacta' is a first-class plant for dry positions, with its lanceolate, pointed leaves. Its eight-inch (20 cm) high tufts have yellow daisies in summer and their symmetrical appearance is attractive between paving-stones. *I. glandulosa* (*orientalis*) is looser in growth, and stands up to two feet (50–60 cm) high. It has large, narrow-rayed, orange-yellow flowers, and looks well near blue geraniums in wild places.

Iris (Iridaceae)   pp. 19, 47, 141

There is a whole world of beauty to be found under the heading 'Iris'. The four-inch (10 cm) early-flowering bulbous iris from the Near East (Reticulata Section) are quite delightful. These include the bright yellow *I. danfordiae* and the soft yellow *I. winogradowii*. *I. reticulata*, of which many hybrids and selections have been made, is available in violet, bright-blue and purple. The earliest of all is the dark-blue, large-flowered *I. histrioides* 'Major', and this is soon followed by the skyblue *I. histrio aintabensis* with dark spots. *I. bakeriana* is pale blue marked with purple and white. It grows best with some protection in the bulb-frame, as does *I. vartanii*. This can be light blue but is usually available in its white variety. The hybrid 'Katharine Hodgkin', however, grows perfectly well in the garden and seems to prefer not being dried out in summer. Its flowers are an unusual blend of pale blue and soft yellow. All these flower in February and March, when they will continue to bloom in spite of frost and snow. All the bulbous iris must be planted in autumn. Those who possess an alpine-house are recommended to plant them in pots, so that they will flower earlier and develop their full beauty undamaged by wintry weather.

The one to two feet (30–60 cm) irises from Central Asia are unusual and decorative (Juno Section). These are bulbous plants with fleshy roots and leek-like leaves. The bright-cobalt-blue *I. graeberiana*, the pale-yellow *I. bucharica*, and the chrome-yellow *I. orchioides*, all of which flower in April, and are quite easy to grow, belong to this group. The smaller Junos can be exquisite but all these are very difficult plants, for the experienced grower.

The crested irises are lovely (Evansia Section), and include *I. cristata* and the even smaller *I. lacustris* from North America, only two to three inches (4–8 cm) high. Their rhizomes creep along the surface of the soil and from these spring pale mats of leaves and mauve-blue flowers. The lavender *I. gracilipes*, the taller *I. tectorum*, and its lovely white form are related East Asian species. These Evansias need a loose, gritty soil, very rich in humus, with some shade, and dislike drought.

Another small spring flowering iris is bright-yellow *I. humilis* (*I. flavissima*, *I. arenaria*). It does best in a very gritty, sandy mixture. This little iris from the steppes of eastern Europe is one of the bearded irises (Pogoniris) and is considered close to the taller Regelia Irises from Central Asia. Both these and the Oncocyclus Irises, from Turkey, Israel and Iran, with which they hybridize, need to be planted out in a raised bed, covered to protect them against the rain both in summer and winter. These are among the most spectacular of all plants but are not easy to grow unless the enthusiast lives in a climate to their liking, such as in Arizona or New Mexico.

The many differently coloured dwarf hybrids are easier bearded irises and flower well when planted in dry ground in the sun or even grown in dry-stone walls. *I. pumila* and *I. reichenbachii* from south-east Europe are other beautiful, irises which like dry conditions, and have yellow or purple flowers. The irises of the Apogon Section grow in quite a different manner, their foliage forming grass-like clumps. Among these are blue and purple *I. graminea*, which smells of plums, *I. sintenisii*, *I. ruthenica* and *I. pontica*, and the one to two feet (30–60 cm) Chinese species, *I. forrestii* and *I. wilsonii*, which have yellow flowers, and *I. chrysographes*, with dark-violet blossoms. These are especially suitable for planting along the edges of streams.

Jankaea see **Haberlea**

Jasione, Sheep's Bit Scabious (Campanulaceae)
J. perennis forms fresh-green, turfy clumps, which are dotted in summer with round heads of cornflower-blue flowers on eight-inch (20 cm) stems. It looks very effective amongst pink and purple thymes but is a lime-hater.

Jeffersonia (Berberidaceae)
J. dubia is a lovely, eight-inch (20 cm) harbinger of spring from Manchuria with delicate, coppery new foliage and soft blue flowers. Its only disadvantage is that these fade all too quickly. It likes the shade and should be planted with daphnes or other small woodlanders in peaty soil. *J. diphylla* from the eastern USA is similar but white-flowered and not so striking.

Kelseya (Rosaceae)
K. uniflora is one of those cushion-forming, dry-climate cliff plants which, like *Dionysia*, are best grown in the alpine-house throughout the year. It is restricted to a few limestone canyons in the northern Rockies and forms close hummocks of tiny, silky, silver-green rosettes starred with equally tiny pinkish white flowers, if the grower is lucky or skilful enough.

Kirengeshoma (Saxifragaceae)
With its unusual maple-like leaves and distinctive flowers, Japanese *K. palmata* makes a very special feature in shaded places, when it flowers from September on. Its waxy, pale yellow, bell-shaped flowers, on dark stems, hang slightly downwards, so it is a good idea to plant this three-foot high plant in a slightly elevated position. *K. koreana* is very similar, though somewhat dwarfer and earlier, but holds its flowers upright. Both are woodland plants, disliking lime, for cool, moist, rich soil.

Kniphofia, Red-hot Poker (Liliaceae)
The only species suitable for the rock garden is

K. triangularis. Forms of this South African species are grown in gardens as *K. nelsonii* and *K. macowanii*, in bright orange-red, and *K. galpinii* in a lovely soft orange. They have narrow, grassy foliage in clumps, from which the two-feet (60 cm), dainty orange 'pokers' rise in autumn. They look well with yuccas and blue-grey grasses but also enjoy damp conditions in summer, though they will not stand being wet in winter when they may need protection from frost and rain.

Lamium and Lamiastrum, Dead Nettle (Labiatae)

L. galeobdolon has striking, silver-marked foliage, but it is so rampant that it is only suitable ground-cover for rough shady slopes in large gardens. The eight-inch (20 cm) 'Silver Carpet' is less dangerous, and has white leaves sprinkled with green. Both of these are only of interest for their ornamental leaves. The garden forms of the spotted dead nettle *L. maculatum* are attractive for both flowers and foliage: 'Album' with white flowers, and 'Roseum' with lovely, pink flowers. Most striking is 'Beacon Silver' with almost wholly silver leaves. All are suitable for covering the wilder shady places. *L. orvala* is an upright dead nettle some two feet (60 cm) tall from southern Europe, with large, brownish-pink flowers and recommended to lovers of unusual wild plants. All are easy to grow, and will thrive amongst shrubs.

Lathyrus, Bitter Vetch (Leguminosae)

The long-flowering, handsome *L. vernus* will grow about eighteen inches (30–50 cm) high in a shaded corner. Its bright-pink variety 'Roseus' is a must alongside daphnes and primulas. There are also purple, white, pink and white and blue forms—all charming and neat in spring.

Leontopodium, Edelweiss (Compositae)

To those who have seen it in nature, *L. alpinum*, the alpine edelweiss, is a disappointment in the garden, where its felted stars are nearer grey than white. It is a common enough plant in the wild and very easily grown in the rock garden. Like most widespread alpine plants, it is extremely variable and the very dwarf races are especially attractive. Such is the form of *L. alpinum nivale* from the Bulgarian Pirin Mountains, grown as *L. crassense* and a coveted alpine-house plant. There are a number of Asiatic species which have excellent, copious, white blossoms, like *L. calocephalum*, *L. souliei*, and *L. palibinianum*. All these need plenty of light and free-draining loamy soil with lime-rubble, and not too much food. They should be divided every second year and replanted.

Leucanthemum and Leucanthemopsis see Chrysanthemum

Leucogenes (Compositae)

L. grandiceps and *L. leontopodium* are aptly called New Zealand Edelweiss. Their gold and white-felted flower-heads are very similar in pattern to the European edelweiss but their neat, silver foliage makes them much choicer plants. They need well drained, gritty, peaty soil, which does not dry out, but sun to keep them compact. Like many New Zealand plants they grow best where summers are cool.

Lewisia (Portulacaceae)   pp. 23, 51, 59

L. cotyledon and its hybrids like rich, lime-free soil in cool crevices amongst stones; they dislike moisture round the necks of their evergreen rosettes and develop their maximum beauty in the alpine-house. 'Sunset Strain' are among the best mixed hybrids in shades of pink to orange and yellow. 'George Henley' has strawberry-red flowers and, like other named hybrids, must be propagated from cuttings, so is not so easily obtainable.

Apart from *Phlox*, *Lewisia* is possibly the most important of the exclusively North American genera for the rock gardener. Most come from the drier ranges of the western mountains and in wetter climates need the protection of an alpine-house. There are several dwarf, white-flowered species such as *L. brachycalyx* and *L. nevadensis*. These become dormant in late summer as does the sumptuous *L. rediviva*, which does not open its soft-pink, water-lily-like flowers until its fleshy leaves have shrivelled up. It needs to be dry in summer and treated like the spring-flowering bulbs. *L. tweedyi* needs a similar cycle of seasonal watering but retains its dark rosettes of leaves. Its large flowers are usually creamy pink but there are deeper pink ones, 'Rosea', and a pure white.

Limonium, Sea Lavender, Statice (Plumbaginaceae)

L. latifolium is a very long-lasting plant with prostrate rosettes of foliage and two-foot (60 cm) lilac-blue veils of flowers from July to September. It is a native of the dunes, and looks best amongst grasses and sea holly. *L. gougetianum* and *L. minutum* are charming, dwarf species for the alpine-house or trough.

Linaria, Toadflax (Scrophulariaceae)

Some species of this genus spread dangerously quickly. One should never be tempted into planting the pretty *Cymbalaria muralis* (*L. cymbalaria*), Ivy-leaved Toadflax, in the rock garden, or it will become a menace. It is useful, however, when used by itself on shady walls by waterfalls or fountains. The larger-flowered *Cymbalaria* (*Linaria*) *pallida* is also not to be despised and can be planted in dry-stone walls, where it will soon fill all the crevices with leaves and violet flowers. Violet, orange-lipped *L. alpina*, the alpine toadflax, is harmless and delightful, thriving in free-draining, gravelly ground and seeding itself. A number of other dwarf Spanish species will also make themselves at home in scree conditions and are worth experimenting with in the less formal rock garden.

Linum, Flax (Linaceae)   p. 39

Though growing to over eighteen inches (50 cm), *L. narbonense* is graceful with flowers of the finest, deepest blue. *L. austriacum* and *L. perenne* are similar but paler. The last has a large-flowered variety, 'Tetra', but these latter species have the disadvantage that their flowers never last later than noon. Other attractive species are *L. hypericifolium* from the Caucasus, with large, lilac-pink flowers; *L. flavum* 'Compactum', the yellow flax; the four-inch (10 cm) deep yellow 'Gemmells Hybrid'; and shining-yellow *L. elegans* from the Balkans. The dainty *L. salsoloides* with needle-shaped leaves on prostrate shoots has pearly-white flowers.

All of these will thrive as long as they have good drainage and plenty of sun. The blue-flowering species look lovely next to yellow.

Lithodora (Lithospermum), Gromwell (Boraginaceae)

There are some fine plants among these semi-shrubby species, such as the small, running *L. oleifolia* from Spain, with sky-blue flowers. However, the finest of the genus is *L. diffusa* 'Heavenly Blue', the blossoms of which are of the purest, deepest and most luminous blue. Unfortunately this beautiful plant is not completely hardy in severe climates and, moreover, it will only really thrive in lime-free soil. It is worth any trouble, however, and will look quite glorious if its gentian-blue flowers are planted in front of crimson Japanese azaleas.

There are also white and pale blue varieties. It is alone in its lime-hating quality among a genus of lime-lovers. More tender and more obviously shrubby are two fine Mediterranean cliff plants, pale blue *L. zahnii* and gentian-blue *L. rosmarinifolia*. These both make good alpine-house plants, growing to about one foot (30 cm) and flowering in winter and early spring.

Lobelia (Campanulaceae)

Although the dwarf form of the pale blue,

autumn-flowering American *L. syphilitica* 'Nana' is a pleasant little plant, the choicest species is the New Zealand *L. linnaeoides*. This is a prostrate, creeping plant with delicate white flowers for gritty peat in cool climates.

Lotus, Bird's-Foot Trefoil (Leguminosae)

The double variety of the bird's-foot trefoil, which grows only four inches (10 cm) high, *L. corniculatus* 'Plenus', is covered in summer with long-lasting golden flowers.

Lychnis, Campion (Caryophyllaceae)

L. viscaria 'Plena' is a double, crimson-pink, early summer flower and a real eye-catcher. It looks best in formal surroundings. There is a dwarf member of the genus, *L. alpina*, which grows only four inches (10 cm) high. In May it produces bright-purple heads from its grassy tufts of foliage. It is a lime-hater for a sunny position in acid soil with arnica, and dwarf rhododendrons.

Lysimachia, Creeping Jenny (Primulaceae)

The best species is the creeping *L. nummularia*, with dull-yellow flowers, delightful planted between paving-stones in damp places. *L. nummularia* 'Aurea' forms flat, golden-leaved mats.

Marrubium (Labiatae)

M. supinum from Spain, *M. incanum* from Italy and *M. velutinum* from Greece all have insignificant flowers but their soft, woolly, rounded leaves, like silver-green velvet, are so attractive that is a pleasure to grow and touch them. Their shrubby clumps like the full sun and a dry position.

Matthiola, Stock (Cruciferae)

M. valesiaca, with its grey-green foliage and bright-lilac, scented flowers, is worthy of note. It grows six inches (15 cm) tall and can be left to wander at will in really gravelly soil. The closely related Spanish *M. perennis* and its race from the Moroccan High Atlas *M. perennis anremerica* (*M. scapifera*) are larger-flowered, mauve-pink and form tighter clumps, if given a starvation diet in a hot, dry place.

Matricaria see Chrysanthemum

Mazus (Scrophulariaceae)

Himalayan *M. reptans* and *M. stolonifer* from Japan like damp, peaty soil, which they thickly cover with fresh-green carpets of small leaves and dainty, gold-speckled, lilac flowers. *M. radicans* from New Zealand forms a flat carpet of leaves almost earth-brown in colour and has white flowers. Enthusiasts can plant their peat beds and damp banks with these alongside orange *Mimulus cupreus* and yellow *Calceolaria*.

Meconopsis, Welsh Poppy, Blue Poppy (Papaveraceae)

M. cambrica has orange or yellow flowers and grows only too easily. Its relatives from the high mountains of Asia are more spectacular, temperamental plants, with silky flowers and hairy rosettes of leaves. All like a cool, humid position and must be shaded from the midday sun; the soil should be free-draining but rich in humus, and moist in the growing season. Many species are monocarpic and die after flowering. Such are the yellow-bristled, steel-blue *M. horridula* and *M. integrifolia* from Tibet and China, a very striking beauty with enormous, yellow-silk flowers. *M. napaulensis* with its pink to purple or wine-red flowers, and *M. regia* with its pure-yellow candelabra, both from Nepal, grow to the height of a man. The last species has lovely golden-haired rosettes, and is best protected from winter rain by covering it with a cloche. The fine, blue-flowering *M. grandis*, *M. betonicifolia* (*M. baileyi*) and their attractive hybrid *M.* × *sheldonii*, which is also pure blue, are all long-lived, about four feet (120 cm) high.

Planted next to rhododendrons in the shade of a maple these sky-blue poppy-like flowers provide a sight of ethereal beauty in the June garden. Dwarfer and more suited to the peat garden is the harebell poppy, *M. quintuplinervia* with pendant, mauve-blue flowers on one foot (30 cm) stems. It is also a good perennial.

Melandrium see **Silene**

Mentha, Mint (Labiatae)

Those who like fragrant herbs should plant the tiny species *M. requienii* from Corsica in moist crevices between rocks or paving, which it will soon cover with mossy green. When its flat carpets of leaves are touched, they fill the air with a refreshing scent.

Mertensia (Boraginaceae)

The lovely *M. virginica* from North America grows just over one foot (30 cm) high, thrives in semi-shaded positions and has sky-blue bells at the end of April. Smaller *M. primuloides* from the Himalayas grows only six inches (15 cm) high, thrives in the sun and bears gentian-blue flowers over its mats of leaves. *M. maritima* from northern coasts has beautiful fleshy, blue foliage and turquoise flowers from pink buds. It needs care in cool gritty soil and is a plant for the experienced grower, as are the tiny alpine species from the Rockies, such as *M. lanceolata*.

Meum (Umbelliferae)

M. athamanticum is a good plant for the informal rock garden, with its clumps of fresh-green, finely-cut foliage and white umbels in June. It likes deep, lime-free soil. *Eryngium alpinum*, *Crepis aurea*, *Gentiana lutea*, *Genista pilosa* and *Hieracium* species all look good alongside it.

Micromeria (Labiatae)

M. croatica, *M. microphylla* and others are neat, shrubby tufts from the Mediterranean area, about six inches (15 cm) high. They have tiny, grey aromatic leaves with pink flowers among them in summer, and will grow happily in sunny, well-drained crevices or in troughs.

Mimulus, Monkey Flower, Musk (Scrophulariaceae)

The pure orange-yellow of the true *M. cupreus* is undoubtedly one of the loveliest colours among flowers. It grows only four inches (10 cm) high, and may be planted in moderately damp but sunny positions among rocks or on the banks of streams beside *Houstonia* or *Mazus*. If it likes the spot it will seed itself. The rampant *M. luteus* should be avoided but its hybrid *M. × burnetii* is neater and worth growing, as are the named, brilliant red varieties, like 'Whitecroft Scarlet'.

Minuartia (Caryophyllaceae)

One of the most worthwhile species is *M. laricifolia*. It is undemanding as to soil and position, and covers its dull-green, needle-leaved mats, from June to September, with white flowers. The four-inch (10 cm) *M. verna* is also pretty, with tiny white stars on rounded cushions. It thrives in cracks in the rock but likes an acid soil. *M. graminifolia* (*Alsine rosanii*) is not so free-flowering but is worth growing in crevices for its large, thick, mossy cushions.

Mitchella, Partridge Berry (Rubiaceae)

M. repens is a beautiful evergreen from North America, with creeping shoots which cover the ground with oval leaves. Its pink flowers are followed by glistening, scarlet berries. It likes a cool, shady position and a peaty soil, thriving in peat beds beneath rhododendrons.

Mitella, Mitrewort (Saxifragaceae)

Like *Tiarella cordifolia* and the long-flowering, pinky-white *T. wherryi*, *M. caulescens*, *M. diphylla* and *M. pentandra* are pretty American shade-loving plants for woodland soil; they will quickly cover stones and earth, and bear dainty, white spires from May to June.

Moehringia (Caryophyllaceae)

M. muscosa may be planted in shady crevices next to *Ramonda* and small ferns. In summer its dainty, fresh-green bushes are decorated with four-rayed, white, starry flowers.

Morina (Dipsaceae)

Nothing could be more decorative than *M. longifolia* in the large rock garden or wild garden when, in early summer, it puts up three-foot (one metre) pink-and-white candles over its spiny clumps of thistle-like foliage. *M. persica* is more unusual and less adaptable but both will grow well on free-draining soil. Plants of striking architectural value such as these look best standing alone or against a background of prostrate conifers.

Morisia (Cruciferae)

M. monanthos (*hypogea*) is a valuable early-flowering plant for troughs or the alpine-house. It comes from Corsica and Sardinia and forms flat rosettes of ferny, dark green foliage, on which the clusters of yellow flowers sit. It needs a sandy, very well-drained soil.

Myosotis, Forget-me-not (Boraginaceae)

The dwarf Alpine *M. rehsteineri* can be planted in shallow water, where it forms beautiful clumps of blue a few inches (2–5 cm) high, with pink *Primula rosea* and marsh-marigolds as neighbours. *M. decora*, *M. saxosa* and others from New Zealand are also only one to two inches (2–5 cm) high but are quite different in habit. They have rosettes of bristly leaves and white flowers, like to grow in peaty scree and dislike wetness in winter.

Nepeta, Cat Mint (Labiatae)

N. × faasenii, the well known foot-high (30 cm), mauve-blue plant, is very undemanding and suitable for lending colour to large, sunny slopes in summer. 'Blue Dwarf' grows only eight inches (20 cm) high. These are obviously rather large or strong-growing and floppy for small rock gardens but look splendid beside paving or gravelled areas.

Nierembergia (Solanaceae)

N. repens (*N. rivularis*), from Argentina, likes damp ground, where it will quickly spread, covering its prostrate bright-green mats of foliage with large, white cups which almost rest on the leaves. *N. caerulea* needs protection in winter. It will grow easily in a drier place, making six-inch (15 cm) bushes covered all summer with deep purple bells.

Oenothera, Evening Primrose   p. 69
(Oenotheraceae)

One of the best of these is the well-known *O. missouriensis*. It needs plenty of space in which to extend its trailing shoots with their huge, yellow flowers. It can be planted in beds above dry-stone walls to hang down. Choice, grey-leaved *O. caespitosa* opens its large, green-throated, white flowers at night, and looks well near yuccas and opuntias; it will spread without becoming a nuisance. *O. tetragona* has reddish foliage and yellow flowers in great profusion, which look well beside blue delphiniums. The variety 'Fireworks' is especially colourful, with red buds and yellow flowers.

Omphalodes, Navelwort (Boraginaceae)

O. verna may be left to cover shady ground, where it will give pleasure each spring with its sky-blue flowers. *O. cappadocica* from the Caucasus is a sun-loving plant, four to six inches (10–15 cm) high, and a good grower, whilst choice *O. luciliae* is a lovely limestone cliff-plant with blue-grey leaves and porcelain-blue flowers. It does best in rich, gritty soil, in a narrow, shady cranny, from which it will flow out. Protect from snails and wetness in winter. It makes an especially lovely alpine-house plant with a long flowering season.

Omphalogramma (Primulaceae)
These are essentially plants for gardeners in climates with cool, moist summers and cold winters. They are all from the eastern Himalayas and south-west China and need rich, moist soil in the peat bed. *O. vinciflorum* with exotic, deep violet flowers is possibly the easiest, but purple *O. minus* and *O. elegans* are also grown. They flower at about six inches (15 cm) high and die back to scaly resting-buds in winter.

Onosma, Golden Drop (Boraginaceae)　　**p. 77**
Most of the species have yellow flowers, and of these two of the best are *O. stellulatum* and *O. tauricum*. *O. cinerara* (*O. albo-roseum*) has striking, large, white flowers flushed with pink, and grows in bristly clumps, whilst the rare *O. sieheanum* has flesh-pink flowers; both come from Turkey. All species like dry positions with as much warmth and sun as possible. They do well on dry-stone walls, protected from winter rain, or in the alpine-house.

Opuntia (Cactaceae)
Hardy cacti which will withstand up to 30°C of frost (−22°F) are something of a rarity. The appearance of these wrinkly, spiny plants is unusual too. They awake from their dormant period only in the heat of summer, when they produce shining, silky flowers of large dimensions. These come from as far north as the Bad Lands of South Dakota and look best with other succulents, yuccas, *Caragana jubata* and other desert plants, in the sunniest corner of the garden. The best known are the yellow-flowering *O. phaeacantha* (*O. camanchica*), *O. polyacantha* (*O. missouriensis*) and the crimson *O. rhodantha* in different varieties, together with the pinkish-red *O. rutila*. All of them need very well-drained, sandy or gravelly soil and will not withstand wet conditions, especially in winter. There are other high-altitude species from the Andes worth the attention of the unprejudiced alpine-house enthusiast.

Orchids (Orchidaceae)　　pp. 59, 81
Wild orchids are generally under legal protection, and however charming and desirable they may seem, one should never be tempted into digging them up and bringing them home. Most of them will in any case not last long in the garden.

One of the easiest hardy orchids to grow is *Bletilla striata* from China. Although it will require a good covering of leaves in the winter, it will grow in any soil in any position flowering best in well-drained loam and peat, planted in the sun. It has bamboo-like leaves, between which appear lovely crimson-pink flowers, with white markings on their lips, on twelve-inch (30 cm) stems during the summer.

Although the Lady's Slipper orchids (*Cypripedium*) can be grown with patience in humus-rich soils or peat-beds, plants offered for sale have almost invariably been collected in the wild, so it is a matter of personal conscience whether or not to attempt to grow such material.

The varieties of *Pleione bulbocodioides* grown in gardens as *P. limprichtii*, *P. formosana*, *P. pricei* and *P. pogonioides*, are humus-loving rock plants from China, with flowers varying from white to deep carmine pink. They need plenty of water in summer and must be absolutely dry in winter. Although they look like tropical plants they have proved to be perfectly hardy if covered with a thick layer of dry peat in autumn. In case of uncertainty, the pseudo-bulbs can be lifted in autumn when the leaves drop, and wintered in the cellar, to be replanted again in early spring. The Indian species are not hardy nor so easy: *P. hookeriana*, pale lilac; *P. humilis*, white with black-flecked lips; and also Chinese *P. forrestii*, with yellow flowers. *P. praecox* and *P. maculata* flower in autumn at the end of their growing season and start growing again in March, when they need careful watering. *P. yunnanensis* is quite a hardy species which seems to prefer cooler conditions in summer and is unusual in liking its pseudo-bulbs covered. The others should only be half-buried when repotted in January in shallow pans. All of these lovely orchids are suitable for the unheated or frost-free glass-house, where they will bloom early in the year. The recipe for success in cultivating them is: dry in winter, wet in summer. Their soil should be loose and rich in humus. They grow well in shredded bark with regular weak liquid feeding when in growth to build up the pseudo-bulbs for the following season.

Origanum, Marjoram (Labiatae)

O. *vulgare* 'Compactum' grows into small bushes, eight inches (20 cm) high at the most, with dense, pinkish-lilac flowers in summer, and provides a great attraction for bees and butterflies. It looks very well with thymes, heathers, asters and junipers. O. *amanum* is a choicer species from Turkey. It forms small rounded bushes hardly four inches (10 cm) high, which are decked for weeks with long-tubed, pink flowers in summer. It is a lovely plant for the alpine-house but, where summers are hot, can also be grown in a sunny position in the rock garden. O. *hybridum* is a lovely plant, which smells of marjoram. Its twelve inch (30 cm) wiry stems bear clusters of grey-haired leaves and end in loose, purple hop-like flower-heads. It looks especially attractive in the alpine-house, where it will bloom from July until Christmas. O. *tournefortii* has similar attractions, while Turkish O. *laevigatum* is proving its worth as a garden plant with its clouds of tiny red-purple flowers on one foot (30 cm) stems all summer.

Another delightful species for the alpine-house or a very well-protected, sunny crevice, is O. (*Amaracus*) *dictamnus* from Crete. Its stalks are four to six inches (10–15 cm) long and carry rounded, white-haired leaves and nodding, pink heads of flower peeping from pink bracts.

Orostachys (Crassulaceae)

O. *spinosa* from Mongolia resembles a spiny Sempervivum and does well in tufa blocks in full sun or half-shade. It has yellow flowers. Chinese O. *chanetii* is pink and is best protected from excess moisture.

Osteospermum Compositae

These long-flowering South African daisies, usually grown as *Dimorphotheca*, are useful plants in climates with mild winters. Most garden plants are hybrids, mainly involving O. *jucundum* (*Dimorphotheca barberiae*) and O. *ecklonis*, in shades of pink and white, and too strong-growing for small areas, though most are low-growing or prostrate. There is, however, a very dwarf plant, O. *jucundum compactum*, from a high altitude in the Drakensberg Mountains. This has bright-pink daisies in summer on stiff erect stems only six inches (15 cm) high from neat clumps of fleshy leaves. This is the hardiest and slowest growing form but unfortunately it is difficult to obtain the true plant, as larger plants are often sold under this name.

Ourisia (Scrophulariaceae)

These are mat-forming plants for cool, moist growing conditions. The New Zealand species are all white-flowered and range from the prostrate, minute-leaved O. *caespitosa gracilis* to the coarser leaved tufts of O. *macrocarpa* and O. *macrophylla* which reach about one foot (30 cm) when in flower. The South American species are little known apart from O. *coccinea* (*elegans*), which has scarlet, tubular flowers. Chilean O. *microphylla* is a very choice plant for the alpine-house though it prefers cool conditions plunged outside in summer. It forms a carpet of thready stems clothed in tiny, round leaves and covered with lilac-pink flat flowers in early summer. There are also two Scottish hybrids: white 'Snowflake' and pink 'Loch Ewe', which links the two continents in its parentage. Almost all will do well in peat-bed conditions.

Paeonia, Paeony (Ranunculaceae)

Most paeonies are not rock garden plants but *P. tenuifolia* from south-east Europe and Russia grows about one foot eight inches (50 cm) high with single, blood-red flowers, over finely divided clumps of leaves. It may be planted at the foot of dry-stone walls, where it will resemble a crimson *Adonis*, blooming as early as May. Compact *P. veitchii* in soft magenta-red and its light pink race *P. v. woodwardii* from China are about the same height. Their large, nodding flowers open later above beautiful, glossy divided foliage. The smallest of all is *P. cambessedesii* from Mallorca with rose-pink flowers over lead-green, crimson-backed leaves. It is best grown in the shaded alpine-house, where it is valued as a pot-plant, in the company of *Helleborus lividus* and *Cyclamen* species. White *P. clusii* from Crete and *P. rhodia* from Rhodes merit similar treatment.

Papaver, Poppy (Papaveraceae)

The Iceland Poppy, *P. nudicaule*, is one of the most loved species for the rock garden. Its gay poppies vary from white to yellow and orange shades. It can be planted anywhere in sun, the only danger being that it will spread too far by self-seeding. The true Alpine Poppies, *P. alpinum* with its many different white and yellow races, are dainty but delicate scree-dwellers, and will only thrive in gravelly mixtures. Soft orange *P. rupifragum* and *P. atlanticum* from Spain and Morocco are suitable for hot, dry sites, whereas the little, lemon-yellow Japanese *P. miyabeanum* is best in cooler scree.

Paradisea, St Bruno's Lily (Liliaceae)

P. liliastrum is a fine and precious plant from the southern Alps with white trumpets on thin stalks rising over grassy foliage. It looks particularly lovely amongst blue flax and does best in lime-free soil. It is so abundant in some Alpine meadows that it makes the whole area shine white.

Paraquilegia (Ranunculaceae)

P. grandiflorum is a variable species widespread along the length of the Himalayan ranges but always local and restricted to cool cliffs. It is best known to alpine enthusiasts in the form established in Scotland from material collected in Bhutan. This has filmy, deep violet flowers over tufts of delicately cut, blue-grey foliage. The colour can vary to paler shades but in all forms it is one of the world's truly beautiful alpines. It is best grown in shaded alpine-house conditions in rich, gritty soil with careful, even watering and not allowed to become too dry during its winter rest.

Parnassia, Grass of Parnassus (Saxifragaceae)

P. palustris has white, pearl-like buds and finely veined petals. It should be planted in a damp position in the peat bed if it is to thrive and flower in late summer. North American *P. fimbriata* and the taller, eight-inch (20 cm) Himalayan *P. nubicola* are similar plants for similar places.

Parochetus, Shamrock Pea (Leguminosae)

P. communis is a widely distributed mountain plant from India, the East Indies and the equatorial mountains of East Africa. Its creeping shoots cover the ground during the course of a single season, spreading mats of pretty clover-leaves. Its solitary, brilliant turquoise-blue flowers appear in late summer and autumn. It likes a somewhat damp, shady position and needs protection in the winter, or pieces may be potted up and overwintered under glass.

Paronychia (Caryophyllaceae)

P. capitata, *P. argentea* and *P. kapela* are easy plants which form cushions which cling closely to the ground, and bear heads of silvery-white, papery bracts. The fast-growing *P. kapela serpyllifolia* is perhaps the best, with its brown autumn colouring.

Patrinia (Valerianaceae)

P. scabiosaefolia has heads of flowers resembling valerian, but yellow in colour, on stems three feet (one metre) high; it looks very well amongst blue aconites and Jacob's Ladder, between mountain pines. *P. triloba* (*P. palmata*), in contrast, is a modest, eight inch (20 cm) dwarf suitable for half-shady positions. It has palmate leaves and yellow flowers in summer.

Pelargonium, Stork's-Bill (Geraniaceae)

P. endlicherianum is a unique, hardy pelargonium from Turkey with strange, crimson-pink, dark-veined flowers for a very sunny crevice, well protected from the rain. It likes a very free-draining soil and is highly recommended for dry-stone walls or the alpine-house.

Penstemon (Scrophulariaceae)

A great number of species and varieties of these North American plants, some of which are shrubby, are available, so that it is difficult to survey them and make a selection. Some of the best are *P. alpinus*, purple-blue; *P. barbatus* 'Nanus', red and pink; *P. caespitosus*, turquoise; *P. newberryi*, magenta; *P. hallii*, shining-blue or purple; *P. hirsutus pygmaeus*, lilac-pink; *P. linarioides*, lilac; *P. scouleri*, lilac-purple; *P. pinifolius*, scarlet; *P. rupicola*, rose; *P. menziesii microphyllus*, prostrate, violet-blue.

All species like plenty of light and sun and a free-draining, preferably acid soil. Many of them are rapid growers but these are often not very long-lived. Their appearance makes them best suited to growing next to other American alpines: *Eriogonum*, *Eriophyllum*, *Heuchera* and *Phlox*. They can be grown in hot, dry gardens, where their reds and blues will enliven the greys of artemisias and the dull, leaden shades of agaves, sedums and yuccas.

Petrocallis (Cruciferae)

P. pyrenaica comes from high in the Alps and Pyrenees but it makes itself at home, on sunny, stony ledges, at low altitudes as well, or in stone troughs, where its tiny pale-lilac or white cushions of flowers can be fully appreciated.

Petrocoptis (Caryophyllaceae)

P. pyrenaica is a modest little plant, some four inches (10 cm) high, with blue-green leaves and pale-pink flowers. It likes shady, humus-filled crevices, and blossoms from spring until summer. The somewhat larger, pink *P. glaucifolia* (*P. lagascae*) from the mountains of northern Spain has the same requirements.

Phlox (Polemoniaceae) pp. 39, 43, 153

This North American genus is quite indispensable. Our gardens would be unthinkable without the glories of the tall border phloxes and the same is true of the dwarf phloxes in our rock gardens in April and May. The hybrids of *P. subulata* and *P. douglasii* come in every shade of crimson, pink, lilac and white, spreading over walls, terraces and slopes. The exuberance and gaiety of their colours are almost too vivid for the rock garden and look better in a more formal setting.

The best pinks and reds are 'Atropurpurea', rose-red; 'Betty', bright-pink; 'Rosette', dark pink, with thick cushions; 'Alexanders Surprise', 'Samson', warm pink; 'Scarlet Flame', 'Red Wings' and 'Temiscaming', vivid reds. Recommended white varieties are 'May Snow' and the strong-growing 'White Delight'. The slate-blue, old-fashioned but still irreplaceable 'G. F. Wilson' is also a strong grower.

Other species with abundant flowers are the eight to twelve inch (20–30 cm) *P. amoena*, pink to crimson; *P. divaricata*, lilac-blue; *P. stolonifera* 'Blue Ridge', heliotrope-blue; the slate-blue crimson-eyed 'Chattahoochee', and *P. reptans*, with pink flowers. All look well planted next to other strongly coloured plants such as saxifrages, candytuft, and dwarf iris hybrids. *P. hoodii*, *P. caespitosa*, *P. missoulensis* and *P. bryoides* are choice cushion-plants with close, grey needle-leaves and pale lilac, blue or white flowers. They need careful cultivation in troughs, raised beds or the alpine-house, as does the sumptuous *P. nana* (*P. mesoleuca, triovulata*) from the south-western USA. This has a sprawling habit but splendid pink flowers. Similar in flower and growth is *P. adsurgens* and its variety 'Wagon Wheels' but this needs entirely different conditions in cool, gritty, lime-free soil with some shade.

Phuopsis (Rubiaceae)

P. stylosa (*Crucianella stylosa*) grows eight inches (20 cm) high. It is not particularly attractive and can become a menace through its rampant growth. It is useful, however, in larger gardens where its flat pink heads (or purplish-red in the case of the variety 'Rubra') look their best in May-June.

Physaria see Coluteocarpus

Physoplexis and Phyteuma
(Campanulaceae) p. 89

Physoplexis comosa (*Phyteuma comosum*) is a very strange plant from the Dolomites, which tumbles out from vertical cliffs and bears bluish-white clusters of flowers with violet claws. To grow it well is the dream of many an enthusiast. It is best established as a young pot-grown plant in narrow crevices in tufa. Protect from slugs and snails. The Phyteumas of the Alpine meadows, *P. orbiculare*, with round, blue heads, the darker *P. scheuchzeri* and others are less spectacular but pleasant slow-growing plants some six to eight inches (15–20 cm) high, good for planting amongst different small grasses.

Platycodon, Balloon Flower, Chinese Bellflower (Campanulaceae)

P. grandiflorum is a shallow-cupped bellflower from East Asia; 'Mariesii' is a sixteen inch (40 cm) variety with lilac-blue or white flowers,

whilst 'Mother of Pearl' is pale pink. The best for the rock garden is *P. grandiflorum* 'Apoyama' from Hokkaido, Japan, which grows into eight inch (20 cm) high clumps with huge, violet-blue flowers. All are excellent summer flowers.

Pleione see Orchids

Polemonium, Jacob's Ladder (Polemoniaceae)

These are pretty, spring flowers with fresh-green, pinnate leaves and pale-blue flowers, from the mountains of Europe and North America. The hybrid *P.* × *richardsonii* grows about eighteen inches (40–50 cm) high and has sky-blue flowers. It does best in a slightly moist place in sun or half-shade. It also has attractive white ('Album') and violet-blue ('Superbum') variants. Other useful species are *P. reptans*, only twelve inches (30 cm) high, with pale-blue flowers, its variety 'Blue Pearl' and the flesh-coloured *P. carneum*. Both of these come from the mountains of North America, as do several choicer species like straw-yellow *P. brandegei* and the high-alpine *P. confertum*, *P. viscosum* and their allies, all exquisite but temperamental plants, with blue flowers for rich, gravelly soils.

Polygonatum, Solomon's Seal (Liliaceae)

P. odoratum, *P. officinale* and *P. verticillatum* are one foot to one foot eight inches (30–50 cm) woodland plants, which are slow but easy to establish in shade beneath shrubs or mountain pines. The same goes for *P. falcatum* from Japan which is only six inches (15 cm) tall. *P. hookeri* from the Himalayas grows only an inch or so (3–5 cm) high, and is quite different with upright, lilac-pink flowers in the axils of its leaves in April. It likes damp humus, building up dense colonies in time.

Polygonum, Knotweed (Polygonaceae)

One of the best species is the creeping

Himalayan knotweed, *P. affine*, with its varieties, 'Darjeeling Red' and 'Donald Lowndes'. Their pink spires jostle over thick mats of foliage well into autumn. They are very useful for topping dry-stone walls. *P. vacciniifolium* is a smaller version of these which looks well with heaths in acid soil. *P. tenuicaule* is a dwarf species from Japan, with upright white spires from mats of dull-green leaves, shaded reddish-brown on the undersides. It flowers in April, grows hardly more than four inches (10 cm) high and likes a shady, moist position, where it will soon form small, turfy clumps with its thick, flat, creeping stems. Similar *P. milletii* and *P. sphaerostachyum* from the Himalayas have quite different growth, with dark-green rosettes and crimson, one foot eight inch (50 cm) spires of flowers. They flower in late summer and are neat, well-behaved plants for moist, rich soil or the peat bed.

Potentilla, Cinquefoil (Rosaceae)

P. nitida with its rich, clear rose-pink flowers will have delighted the eyes of anyone who has walked through the Dolomites in early summer. Unfortunately, it seldom flowers so copiously in the garden and one must be content with its silver-grey cushions of foliage, which cling tightly to the rock. *P. speciosa* from Turkey has even shinier silver leaves, forming little clumps in sunny crevices. Of the small, mat-forming species, *P. aurea*, in particular its subspecies, *chrysocraspeda* (*P. ternata*) with yellow flowers, is delightful next to *Veronica prostrata*. *P. ambigua* from the Himalayas, with golden-yellow flowers, is another indispensable species, along with the compact, grey leaved, yellow *P. fragiformis* and the early-flowering *P.* 'Verna Nana' (a form of *P. crantzii*) which is only two inches (5 cm) tall. The eighteen inch (40–50 cm) species from the Himalayas, which have silky strawberry-like leaves and attractive blossoms, are also valuable: these are the yellow *P. argyrophylla*; the dark red *P. atrosanguinea*, with

its scarlet hybrid 'Gibson's Scarlet', the cherry-pink *P. nepalensis* 'Miss Willmott' (which looks superb behind *Gentiana farreri*), and the rich-flowering 'Flammenspiel', with red blooms edged with yellow. Nor should the slightly smaller (30–40 cm) species be forgotten, the profusely flowering, pale yellow *P. recta* 'Sulphurea' and the white *P. rupestris* 'Pygmaea'.

All potentillas may be recommended for the length of their flowering season in summer and they fit well into any scheme.

Pratia (Campanulaceae)

These are prostrate mat-forming plants with lobelia-like, white, violet-streaked flowers followed by purple berries. *P. angulata* (*treadwellii*) and *P. macrodon* come from New Zealand and *P. repens* is South American. All enjoy a cool, moist, gritty, peaty soil.

Primula (Primulaceae)   pp. 43, 117, 121

Primulas include some of the loveliest flowers in nature. There are hundreds of species, most of which are natives of East Asia, and many of them are highly prized garden plants. The primulas of the Auriculastrum Section from the

Many kinds of primulas are found in the mountains of Europe and Asia. They vary in appearance and in their choice of natural habitat. Many species thrive on rocks, whilst others adorn meadows or grow in woods. They are lovely and desirable flowers, but not all of them will do well in the garden. Among the permanent guests in the rock garden we see here (1) *Primula auricula* which flourishes between limestone rocks, (2) *P. vulgaris sibthorpii*, which flowers in February, and (3) *Primula denticulata* from the Himalayas, several varieties of which are available in lilac, pink, and white.

European Alps are not always easy in cultivation at low altitudes. Among those which will grow and flower well are *P. auricula* with mealy leaves and large, yellow flowers and *P. marginata* with white-powdered, sharply toothed leaves and lilac flowers. Both of these grow best in crevices and on rock ledges and will thrive in dry-stone walls facing either east or west. The sweet-scented garden auriculas in their delicate shades of yellow, lilac and brown, also grow best in shady positions. The dwarfer garden hybrids of the European auriculas are the most satisfactory for the rock garden, however. These are usually listed in catalogues under *P. × pubescens* and include many vigorous free-flowering plants under six inches (15 cm) high. The older reds, like 'Faldonside', 'Rufus' and 'The General' are still unequalled for colour, and pale-violet 'Mrs J. H. Wilson' is unequalled for vigour, but there are good newer creamy-whites like 'Harlow Car' and fine deeper violet hybrids like 'Christine'. All like a cool, rich, gritty soil and make easy plants for the alpine-house if kept free from greenfly and root aphis. The alpine-house Primula par excellence, however, is *P. allionii*, a plant beloved by English enthusiasts who grow it to perfection. It is a very slow-growing, limestone-cliff plant, happiest grown under glass throughout the year. It needs little water in summer and winter but will take quite moist conditions when the roots are active after flowering in spring and in early autumn. It is a very local plant in nature, only growing in a small area of the Maritime Alps, but its popularity in cultivation is shown by the many named forms. Among the more distinct are white 'Snowflake' and 'Avalanche', luminous carmine 'Crowsley' and the robust 'William Earle'.

Of the European alpine-meadow primulas, *P. farinosa* and the larger *P. frondosa* from Bulgaria do best in the peat bed, whilst *P. halleri* (*P. longiflora*) prefers turfy soil with lime rubble. The soft-yellow wild European primrose, *P. vulgaris* (*P. acaulis*) is very easy to establish. This, and its lilac-pink eastern subspecies *sibthorpii*, are among the earliest to flower, bringing joy as early as February. The lovely hybrids of *P. vulgaris* and *P. elatior* come in all colours, and wonderful effects can be achieved with them. *P. juliae* from the Caucasus looks well everywhere, covering its mats of foliage in April with purple flowers. The many strong, purple Juliana hybrids (*P. × pruhoniciana*) stem from this species and do very well if they are kept moist enough.

Of the Asian primulas, it is impossible to be without the early-flowering spherical heads of *P. denticulata*, ranging from lilac through violet, pink, crimson and purple to pure white, or the vivid carmine-pink *P. rosea*. The latter, especially, requires plenty of moisture. The Candelabra primulas, *P. aurantiaca*, *P. beesiana*, *P. bulleyana*, *P. cockburniana*, *P. helodoxa*, *P. japonica*, *P. pulverulenta* and their hybrids, are excellent and colourful early summer flowers for moist areas near water, as are the members of the Sikkimensis Section, *P. alpicola*, *P. sikkimensis*, and *P. florindae*, with their profuse heads of pendant flowers. *P. capitata*, *P. flaccida* (*nutans*) and *P. vialii* are exquisite plants for the peat bed as are two similar tiny alpine species, with pink flowers in March, *P. clarkei* from Kashmir and *P. warshenewskiana* from Afghanistan. Both need plenty of moisture in gritty, peaty soil.

All primulas prefer to be damp rather than dry during their growing season but many of them detest winter wetness. Robust species like *P. japonica* and *P. florindae* will thrive in any soil, but the more delicate ones can require much care. Most Asiatic primulas dislike lime and they all like a cool, humid atmosphere, flourishing near water and in the half-shade for that reason.

Those wishing to try some of the choicer species, many of which can be easily obtained by raising them from seed, should bear these basic rules in mind and adapt their gardening to suit them and their local climate. The Cortusoides Section are mainly rather hairy woodlanders, and Chinese *P. polyneura* is one of the easiest. *P. sieboldii* has long been grown in Japan and many named selections are available. The Petiolares Section are rather like aristocratic versions of the European primrose, often dusted with yellow farina. They can be grown in peat beds if protected from winter wet. Lilac-pink *P. gracilipes* and ice-blue *P. whitei* are two of the easiest of these difficult plants. Of the Soldanelloideae Section, apart from the more robust, pale violet *P. flaccida* (*nutans*), the easiest to start with is *P. reidii* in its sturdier Nepalese variety *williamsii*, with scented white or blue bells on six inch (15 cm) stems. Among the Nivales Section, cream *P. chionantha* and violet *P. sinopurpurea* are not too difficult in the peat bed. The American species are few but the distinctive *P. suffrutescens* from California is outstanding with its shrubby stems and rose-pink flowers. It can be tried in a raised bed or the alpine-house, as can the New Mexican *P. ellisiae* and *P. rusbyi*, with heads of lilac-blue or red-purple flowers from neat basal foliage.

Prunella, Self Heal (Labiatae)

These are undemanding, long-flowering plants with whorled heads from July to September on thick mats of foliage. The most attractive are the large-flowered *P.* × *webbiana* in violet-blue and the forms of *P. grandiflora*, bright-lilac 'Loveliness', pink 'Rosea' and white 'Alba'. 'Rotkappchen' ('Red Riding-hood') is a very deep carmine-pink. All will succeed in sun or part shade.

Pterocephalus (Dipsaceae)

P. parnassi from the mountains of Greece forms flat, grey-green mats of foliage adorned in summer with pink, scabious-like flowers on short stems. It likes the sun and a dry position, and is happiest when it can spread over stones.

If obtainable, other species can be grown in similar places.

Pulmonaria, Lungwort (Boraginaceae)

P. angustifolia, narrow-leaved with azure-blue flowers, is one of the loveliest of these easy, spring-flowering shade-loving plants. *P. saccharata* 'Margery Fish' and coral-red *P. rubra* should be planted by anyone with sufficient space available.

Suitable neighbours include pink and yellow *Epimedium*, Christmas and Lenten roses, golden *Eranthis* and the smaller ferns, as well as white *Leucojum vernum*, snowdrops, and dog-tooth violets.

Pulsatilla, Pasque Flower (Ranunculaceae)   p. 65

P. halleri slavica is one of the earliest and largest, unfolding its big, star-shaped, violet blossoms as early as March from fat, silvery-haired buds. *P. albana* has nodding, lilac bells or soft yellow in the garden form 'Caucasica'. *P. montana* and *P. pratensis* surround their violet-black bells with tall, silky-haired leaves. Garden hybrids of these species with *P. vulgaris*, the Pasque Flower, have produced a wide range of shades from white ('White Swan') and pale lilac through salmon-pink (Canadian 'Bartons Pink' is a good strain), red ('Rote Glocke'), to reddish violet and brownish red. All like free-draining, limy soil, an airy position and sun. Of the wild forms, the English race is one of the dwarfest and the eastern *P. v. grandis* the largest in flower, always opening its buds before the leaves unfold. Taller *P. alpina* also likes lime but pale yellow *P. alpina apiifolia* (*sulphurea*) does not. Nor does the dwarfer, pure-white *P. alba*. These should be planted as young seedlings and take time to establish. The beautiful *P. vernalis*, a diminutive plant with white bells covered with golden hairs, is even more of a challenge in the garden.

Ranunculus, Buttercup (Ranunculaceae) **p. 65**
One of the loveliest is *R. calandrinioides* from the Atlas Mountains of Morocco. It opens as soon as the snow has melted, producing pinkish-white flowers above its grey-green leaves. It likes to be damp in winter and dry in summer so is usually grown under glass. The eight inch (20 cm) Pyrenean *R. amplexicaulis* is also pretty, with its silvery-white cups in May-June. It likes loamy soil and should not be allowed to dry out.

   R. aconitifolius, taller and with many smaller, white flowers, grows equally well in sun or half-shade and looks in place beside pools and streams. *R. gramineus* enjoys dry, sunny positions, where its vivid yellow flowers can contrast with blue *Linum alpinum*. The glorious, three-foot (one metre) yellow *R. lingua* is excellent for the boggy edges of large pools whilst *R. aquatilis* should be planted in deeper water, where its leaves will float charmingly on the surface. The white-flowered, high-altitude buttercups from the European ranges are by no means as impossible to grow as the fabulous and unattainable *R. glacialis*. *R. alpestris* and *R. crenatus* are usually successful in moist, gritty peat with a little shade in summer. The New Zealand species are more difficult, succeeding best in cool moist summers. The large white *R. lyallii* and yellow *R. insignis* are perhaps the most magnificent of all buttercups but like the other dwarfer alpines are not the most permanent of garden plants. The Australian alpine *R. muelleri* with varnished yellow cups seems to be proving more accommodating.

Ranzania (Berberidaceae)
R. japonica is yet another distinguished Japanese woodland plant quite unlike anything else. Its pale-green, lobed leaves eventually reach about eighteen inches (50 cm) but it opens its cool lilac flowers early nearer the ground. This is a plant for the peat bed.

Raoulia (Compositae)
pp. 39, 43
Those usually seen in gardens are carpeting plants from New Zealand which grow quite flat on the ground. *R. hookeri* and *R. australis* are silvery-white and, without doubt, the most effective but *R. glabra*, *R. tenuicaulis* and the tiny *R. lutescens* are also desirable. They require free-draining, gritty soil, a sunny position, and above all, protection from winter rain. Their minute rosettes form carpets of foliage for trough gardens and small beds. The beginner should not be misled into thinking all species are as easy as these. The famous Vegetable Sheep, which form great white or silver hummocks high on the New Zealand mountains, are among the most difficult plants. The specialist will want to try species like *R. eximia*, *R. mamillaris* and *R. buchananii*, which need cool, moist summer conditions and more water than their woolly appearance would suggest, but very careful watering in winter.

Ricotia (Cruciferae)
R. davisiana is a very unusual scree plant from southern Turkey for deep, gravelly soil and full sun in a raised bed or the alpine-house, where it can be protected from excess moisture. Its six-inch (15 cm) stems of soft-pink flowers blend beautifully with its lobed, fleshy blue-grey foliage.

(1) *Primula vialii* from west China is one of the loveliest of all primulas, an exotic beauty. It needs humus soil and a cool, moist position. (2) *P.* 'Linda Pope' is a large-flowered variety or hybrid of *P. marginata*, the slate-blue cliff auricula from the Maritime Alps. (3) *P. clarkei* is a delightful miniature primula (lifesize illustration) from Kashmir, which likes moist humus and flowers in April.

Romanzoffia, Mist Maidens
(Hydrophyllaceae)
These small, saxifrage-like plants come from the moist, shady rocks of western North America and north-east Asia and are all similar in their fleshy, rounded leaves and pearly-white cups. They need cool, damp shade and will die back to tuberous bases when it is too hot, dry or cold. *R. sitchensis* is the most often available.

Rosularia (Crassulaceae)
R. pallida from Turkey forms thick mats of fleshy, hairy rosettes of leaves and bears pale-yellow flowers. It is a plant for the specialist, and does best in the alpine-house. Others flower in pink or white and need similar conditions.

Rupicapnos and **Sarcocapnos**
(Papaveraceae)
These two genera are all small cliff-plants from Spain and north-west Africa, forming rounded tufts of greyish filigree-foliage with many small *Corydalis*-like flowers. They are best established from seed and several will sow themselves happily in the grit or gravel of the alpine-house staging, where they find the well-drained, slightly shaded conditions to their liking. *R. africana* has pink, maroon-tipped flowers. All the *Sarcocapnos* are white, tipped with yellow. *S. enneaphylla* is the easiest and *S. crassifolia* the choicest, slowest-growing and most difficult.

Sagina (Caryophyllaceae)
S. subulata is useful if low, dull-green mats of foliage are wanted between paving-stones and elsewhere. It does best out of the direct sun, and looks particularly well in summer when it is covered with white flowers. There is a mossy, yellow form, 'Aurea'. These should be divided, and replanted in fresh soil occasionally. *S. boydii* is a very tiny, polished ebony-green hummock for troughs. It is a very strange plant collected once in Scotland and never found again in the wild.

Salvia, Sage (Labiatae)
S. multicaulis from Turkey and Iran, with roundish-oval, grey-green foliage, and reddish calices, and *S. bulleyana* from China, with yellow and maroon flowers, grow less than two feet high (60 cm) and are pleasant plants for the wild garden or the perimeter of the larger rock garden. The only really dwarf sage available, however, is *S. caespitosa* from Turkey. This forms low, shrubby mounds of cut, hairy, greyish foliage with pale lilac hooded flowers clustering tightly to the rosettes. It is usually grown in the alpine-house but, provided that really hot dry conditions can be supplied and some protection given against winter wetness, it will enjoy the free root-run of a raised bed outside and make a wide cushion of foliage.

Sanguinaria, Bloodroot (Papaveraceae)
S. canadensis is a spring flower from North America, whose buds push through the earth wrapped in the scrolls of its grey leaves. Unfortunately its snow-white stars drop all too quickly. The double *S. canadensis* 'Flore Pleno' is longer-lasting. The rounded, veined leaves look charming up until summer. It likes acid soil with plenty of humus, in half-shade. Its rhizomes are brittle and 'bleed' orange-red droplets if damaged; they should be planted only an inch or two (a few cm) deep and left undisturbed.

Saponaria, Soapwort (Caryophyllaceae) p. 23
The best known species is *S. ocymoides*, whose trailing stems of pinkish-red flowers appear in early summer. It sows itself and care must be taken to prevent it getting out of hand. The fresh-pink *S.* 'Bressingham Hybrid' is a smaller plant but a profuse flowerer. *S. pumilio* from the eastern Alps and *S. caespitosa* from the Pyrenees have turfy mats of foliage with pink flowers. They are the parents of *S.* 'Olivana' which forms thick, green cushions of foliage covered in May with large, silky-pink, almost stemless flowers.

This is one of the best of all easily grown alpines. The foot-high (30 cm) *S. haussknechtii*, a late-summer flower with large, lilac-pink blossoms, and its attractive, pink, long-flowering hybrid, *S. × lempergii* (*S. haussknechtii × S. cypria*) look well next to *Satureja montana*. *S. cypria* grows in loose clumps but has large, flesh-pink flowers. It can only be recommended for the alpine-house, as can the tight tuffets of rose-pink *S. pulvinaris*.

Sarcocapnos see Rupicapnos

Satureja, Savory (Labiatae)

The heavy scent of *S. montana*, the winter savory, proclaims one of the loveliest of late summer flowers in the rock garden. Its broad bushes bear white flowers which are covered with bees for weeks on end. *S. montana illyrica* ('Pygmaea') is a smaller plant, some twelve inches (30 cm) high, with lilac-blue flowers. The alpine calamint, *Acinos alpinus* (*Satureja alpina*, *Calamintha alpina*) is not particularly striking but is worth growing for its neatly marked, purple-violet flowers and prostrate habit. It looks well beside pink *Gypsophila repens*.

Saxifraga (Saxifragaceae) pp. 43, 125, 129

The very name *Saxifraga*, 'the rock breaker', makes it clear that these are rock garden plants. There are over three hundred species of saxifrage and hundreds of garden hybrids, making the genus a treasure-trove for the alpine gardener. Karl Foerster said that one needs a rock garden just to grow the saxifrages, and how right he is. The various sections include a wide range of habits and shapes. Some form rounded, mossy cushions, some grow into firm mounds of small or large rosettes and others have soft, fleshy leaves. The flowers may appear singly, in small sprays on short stalks or massed into long spikes. Only a selection of some of the loveliest of the many saxifrages can be made here.

One of the earliest to flower is *S. oppositifolia* with mats of creeping shoots and purple-pink flowers soon after the snow has melted. It needs gritty, peaty soil and a cool position. There are many geographical and garden forms, of which compact *latina* and 'Ruth Draper' are outstanding. The early-flowering saxifrages of the Kabschia and Engleria Sections cover their firm cushions and mats of small rosettes with flowers in March-April.

Listed below is a small selection of the many species and varieties which can be had from specialist nurseries, including some of the most profuse-flowering and attractive plants. White: *S. burseriana* and varieties, 'Crenata', 'Gloria', and 'Magna'; *S. marginata* and *S. marginata rocheliana*; 'Marie Louise'. Pale-yellow: *S. × apiculata*, *S. diapensioides* 'Lutea', 'Primrose Bee'. Deep-yellow: *S. ferdinandi-coburgi pravislavi*, 'Haagii', *S. juniperifolia sancta*. Pink: 'Arco-Valleyi', 'Cranbourne', 'Delia', 'Irvingii', 'Kellereri', 'Mother of Pearl', 'Myra'. Crimson: *S. × biasoletti*, *S. grisebachii* 'Wisley', *S. sempervivum*, 'Tristan', 'Winifred'.

These saxifrages do not like the full sun and prefer an east or north-east facing corner of the rock garden, on steeply sloping or even vertical surfaces planted in deep, narrow crevices.

The white, May and June flowering, encrusted saxifrages of the Euaizoonia Section, with their rosettes of silvery leaves like more sun. The following may be particularly recommended: the varieties of *S. paniculata* (*aizoon*), with white or pink flowers, *S. cochlearis* with its compact form 'Minor'; *S. cotyledon* 'Pyramidalis' (not too dry, acid, humus), *S. hostii*, and *S. callosa* (*lingulata*). *S. longifolia* is a beautiful, choice plant with a symmetrical rosette of foliage, which produces its glorious spike only once after many years, and then dies away. This is the king of the saxifrages from the Pyrenees, and does very well in crevices in dry-stone walls. The English hybrid 'Tumbling Waters' is no less splendid and is perennial, forming side rosettes after flowering, from which it should be propagated as seed will not come true.

The mossy saxifrages of the Dactyloides Section need a much shadier, cooler position. Their rosettes of soft foliage form large cushions adorned in spring with a real froth of flowers. There are many garden hybrids such as white 'Pearly King', cream 'Flowers of Sulphur' and blood-red 'Triumph'. Among the easier species are S. trifurcata with its dense, white foam of flowers and S. hypnoides with bronze-red autumn colour. Many mossies are difficult to grow well and the alpine-house is the safest place for the Spanish species like S. pubescens iratiana or the Moroccan S. demnatensis.

The shade-loving saxifrages of the Robertsonia Section include S. × urbium, the London Pride. A charming, deep pink miniature version of this is S. umbrosa 'Clarence Elliott'. S. cuneifolia with dense rosettes of wedge-shaped leaves and the glorious, salmon-pink S. 'Primulaize Salmon' also enjoy shade. In June the double flowers of the meadow saxifrage, S. granulata 'Plena' recall white stocks and in October S. cortusifolia fortunei brings us to a conclusion. It is the last to flower, and has white sprays above its glossy, olive-green foliage. It needs a sheltered position to help to delay the night when it will be blackened by the first hard frost. Its variety 'Rubrifolia' flowers slightly earlier and has rich ruby-red leaves and flower-stems.

Scabiosa, Scabious (Dipsaceae)
S. graminifolia, with its narrow leaves and bright lilac flowers, is an indispensable plant for sunny dry-stone walls and south-facing slopes. S. japonica alpina and S. lucida also grow six to eight inches (15–20 cm) high with violet-purple heads in summer.

Schizocodon see **Shortia**

Scutellaria, Skull Cap (Labiatae)
One of the prettiest of the smaller species is S. orientalis pinnatifida with loose carpets of grey foliage and attractive, yellow flowers. The eight inch (20 cm) violet-blue S. scordifolia from north-east Asia and S. indica japonica from Japan flower in July and August. The bushy green S. alpina is a lime-tolerating plant with lovely purple and white-lipped flowers. All will thrive if they get sufficient sun, and prove satisfying, long-flowering plants.

Sedum, Stonecrop (Crassulaceae) pp. 59, 133
Countless walls adorned with S. acre, S. album, S. reflexum and S. spurium reveal how easy these succulents are to grow. There are many other species which flourish in dry, poor conditions and can be used to beautify garden walls or cracks between paving stones. S. cauticolum, S. ewersii, S. pluricaule and S. sieboldii are all pink flowered species from eastern Asia forming clumps of fleshy, rounded grey leaves. They are among the best late-flowering plants.

Indispensable mat-forming sedums for sun and half-shade are orange-yellow S. aizoon kamtschaticum, S. floriferum and its lovely variety 'Weihenstephaner Gold', and best of all, the crimson to white varieties of S. spurium. All of these have profuse flowers in summer and provide plenty of nectar for bees.

Two of the finest, most compact sedums are the western American S. spathulifolium

Kabschia saxifrages. These small, en-crusted, cushion-forming plants with large flowers are some of the gayest plants in the rock garden. They burst into bloom at the first notice of spring. The first to flower is (3) *Saxifraga burseriana* from the eastern Alps. The pure species are matched by the great beauty of some of the *lilacina* hybrids: (1) 'Myra', (2) 'Irvingii' (4) 'Rubella'.

walls and will tumble out in a charming fashion. Its white blossoms open only at night, folding up during the morning. *S. maritima*, with mats of grey foliage, has a short-stemmed, white form 'Whitethroat', a lovely double 'Plena', and a pale-pink variety, 'Rosea'. The spectacular species from western North America are not often successful or long-lived in Europe. Fiery scarlet *S. laciniata* and *S. californica* can be tried in hot raised beds but are large for the alpine-house. *S. hookeri* and its subspecies *bolanderi* and *ingramii* are dwarfer with fringed flowers in pinks and white above grey, downy foliage.

Sisyrinchium (Iridaceae)

The most easily grown species, e.g. blue *S. angustifolium* and yellow *S. brachypus* from North America, are by no means the best and often tend to seed themselves rather too freely. The dwarf white form of *S. bellum* grown as *S. macounii* and compact forms of violet *S. montanum* are among the better, neater ones available. *S. douglasii* is outstanding among the North Americans with rush-like foliage and silky purple bells. Its white form is more vigorous but both will grow in a sunny, well-drained place if moist in spring. *S. filifolium*, with veined, pearly white cups, needs similar treatment. Both this and the taller *S. odoratissimum* (*Symphyostemon biflorus*), with cream purple-streaked trumpets, come from southern Argentina. These are all dwarf plants from three inches to a foot high (10–30 cm).

Soldanella (Primulaceae)

These are among the loveliest of mountain-flowers. The most vigorous are *S. montana* and *S. carpatica* from eastern Europe and *S. villosa*, which is similar but with red hairy stems and spreads by means of thin stolons, from the Pyrenees. These will thrive in moist shady positions, in gritty peat or leaf-mould, and bring a look of the mountain woodlands to the garden in April with their violet flowers, if planted next

to daphnes, Christmas and Lenten roses and ferns. The small, higher altitude species, *S. minima* and *S. pusilla* with their fringed lavender or white bells are too tiny even for the peat garden and are best grown in pans of gritty peat plunged outside in summer. *S. alpina* and *S. pindicola* tend to be the shyest flowering.

Solidago, Golden Rod (Compositae)

The varieties of golden rod which look well in the more formal terraced garden in late summer are the dwarfer hybrids of *S. cutleri* (*brachystachys*) such as 'Golden Thumb', 'Goldenmosa', 'Crown of Rays', and many others. *S. caesia* and *S. virgaurea* 'Nana' go well with junipers in less formal surroundings.

Spigelia (Loganiaceae)

S. marilandica is an unusual, foot high (30 cm) plant from North America with heads of pointed, gentian-like flowers that are red on the outside and yellow inside. It flowers in summer and needs a damp, sandy loam.

Stachys (Labiatae)

S. olympica (*S. lanata*) is excellent beside paving in large gardens, especially in its non-flowering variety 'Silver Carpet', with mats of strong-growing, grey-felted foliage. It looks very well beside dwarf berberis. Of the smaller species, *S. lavandulifolia* from Turkey is notable. It is a rampant plant and needs at least half a square yard (metre) of ground in the full sun but its silken, hairy, purple-red heads are too lovely to miss. *Allium christophii* can be planted in its grey-green carpets of foliage. For the alpine-house, *S. candida* with its white-felted leaves makes an excellent foliage plant.

Symphyandra (Campanulaceae)

Biennial *S. hofmannii* from Bosnia will seed itself once it has become established. In June it sends up its two foot (60 cm) spires of close-packed, yellowish-white bells from every available crevice. *S. wanneri* from the Balkans is perennial and likes a shady crevice, where it will produce large, lilac-blue bells. This is a dwarfer, eight-inch (20 cm) plant, as is *S. armena* from the Caucasus, which is perhaps the choicest.

Synthyris (Scrophulariaceae)

S. reniformis and the more compact *S. stellata*, which is often grown under the former name, come from the woods of the Rocky Mountains. They are low-growing plants which flower at the beginning of April with lilac spikes which last until May. They like a humus-rich soil and some shade. *S. pinnatifida* and its variants, like the densely hairy *lanuginosa*, on the contrary, need very well-drained conditions in full sun. These are beautiful alpine scree-plants but tend to form their buds in autumn so it is a challenge to encourage them to produce their purple-blue spikes.

Talinum (Portulacaceae)

These succulent relatives of *Lewisia* have at least two hardy species from the western USA. Both form flat, slow-growing cushions of fleshy needles in a very sunny, well-drained place. *T. spinescens* has four-inch (10 cm) sprays of magenta flowers and *T. okanoganense* is dwarfer with shell-pink cups. The pink hybrid between them, 'Zoe', is especially lovely and flowers over a very long period in summer. These little plants can be best seen and enjoyed in a trough or the alpine-house.

Tanacetum see Chrysanthemum

Tanakaea (Saxifragaceae)

Almost complete shade and cool, moist, peaty soil are ideal conditions for slow-growing, *T. radicans* from Japan. Clumps of leathery, dark-green leaves send out wiry runners and produce sprays of white Astilbe-like flowers on four-inch (10 cm) stems in summer.

Thalictrum, Meadow Rue (Ranunculaceae)

Between shrubs or on the edge of pools, the tall species will make a wonderful effect where there is space. Lilac-pink or white *T. aquilegifolium*, lilac-blue *T. delavayi (dipterocarpum)* and *T. diffusiflorum* all grow about six feet (2 m) high. *T. alpinum*, four inches (10 cm) high, is a modest plant with delicately divided leaves, effective in the peat bed running amongst *Primula farinosa*. *T. kiusianum*, from Japan, is only four inches (10 cm) high, with fluffy, lilac sprays above its dainty, fern-like foliage, which turns purplish-brown in autumn. It likes moist soil with plenty of humus and grit. *T. tuberosum* from Spain and *T. orientale* from the eastern Mediterranean like dry, stony soils. These are very choice, slowly creeping plants with fine white to lilac flowers.

Thlaspi (Cruciferae)

While striking in its native Alps, *T. rotundifolium* is seldom such a success in cultivation. *T. stylosum* is a pleasant enough plant with its early, pale-lilac flowers. It grows only a few inches (3–5 cm) high, likes gravelly soil and goes well with other early flowers, like *Erysimum kotschyanum*, in small beds and troughs.

(1) *Saxifraga longifolia* from the Pyrenees develops into a rosette about six inches (15 cm) across, with narrow leaves, and only flowers after many years. After producing its one foot eight inches (50 cm) rocket-like flower the plant dies. More perennial is its magnificent hybrid, 'Tumbling Waters'. (2) *S. grisebachii*, a jewel from Macedonia. (3) *S. hostii* forms grey-green mats which turn red in autumn.

Thymus, Thyme (Labiatae)

These are plants from exposed, stony slopes and moors, and require sunny dry positions. Most are excellent ground-cover plants and small bulbs can be planted beneath their mats of foliage. The most useful are the different garden forms of *T. serpyllum*, 'Albus', 'Carneus', and 'Coccineus'. This is a vigorous species and it should not be planted near small, slow-growing plants. The Portuguese *T. caespititius* has a similar appearance but is very neat, compact and suitable for troughs.

The woolly-leaved forms of *T. praecox*, grown as *T. hirsutus*, *T. lanuginosus* and *T. doerfleri*, have grey foliage which trails over stones and abundant pink flowers. 'Bressingham Seedling' is a compact, free-flowering selection of this type. The bushy *T. × citriodorus* 'Aureus' and 'Silver Queen' are not always completely hardy in severe climates. Nor are the neat little Spanish thymes, white *T. membranaceus* and pink *T. longiflorus*, whose tubular flowers peep from among decorative pink-tinged bracts. These are choice plants for sunny raised beds, troughs or the alpine-house, as is the magnificent Turkish *T. cilicicus*, possibly the most spectacular of all when its dense cushions are massed with lilac-pink heads in summer.

Tiarella see **Heuchera** and **Mitella**

Townsendia (Compositae)

T. exscapa (*T. wilcoxiana*) from North America is a dwarf plant with disproportionately large flowers, looking like stemless asters. It needs very poor soil between stones to keep it compact. The very early lilac-pink *T. parryi* is similar, whilst *T. formosa* grows four inches (10 cm) high and has violet-blue flowers. All of these are plants for the experienced grower and most of them are not very long-lived.

Trachelium (Campanulaceae)

The Balkan *T. rumelianum* grows about six inches (10–20 cm) tall, forming small clumps, with bright blue heads in summer, ideal for sunny or half-shaded crevices in dry stone walls. *T. asperuloides* is more delicate and is best kept in the alpine-house. It is a Greek plant with rounded cushions which are covered in July with tiny light blue flowers. It is a good idea to clip it after flowering to keep it in shape.

Tricyrtis, Toad Lily (Liliaceae)

T. hirta, *T. macropoda* and *T. stolonifera* from north-east Asia grow about eighteen inches (50 cm) high and like rich soil in the shade, where they produce fascinating yellow or white flowers speckled with maroon in summer and autumn. They appreciate a covering of leaves during winter.

Trillium, Wake Robin (Liliaceae)

These are outstanding North American woodlanders, enjoying peat-bed conditions. *T. grandiflorum* has large, white, three-petalled flowers above whorls of leaves in April. It is a humus-lover and looks lovely beside *Mertensia virginica* in a shady corner. *T. erectum* has a special beauty all its own with its dull-red flowers and dusky, mottled foliage. *T. sessile* has ox-blood coloured flowers, and *T. sessile californicum* (*T. chloropetalum*) white flowers over their whorls of dark-speckled leaves. These reach about one foot high (30 cm) and are the most successful species in most gardens.

Trollius, Globe Flower (Ranunculaceae)

The garden hybrids of *T. chinensis* and *T. asiaticus* make a showy effect with their orange and yellow flowers at the side of large sheets of water. For smaller areas, the dwarf *T. pumilus* and *T. patulus* (*ranunculoides*) from Asia and the late-flowering *T. yunnanensis* with its open, marsh-marigold like flowers, are more suitable and will prove successful in any good moist soil.

Tunica (Caryophyllaceae)
T. (*Petrorhagia*) *saxifraga* is a dainty little plant, scarcely eight inches (20 cm) high. It is extremely easy and resembles a Gypsophila with its long-lasting pink flowers. It is suitable for dry-stone walls or any other sunny spot.

Those who are keen on double flowers will appreciate the attractive *T. saxifraga* 'Rosette'.

Typha, Bulrush (Typhaceae)
T. minima is a dwarf bulrush only just over one foot (40 cm) high, suited to the rock garden pond. It should be planted in water about an inch (1–3 cm) deep.

Uvularia (Liliaceae)
The North American eighteen-inch (50 cm) yellow *U. grandiflora* and *U. perfoliata* and the dwarfer, cream *U. sessilifolia* somewhat resemble Solomon's Seal. These are woodland plants for rich soil in shady positions or the peat bed and they flower in April.

Vancouveria see **Epimedium**

Verbascum, Mullein (Scrophulariaceae) **p. 59**
V. acaule (*Celsia*) from the south of Greece has bright-yellow flowers above its rosettes of primrose-like leaves. It is not reliably hardy but can be kept over winter in the alpine house. *V. dumulosum* is a shrubby, dwarf mullein from Turkey which forms broad, compact, grey-felted bushes only eight inches (20 cm) high, with short, yellow spikes in June. It needs a dry, sunny crevice and achieves its greatest beauty under glass. *V.* 'Letitia' is a hybrid between *V. dumulosum* and *V. spinosum*. Its stiff, branching shoots interlace to form eight to twelve inch (20–30 cm) mounds, covered in summer with dainty, lemon-yellow flowers.

Veronica, Speedwell (Scrophulariaceae)
White-felted *V. bombycina* from Syria grows only an inch or two (a few cm) high. It is very sensitive to damp conditions and best grown in the alpine-house, but almost all the others are easy garden plants. *V. armena* is long-lived and one of the earliest to flower with its pure-blue blossoms, an excellent companion to *Tulipa chrysantha*. The flat, pale-blue *V. repens* is also early-flowering, as are the bushy, bright-lilac *V. schmidtiana* from Japan and deep-blue *V. saturejoides* from the Balkans, which forms green mats of foliage.

V. fruticans (*saxatilis*) has vivid, dark green leaves and lovely sapphire-blue flowers in May–June. The four inch (10 cm) varieties of *V. prostrata* which flower in May–June are indispensable, including the white 'Alba', vivid pink 'Mrs Holt' and 'Spode Blue', as are the taller, gentian-blue varieties of *V. teucrium*, 'Kapitän' and 'Shirley Blue' flowering in June.

V. bonarota (*Paederota bonarota*), with spires of dark-blue flowers, and *V. lutea* (*Paederota lutea*), with yellow spikes, come from the southern limestone Alps and thrive in shady crevices in dry-stone walls. For terraced beds or the fronts of borders, there are also the eight to twelve inch (20–30 cm) varieties of *V. spicata* with slender flower-spires. These include the lavender blue 'Blue Fox', deep rose 'Red Fox', dark-pink 'Erika', wine-red 'Heidekind', pure white 'Icicle' from America and dull-violet English 'Saraband' with silver-grey leaves among the most worthwhile. *V. s. incana* 'Candidissima' is a glorious plant with violet-blue spikes and silver-grey leaves. All these are real sun-lovers and among the most versatile of plants.

Viola, Violets (Violaceae)   **p. 77**
When speaking of violets, *V. odorata*, the fragrant March-flowering violet is the first which springs to mind. Several varieties of this are available, of which violet-blue 'Queen Charlotte' and 'Triumph' are particularly profuse and large. They will flower a second time in autumn. Other colours also exist, 'Alba' is

white, 'Sulphurea' and 'Irish Elegance' apricot-yellow and 'Red Charm' purplish-red. These are not so widely available as they used to be. Among other shade-loving violets are the vigorous American *V. papilionacea* which has no scent, and its white variety 'Immaculata', and white or violet-streaked *V. cucullata* and *V. septentrionalis*. *V. jooi*, the pink Carpathian violet is charming and the yellow alpine violet, *V. biflora* will lighten damp shady places. *V. eizanensis* from Japan with deeply divided leaves and bright-pink flowers enjoys gritty, humus-rich soil. Tiniest of all is the minute Japanese *V. verecunda* 'Yakusimana' with white purple-veined flowers.

The small pansies like an open position but do not like to be alone, preferring the company of other plants. In these conditions *V. cornuta* with its many varieties in mauve, blue and white will grow into mats of foliage covered with blossom from May to September.

The lilac-blue *V. grisebachiana* from the Balkans, the magenta *V. elegantula* (*V. bosniaca*) and *V. stojanowii* from Bulgaria with its small, yellow flowers are all delightful wild pansies. None of them are very long-lived but they may seed themselves, if one is fortunate. There are many of these to tempt the grower, varying in the challenges they offer, from the comparative ease of those mentioned to the difficult high-alpines like *V. cenisia*. Others to tempt the enthusiast are Spanish *V. cazorlensis* and *V. delphinantha* from the Balkans. These similar species form tufts of needle-leaves with bright pink, long-spurred flowers. They are often longer-lived in troughs or raised beds outside, grown in holes bored through tufa and protected from winter wet, than in the alpine-house. The many dry-climate species from the western USA present different problems. They go dormant in late summer and need bulb-frame conditions. Among these are bicoloured, cut-leaved *V. beckwithii* and *V. hallii* and bright yellow *V. pedunculata*. All like to be wet in spring.

Viscaria see **Lychnis**

Vitaliana (Primulaceae)   p. 93
V. primuliflora is a cushion plant from the mountains of southern Europe. It is very like *Androsace* and can be included in this genus but is usually found in garden catalogues as *Douglasia vitaliana*. It is happiest in a gritty scree mixture but does not always produce its bright yellow flowers freely. The southern subspecies are reputed to be the most free-flowering: *praetutiana* from the Appennines and grey-leaved *cinerea* from the Pyrenees.

Waldsteinia (Rosaceae)
These are easy and long-lived plants. *W. ternata* is especially to be recommended, growing only four inches (10 cm) high. It forms a dense carpet of foliage on shady slopes or dry-stone walls and its yellow, strawberry-like flowers are a welcome bonus. *W. geoides* is more vigorous but useful ground cover for shady beds in larger gardens.

Succulents, drought-loving plants with thick skins, are ideal occupants of the rock garden and dry-stone wall. Almost all of them flourish best when they can bake in the sun, especially the Houseleek (*Sempervivum*), which is quite happy with only a handful of soil in crannies and crevices in the rocks. There are many species and hybrids: (1) *S. tectorum* 'Atropurpureum', (2) the colourful variety 'Sunset'. Most of the many species of Sedum are sun-lovers too: (3) *S. spathulifolium* 'Purpureum' (4) *S. cauticolum*, (5) *S. spurium* 'Roseum' and (6) *S. spurium* 'Atropurpureum'.

Wulfenia (Scrophulariaceae)

Although the robust *W. carinthiaca* is the most commonly grown, *W. baldaccii* from the limestone rocks of Albania and *W. orientalis* from Turkey have more elegant, lilac-blue spires between loose rosettes of foliage, as does the hybrid *W. × suendermannii*. *W. amherstiana* from the Himalayas is only four inches (10 cm) high, and bears bright-lilac flowers above its flat, wrinkled rosettes of leaves. All are humus-loving plants which prefer to be damp rather than dry.

Zauschneria, Californian Fuchsia (Onagraceae)

Z. californica is an excellent plant for dry-stone walls and crevices protected from the rain and in the full sun, where it will flower from August to September, with its scarlet, trumpet-shaped flowers. *Z. cana* has longer trumpets, and its narrow, grey-leaved shoots bend under the burden of blossom, so it should be planted in an elevated position. These may need protection in winter in cold areas. They look well when planted beside the blue mounds of *Ceratostigma*.

Bulbs and Corms

Bulbous plants are becoming more popular every year, and more and more seedsmen and garden centres are offering the dwarfer species. Rock gardens and terraced beds are especially suitable for these, and gardeners who possess a small greenhouse can look forward to their first flowers in late winter, while storms and snow may still rage outside. Early crocus, dwarf iris, wild tulips, dwarf narcissus and other bulbs can be planted in autumn in containers which are then well watered and plunged in the garden. They should only be brought inside when the bulbs have taken root, in November or December, and then preferably plunged in peat. The plants will burst into flower with the first warmth of the year. Many of these tiny flowers can be best appreciated when raised nearer to eye-level.

With the steadily increasing interest in bulbs, the bulb-frame has become a feature of many amateurs' gardens. This is simply a raised bed which can be covered with frame-lights or plastic sheeting in summer and winter to keep off excess wetness. The covering is removed in late summer to tidy the frame and give a good watering to start root growth and again in spring when the weather improves, remaining off till the foliage yellows. This bed can be as decorative or as practical as one wishes, though the only efficient way for the specialist to maintain a wide collection is to grow each species separately in pots, when they can be kept segregated and given individual attention. If obtainable, clay pots are preferable, as they allow one to make many more mistakes with watering in winter. Repotting should be done just before the first watering. For many bulbs, such as *Narcissus* and *Fritillaria*, this is only necessary every second year. *Crocus*, *Colchicum* and *Tulipa* should be repotted annually but *Cyclamen* need only be disturbed when they burst out of their pots.

Outdoors there are bulbs which will flower all through the garden year. This begins in February–March with crocus and snowdrops, and finishes in October–November with autumn crocus and meadow saffron. Between these two periods come all the bulbs which are described below.

Allium (Liliaceae)

One of the earliest to flower is *A. karataviense* but its pleated, blue-green and reddish-brown leaves are showier than its greyish-pink balls of flowers. *A. narcissiflorum* has nodding, reddish-pink heads and *A. oreophilum* (*A. ostrow-skianum*) crimson ones: these are two of the loveliest species. *A. beesianum* and *A. cyaneum* are also charming with tufts of bright-green foliage and sky-blue flowers. *A. caeruleum* has small, blue ball-shaped heads on knee-high stems. Other striking alliums are the vivid lilac starry globes of *A. christophii* (*A. albopilosum*), and the flatter, dark-purple heads of *A. atropur-pureum*, especially attractive if it is planted near *Stipa pennata*. *A. moly*, which can be rampant, has golden flowers which go well with blue *Veronica*. *A. pulchellum* and *A. flavum*, with the dwarf *A. flavum* 'Minus', like the minimum of nourishment and water. They do best in narrow crevices, and open their lilac-pink and bright-yellow flowers like fireworks on wiry stems for weeks on end during the summer. *A. senescens* is a late-flowering species popular with bees and butterflies in August and September. It has lilac-pink heads on foot-long (30 cm) stems above its grey-green foliage.

All these are easy to grow and their demands are few. Do, however, be warned against *A. ursinum*, *A. paradoxum* and *A. zebdanense*, which will take over the garden in the space of a few years.

Alstroemeria (Alstroemeriaceae)

There are at least two dwarf plants in cultivation from this spectacular South American tuberous genus. *A. hookeri* is like a one foot high (30 cm) version of the tall pink garden hybrids, but the plant grown as *A. pygmaea* is only an inch or so high with brilliant orange-yellow flowers and narrow bluish foliage. It goes dormant in late summer and can be grown in gritty soil in the alpine-house or a raised bed.

Anemone see page 72

Arisaema (Araceae)

These are unusual tuberous plants which belong to the arum family. They are all suitable for shady beds with other woodland plants. *A. speciosum* from the Himalayas has decorative leaves and startling, long-tailed, brownish, cowl-shaped spathes. *A. triphyllum* from North America has zebra-striped, hooded spathes, with drooping tips, hidden between its spreading leaves. *A. consanguineum* from China first pushes up a stiff, yard-high (metre) stem, on the end of which the large and much divided leaves appear. The green spathe is inconspicuous but in autumn its hanging clusters of brilliant red berries make a fine show below the yellowing canopy of leaves. The most beautiful of these strange plants is *A. candidissimum* from China, which has cowled spathes striped in white, pink and green. All species like humus-rich soil, shade and protection from wind and look well amongst ferns.

Arisarum, Mouse Plant (Araceae)

These tuberous Mediterranean shade-lovers spread carpets of arrow-head leaves in well-

135

drained, shady places. *A. proboscideum* hides its brown spathes, leaving only the whitish tips exposed—like the long tails of mice diving for cover. *A. vulgare* is less hardy and likes drier conditions but is no less fascinating with its striped spathes.

Arum (Araceae)

The dark spathes of *A. dioscoridis, A. palaestinum* or *A. petteri* (*nigrum*) from Dalmatia should not be missed. The tubers should be planted in a warm, sheltered, slightly shaded position. The purple-maroon spathes which appear in the early part of the year are unusual and striking. They need protection in the winter to keep them dry. *A. italicum* is prized for its decorative, marbled, white-and-green, arrow-head foliage which appears in autumn and remains throughout the winter. Its fiery-red clusters of berries look striking in summer but, like those of all the species, they are poisonous. Elegant *A. creticum*, with its sweet-scented, pointed, yellow spathes, is the most beautiful of the hardy species and should be planted in a deep, rich well-drained soil in sun.

Bongardia (Berberidaceae)

B. chrysogonum (*Leontice chrysogonum*) from the Near East is a unique plant with long, brown-marked, pinnate leaves, and small, yellow, short-lived flowers on stems some twelve inches (30 cm) long. It dies back soon after it has flowered. Its tubers should be planted about eight inches (20 cm) deep in a dry, sunny, well-protected corner.

Brimeura see Hyacinthus

Brodiaea (Liliaceae)

California is the centre for these bulbs which extend the bulb season into summer. Botanists have split them into many genera and they are found under a variety of names in lists. Most are rather tall for small rock gardens but look well in more spacious, informal surroundings. Among the very dwarf species are *B. coronaria macropoda* (*terrestris*), *B. stellaris* and *B. minor*, all with violet flowers and less than six inches (15 cm) high. *B.* (*Dichelostemma*) *ida-maia* has drooping tubular crimson flowers tipped with green, but needs the protection of a bulb-frame.

Bulbocodium (Liliaceae)

B. vernum is a spring-flowering, Colchicum-like corm from the mountains of southern Europe. Its bright red-purple flowers appear before the leaves expand in early spring.

Calochortus, Mariposa Lily (Liliaceae)

It is a great pity that most of these lovely North American bulbous plants are not hardy in wet or severe climates. Among the best species to try are Californian *C. amabilis*, with rounded, yellow, hanging flowers; Mexican *C. barbatus* (*Cyclobothra lutea*), which has interesting, yellow flowers lined with hairs in summer; and lilac-flowered *C. uniflorus* from Oregon and California. All need plenty of sun and warmth and must be carefully protected from frost and rain, especially in winter. Those fortunate enough to live in climates where these plants will grow outside will soon find out about the other fifty or so species.

Dwarf narcissi. *Narcissus cyclamineus* **from Portugal is a striking flower with long trumpets and reflexing petals in a ruff. There are many hybrids of this species, all early-flowering: (1) 'February Gold' is one of the earliest. (2)** *N. bulbocodium* **comes from Spain and Morocco and grows in mountain pastures, flowering as soon as the snow melts. (3)** *N. asturiensis* **from Spain (enlarged) is the smallest and earliest species. All narcissi like to be moist in spring.**

1

2

3

Camassia, Bear Grass, Quamash (Liliaceae)
This is another exclusively American genus.
The pale-blue flowers of *C. cusickii* look pretty
behind *Dodecatheon*, whilst the later, steel-blue
spires of *C. quamash* (*C. esculenta*) 'Orion' are
not to be despised. They like to be damp when
in leaf, but are a little large and leafy for most
rock gardens.

Chionodoxa, Glory of the Snow
(Liliaceae)
These bulbs from the mountains of Turkey
should be found in every garden. *C. luciliae*,
with its sky-blue starry flowers with white
centres, and its variety 'Pink Giant', start the
flowering season in March, soon to be succeeded
by *C. sardensis* with gentian-blue clusters of
flowers, whilst the last to flower is *C. gigantea*,
with large, blue and white flowers. They make a
most colourful show with *Eranthis*, *Adonis
amurensis* and yellow and white crocus, dancing
charmingly beneath shrubs and amongst cushion plants.

Colchicum, Meadow Saffron (Liliaceae)
These autumn flowers provide one of the last
great moments in the garden year. Some of the
loveliest are the large-flowered species, like *C.
bornmuelleri* and *C. giganteum*, related to *C.
speciosum*, and their garden hybrids 'Lilac
Wonder', 'The Giant' and 'Violet Queen'.
Double varieties include 'Waterlily', *C. autumnale* 'Pleniflorum' and *C. autumnale* 'Alboplenum'. Of the smaller-flowered species, *C.
byzantinum* and *C. cilicicum* are especially good.
The delicate, lilac, spring-flowering *C. brachyphyllum*, *C. libanoticum* of gardens, *C. hungaricum*, *C. triphyllum* and the yellow *C. luteum*
are unusual species for the bulb-frame. All
thrive best in well-drained sandy loam and
should not be allowed to become too damp in
summer. The disadvantage of the larger ones is
their spreading leaves which grow in spring and
die away in the early summer, leaving an empty

space. They combine well with all autumn
flowers and colours in the rock garden.

Corydalis see page 88

Crocus (Iridaceae)   p. 145
The vivid colours of the wild species are much
more charming than the large garden hybrids.
The prettiest orange and yellow spring-flowering species are *C. ancyrensis*, *C. flavus*, *C.
balansae* 'Zwanenberg', and the prolific
varieties of *C. chrysanthus* and *C. angustifolius*
(*C. susianus*). Recommended for blue and lilac
shades are *C. etruscus* 'Zwanenberg', *C. imperati*,
C. sieberi and the *C. tommasinianus* hybrid,
'Vanguard'. White species include *C. biflorus*, *C.
chrysanthus* 'Snow Bunting', *C. fleischeri* (very
early) and *C. versicolor* 'Picturatus' (late).

Most species of autumn crocus are lilac-blue
and flower from September to November. The
best of these are *C. goulimyi*, *C. speciosus*, *C.
salzmannii*, *C. kotschyanus* (*C. zonatus*), *C.
pulchellus*, *C. medius* and *C. banaticus* (*C.
iridiflorus*). Those with bulb-frames or alpine-houses can continue the season into November
and December with *C. niveus*, *C. tournefortii* and
C. vitellinus.

These lovely small plants may be planted all
over the garden, so long as the position is
sufficiently sunny, and their chief enemies—
mice—are kept at bay. The best position of all is
near the house, in rock garden beds, where they
will flower earlier and be close to us. Crocuses
will thrive amongst loose-growing ground-cover plants such as sedums and acaenas. Only
C. tommasinianus will survive for long periods
in lawns.

Cyclamen (Primulaceae)   p. 19
The crimson, pink and white, early-flowering *C.
coum* (*C. orbiculatum*, *C. × atkinsii*) glimmers
like tiny jewels in the snow next to Christmas
roses. In summer the wafting scent of *C.
purpurascens* (*C. europaeum*) invites us to linger

in front of its rosy clumps of flowers, as does the elegant autumn *C. hederifolium* (*C. neapolitanum*). Its profuse pink and white flowers are followed by lovely, white-patterned, ivy-like leaves. *C. repandum* (*C. vernale*) is a pretty ruby-pink spring-flowering species for more temperate gardens, where it enjoys shade in a rich soil. *C. cilicium* prefers a sunny position in a well-drained place, where it will flower in autumn with pink flowers. *C. cilicium intaminatum* is the smallest of all with white flowers and small rounded leaves, and is the most suitable for troughs. Those who can offer some protection can grow the other less reliably hardy species. White-flowered *C. balearicum* and *C. creticum* appear in spring and like a lot of shade. In autumn there are white *C. cyprium*, *C. africanum* and *C. graecum*, which needs hot summer conditions to flower and does best planted out in the bulb-frame where it can extend its strong roots. Perhaps the most spectacular are the spring-flowering *C. trochopteranthum* (*C. coum alpinum*), carmine *C. pseudibericum* and pink *C. libanoticum*, along with the graceful wild parent of the large greenhouse strains, *C. persicum*.

All cyclamen like a slightly shaded but warm position, which should be dryish rather than damp; the soil should consist of limy humus. Their corms must be covered with a few inches (a few cm) of gritty soil. They look well planted alongside dwarf conifers.

Eranthis, Winter Aconite
(Ranunculaceae)
The yellow cups of *E. hyemalis* are surrounded by a green ruff, and when *E. cilicica* blooms ten days later, we know that spring is on its way. The flowering season can be lengthened by planting the large-blossomed, sweet-scented hybrid, *E.* × *tubergenii* 'Guinea Gold'. All species like a semi-shaded position under shrubs. If they are to spread they must not be disturbed or dug up.

Erythronium, Dog's-tooth Violet, Trout Lily
(Liliaceae) p. 65
The European name refers to the shape of the corm and is an ugly name for such a beautiful plant. In America it is known as the Fawn or Trout Lily, from its attractively dappled leaves, and many species grow in the woodlands and mountain pastures of North America. In Europe, the best of these have proved to be *E. revolutum* and its glorious variety 'White Beauty', the clear-yellow *E. tuolumnense*, and the hybrid of these two species, 'Pagoda'. The only European species, *E. dens-canis*, is quite lovely, with pale-pink blossoms. Gardeners in America or those prepared to raise them from seed, can enjoy many more. All erythroniums like light shade and humus-rich soil. They enjoy peat beds if planted at the bases of shrubs.

Fritillaria (Liliaceae)
The best-known species is the three-foot (1 m) *F. imperialis*, the Crown Imperial, the monarch of spring flowers. It looks attractive at the foot of dry-stone walls or in groups in formal terraces. *F. meleagris*, the Snake's-head Lily, with chequered reddish-purple bells likes a damp soil and does well in peat beds. Do not forget to plant the white varieties alongside the darker ones. *F. camtschatcensis* is even more of a peat-lover from north-east Asia and Canada. It has nearly black bells on sixteen inch (40 cm) stems rising out of whorls of foliage.

Other species which will settle down in the rock garden are *F. acmopetala*, *F. pallidiflora*, *F. pontica*, *F. persica* and *F. pyrenaica*, which will give much pleasure with the various shadings and patterns to be found within their different bells. They should be planted in well-drained, gritty soil, in very light shade amongst dwarf shrubs, or in pots in the alpine-house, where they can be admired in comfort from close to. Many specialist growers have become dedicated to this genus which has been given much attention by botanists collecting material in south-west Asia. Among the more recent additions to gardens, the tiny brick-red alpine *F. carduchorum* and the mahogany and yellow *F. michailovskyi*, both from eastern Turkey, seem set to become more widely available. The others remain plants for the specialist, like the western American species, which, apart from *F. lanceolata*, are by no means easily grown, even by enthusiasts in the western USA.

Galanthus, Snowdrop (Amaryllidaceae) **p. 19**
The first flower to appear every year, often in January, is *G. elwesii* from Turkey. The well-known *G. nivalis* only appears when this is already dying away. The latter species has given rise to the pretty, large British varieties, 'Sam Arnott', 'Atkinsii' and 'Straffan'. One can never have too many snowdrops to bring spring into the garden, and they look especially attractive beneath pink and white daphnes. There are many named varieties in English gardens but few are really outstandingly different. There are not so many wild species and some of the more distinct are *G. ikariae* and its taller subspecies *G. i. latifolius*, with bright, glossy leaves, and *G. plicatus* with its hybrid 'Magnet', whose flowers dance on long, wiry stalks.

Gladiolus (Iridaceae)
Purplish red *G. palustris* is an inhabitant of water-meadows and an ideal species to set alongside *Iris*, *Trollius* and *Dianthus superbus* on the moist edges of pools, where it will flower in July. *G. byzantinus* and *G. communis* blossom earlier and have larger flowers; they come from the dry pastures of southern Europe and look well amongst grasses. Most species are South African and are tender, but specialists are finding that many of the graceful, dwarfer species grow well in much the same conditions as Mediterranean bulbs, like the more tender Cyclamen.

Habranthus see **Zephyranthes**

Hyacinthella, Hyacinthus, Pseudomuscari and **Brimeura** (Liliaceae)
The small, vivid blue *Pseudomuscari azureum* (*Hyacinthella azurea*) and its white variety are the earliest and loveliest of these flowers. Planted next to *Draba* or *Iris danfordiae* they will make a charming picture. *Hyacinthella dalmatica* has dense, bright-blue spikes on four inch (10 cm) stems early in spring. The wild *Hyacinthus orientalis* is the origin of the large-flowered florists' Hyacinth. It is a graceful, scented species but is not available commercially. The selections sold as Roman Hyacinths would be the nearest to the wild plant.

Brimeura (*Hyacinthus*) *amethystina* from the Pyrenees is a dainty, late-flowering plant some eight inches (20 cm) high, with loose heads of rich blue, funnel-shaped bells. It is easily grown and should be much more widely planted. *Brimeura fastigiata* (*Hyacinthus pouzolzii*) is an unusual lilac-pink but is best in the alpine-house.

Hyacinthoides see **Scilla**

Ipheion (Liliaceae)
I. uniflorum from Argentina may also be found as *Brodiaea* or *Triteleia*, and is a delightful and easy spring flower. Each petal of its light-blue, starry flowers has a dark stripe running down it. Its leaves appear in autumn and its bulbs should be planted in front of stones or in little sunny hollows. In very cold areas it should be given protection during winter.

Early-flowering Irises of the Reticulata Section: (1) *Iris* 'Katharine Hodgkin' (enlarged), a precious hybrid between *I. histroides* and *I. danfordiae*. (2) *I. winogradowii* from the Caucasus likes to be damp. (3) *I. reticulata* 'Harmony' is a gay, easy flower, much recommended.

Iris for dwarf bulbous iris see page 104

Ixiolirion (Amaryllidaceae)

I. montanum is a foot-high (30 cm) slender-stalked bulb from Turkey with attractive violet-blue trumpets in June. It is hardy if planted deeply and looks at home among cushion-forming plants and dwarf, spiny shrubs.

Lapeirousia (Iridaceae)

L. laxa is a delightful and surprisingly hardy little corm from south and east Africa, which will sow itself in sandy soils in full sun. It grows about six inches (15 cm) high and has soft red flowers, which always attract attention, over a long period in summer. Gardeners in the warmer parts of the USA and New Zealand can experiment with the more tender species.

Leucojum, Snowflake (Amaryllidaceae)

L. vernum, the spring snowflake, likes to be in slight shade but it will also grow in sun if the ground is damp. Alongside *Primula rosea* and marsh marigolds, on the banks of streams or ponds, it will make free-flowering clumps. *L. aestivum*, the summer snowflake, is also at home amongst marsh plants, and flowers in May. There is a robust variety with stems reaching about two feet (60 cm) called 'Gravetye Giant'. Among the dwarf species, autumn-flowering *L. autumnale* is the only reliable garden plant, increasing and flowering well in a warm, sunny, well-drained place. The others enjoy the same conditions as the more tender *Cyclamen* under glass. *L. roseum* flowers in autumn; *L. nicaeense* and *L. trichophyllum* flower in spring. All are white or pink-flushed and grow from four to eight inches (10–20 cm).

Lilium, Nomocharis and Notholirion (Liliaceae)

In the wild garden the different Turk's Cap Lilies are especially suitable, including *L. martagon* with its lilac-pink, mahogany-red and white varieties, the scarlet *L. chalcedonicum*, *L. carniolicum*, *L. pomponium* and *L. pumilum*, the orange-yellow *L. davidii*, *L. hansonii*, *L. henryi* and the yellow *L. monadelphum*, *L. pyrenaicum* and *L. jankae*. There are even lilies for marshy positions, such as the glorious, flaming, reddish-yellow Leopard Lily, *L. pardalinum*, as well as some of the other rarer North American species.

Most lilies are too large for the rock garden, but the Burmese *L. mackliniae* with pendant, white flowers flushed with purple on eighteen-inch (50 cm) stems is quite in place. This comes near *Nomocharis*, a genus between *Lilium* and *Fritillaria*, which is important for gardeners in climates with cool moist summers. These are beautiful bulbs for the peat garden, growing up to about two feet (60 cm) with white flowers flushed with pink or purple and often spotted or speckled with maroon. Most of the cultivated material is now of hybrid origin, derived from *N. aperta*, *N. saluenensis*, *N. mairei* and *N. pardanthina*. The best way to establish these is to grow them from seed, sowing thinly and planting out the clump intact in the peat bed. *Notholirion* is a genus with similar affinities, usually grown in similar places, though more sun and better drainage might be desirable. *N. bulbuliferum* (*hyacinthinum*) with pale lavender trumpets is possibly the easiest.

All lilies do best if shaded by other plants at the bases of their stems. Most species, with the exceptions of the Madonna lily, *L. candidum*, *L. chalcedonicum* and *L. martagon*, are more or less lime-hating, and all need well-drained soil.

Muscari, Grape Hyacinth (Liliaceae) p. 145

The best of the grape hyacinths are *M. armeniacum*, with its pale blue variety 'Cantab', and the two-toned, pale and dark blue *M. tubergenianum* from north-west Iran. Both look delightful amongst the daisy-like carpets of *Matricaria oreades*. *M. moschatum* bears racemes of loosely set bells which are pale-lilac above and dull-yellow below, smelling strangely sweet and with a subtle beauty. It flowers in May and grows eight inches (20 cm) tall. The latest to flower, in June, is *M. comosum*, with its strange violet tufty heads. Among the more distinct of the less eccentric species are china-blue *M. botryoides*, blue-black *M. commutatum* and *M. neglectum*, and the bicoloured indigo and sky-blue *M. latifolium*. These all grow well in any well-drained soil in sun or part-shade.

Narcissus (Amaryllidaceae)   p. 137

There is no other genus of bulbous plants in which so many new hybrids have been intro-duced in recent decades, beautifying our gar-dens more and more each spring with their glory. The large, trumpet, cup-shaped, and poet's narcissi are suitable not only for parkland but also in terraced gardens, where they produce a joyful effect among the fresh green and brown shoots of herbaceous plants, and beside Crown Imperials and dicentras or early-flowering shrubs, such as *Ribes sanguineum*.

In smaller gardens the dwarf, wild narcissi and their garden hybrids will be more appropriate. *N. asturiensis* (*N. minimus*) is the smallest and earliest of the trumpet-shaped daffodils, flowering in March. After this comes the lovely *N. bulbocodium* and the narrow-flowered *N. cyclamineus* with all its different hybrids, such as the two-toned bright-yellow 'Dove Wings'; yellow 'February Gold', 'Little Witch' and 'Peeping Tom', and the ivory-white 'Jenny'. *N. triandrus* with pretty, pale, hanging flowers, has many vigorous hybrids—bright-yellow 'April Tears'; yellow 'Hawera' and 'Liberty Bells'; and white 'Silver Chimes', 'Thalia' and 'Tresamble'. The natural hybrid, *N. × johnstonii*, the Queen of Spain daffodil, is only eight inches (20 cm) high, and also blooms early. The small trumpet daffodils include *N. moschatus*, pale-yellow, and *N. minor* 'Little Beauty' with two-toned, white and yellow flowers, and the later, small-flowered, golden-yellow jonquil, *N. jonquilla*, the scent of which can be smelt far away. The

snow-white *N. watieri* from the High Atlas of Morocco is a delightful flower but it is best planted in pots in the alpine-house.

The winter-flowering Hoop Petticoat narcissi from southern Spain and north-west Africa are also best grown here. These are variable plants usually included in two species, white *N. cantabricus* and yellow *N. bulbocodium*, but they vary between these colours and under glass will flower from midwinter until spring. *N. c. petunioides* has white flowers reflexed until almost flat and *N. b. romieuxii* is a vigorous, free-flowering soft-yellow race. These flower best if dried off in summer.

All the dwarf wild narcissi come from the west Mediterranean region, and need a fairly sheltered, sunny position, but most are mountain plants and, in the early part of the year, like to be moist. In fact, apart from the few alpine-house species, most do not enjoy hot, dry conditions even in Summer.

Nomocharis see **Lilium**

Notholirion see **Lilium**

Ornithogalum, Star of Bethlehem (Liliaceae)

O. umbellatum opens its white, starry heads flat on the ground and looks well with blue grape hyacinths. *O. nutans* spreads rather more than one might wish, and in its place one may use the similar *O. pyramidale*. Its white flowers are striped with green on the back, and they open on their twenty-inch (50 cm) stalks in June.

Oxalis (Oxalidaceae)   p. 51

O. adenophylla has large, silken, lilac-pink flowers, and *O. enneaphylla* pearly-white ones. These look quite charming set on their tufts of divided, grey-green leaves. They come from Chile and southern Argentina and need a peaty, gritty soil, as does another small species, *O. laciniata*, suitable for the alpine-house or trough. It grows only two inches (5 cm) high, and has scaly, pinkish rhizomes from which tiny, metallic grey, fan-shaped leaves appear in spring. In May–June large, purplish blue to pale-blue flowers, netted with dark veins, open. Its hybrid 'Ione Hecker' has similar flowers but is a slightly larger and more vigorous plant. Gardeners in warmer climates are wary of growing any of this genus as several can become inerradicable weeds. This will not be the case with those already mentioned, which are all cold climate plants, but English gardeners also grow several species which are kept in check by the climate. Some of these are quite choice, slow-growing plants even in southern England. Such are the South African O. *depressa* (*inops*) and O. *obtusa*, both with large pink flowers and small grey-green leaves. Chilean O. *lobata* is also rather tender but is unlikely to prove a nuisance anywhere. It is one of the best of the genus with yellow flowers from tufts of bright green leaves in early autumn.

Puschkinia (Liliaceae)

P. scilloides (*libanotica*) is an early spring bulb with light blue darker-striped flowers. It can be planted among cushion-forming plants to good effect but looks well everywhere.

Rhodohypoxis (Hypoxidaceae)

R. baurii ranges from bright crimson to white, forming carpets of blossom all summer. It comes from Lesotho in southern Africa and needs an acid free-draining, peaty soil. It likes to be very moist in summer and dry in winter, which is not always very easy to achieve. It is an excellent plant where it can be suited but even then it will need protecting from wet in the winter and so it is best grown in the alpine-house or special beds. There are many named selections in Britain.

Romulea (Iridaceae)

These close relatives of *Crocus* have never become well-known in gardens. The majority are South African and tender but merit investigation by rock gardeners in climates where winters are virtually frost-free. Bright red *R. sabulosa*, pink *R. rosea* and shining yellow *R. saldanhensis* among others are grown under glass by British gardeners. *R. macowanii alticola* (often grown as *R. longituba* or *Syringodea luteonigra*) comes from extremely high altitudes in the Drakensberg Mountains and is perfectly hardy with yellow flowers in late summer. The Mediterranean species are the more important for European gardeners. The best are those in the variable *R. bulbocodium* group, like white *R. tempskyana*, yellow *R. crocea* and *R. clusiana* and *R. nivalis* with violet flowers shading to yellow and white in their throats. These are all suitable for the bulb-frame or pots in the alpine-house.

Roscoea (Zingiberaceae)   p. 93

These orchid-like plants from east Asia belong to the ginger family. Their fleshy, deep rootstocks push up lush leek-like shoots in May, and flower from June to August. The flowers are two-lipped and topped by high-domed helmets. *R. cautleoides* is bright-yellow, *R. humeana* wine-red, *R. purpurea* (*R. sikkimensis*) purple and *R. procera* has large, lilac-purple flowers with white stripes. All grow twelve to sixteen

(1) *Muscari armeniacum*, a very easily cultivated grape hyacinth. (2) *Crocus imperati*, perhaps the loveliest of all the early spring crocuses, from southern Italy. On the outside it is striped with yellow and brown. The autumn crocuses are far too little known. (3) *Crocus speciosus*, aptly named. (4) *C. banaticus* from Romania. The dwarf tulips of Central Asia are delightful: (5) *Tulipa aucheriana* and (6) *T. urumiensis*.

inches (30–40 cm) high. *R. alpina* is shorter and bears smaller pink flowers but is less spectacular. They thrive in deep, loamy, humus in slight shade. They should be planted deep in the earth and thickly covered with leaves in winter, remembering they do not appear till very late in spring.

Scilla, Squill (Liliaceae)

The earliest to flower is the light-blue *S. mischtschenkoana* (*tubergeniana*) from north Iran which often appears above the snow. The well-known *S. siberica* and its vigorous variety 'Spring Beauty' follow in April with their brilliant deep-blue flowers, as do the dainty, loose lavender-blue stars of *S. bifolia*. After a few weeks the stately *Hyacinthoides* (*Scilla*) *hispanica*, the Spanish bluebell, raises its spikes of dark-blue, pink or white bells, and this is an easy plant for the shade. *S. hohenackeri* from the Caspian woods and *S. lilio-hyacinthus* from western Europe are two more pleasant, early shade-lovers. The latest species to flower is *S. litardierei* (*amethystina*) from Jugoslavia, which blooms in June and bears long-tubed, icy-blue blossoms.

Sternbergia (Liliaceae)

S. lutea is a six inch (20 cm) plant with shiny, dark-green leaves and vivid, yellow, crocus-like flowers in autumn. It looks well beside the autumn colours of *Euphorbia polychroma*, grey-leaved plants and blue autumn crocus. It likes sun and a limy soil which is completely dry in summer. In winter it needs a protected position to prevent its leaves being frosted. *S. lutea sicula*, the smaller narrower-leaved subspecies, is considered to be the most free-flowering. Large *S. clusiana* and spring-flowering *S. fischeriana* need a long, hot summer baking to flower well.

Tecophilaea (Tecophilaeaceae)

This Chilean corm is one of the most coveted plants. Only one species concerns the rock gardener, *T. cyanocrocus*, with intense gentian-blue crocus-like flowers in spring. It is by no means an easy plant and is usually grown in the alpine-house. Where it has succeeded outside this has usually been in areas where winters are temperate and summers warm but not dry, as in Ireland or New Zealand. There are paler blue forms called *leichtlinii* and purplish blues called *violacea*.

Trillium see page 130

Tulipa (Liliaceae)   p. 145

The tulips grow wild from Europe to the Himalayas, centred on central Asia. More than most bulbs, they miss the summer-baking of their native lands and, in wet climates, the bulb-frame provides an excellent alternative to the trouble of lifting the bulbs in summer and storing dry until late autumn. In pots they must be repotted annually as they find their way to the bases of the pots each year and the deepest available pots should be used.

Of the few species which will settle down and increase in the rock garden, one of the best is *T. tarda*, about four inches (10 cm) high with yellow, white-tipped flowers in bunches. *T. sylvestris* is taller but an equally good garden plant, especially in its free-flowering variety 'Tabriz'. *T. s. australis* (*T. celsiana* and *T. persica* of catalogues) is bronze-tinged outside and needs a hotter site or the bulb-frame, as does *T. urumiensis*, which is more or less a dwarfer version of it. Although not the most exciting tulip, the robust race of *T. biflora*, known as *T. turkestanica*, grows and flowers freely with several small white, yellow centred flowers on each eight-inch (20 cm) stem. Other races of this group, grown as *T. polychroma*, need the bulb-frame. *T. sprengeri* is the most successful species in English gardens, sowing itself freely. It is also the last to flower, not opening its elegant orange-scarlet flowers until June. Although the many garden hybrids of *T. kaufmanniana* are dwarf, early-flowering plants, they seem misplaced on the rock garden and are best kept to more formal surroundings near the house. The original species has cream flowers flushed pink outside and will establish and increase in a hot, dry situation.

The twelve-inch (30 cm) *T. praestans* is the only scarlet species which increases and flowers well outside. Its sumptuous taller relatives *T. fosteriana*, *T. eichleri* and *T. tubergeniana* need a more thorough summer baking. The more elegant dwarfer scarlet species are very successful in the bulb-frame: *T. linifolia* (and its earlier flowering and yellow forms, grown as *T. maximowiczii* and *T. batalinii*) and *T. montana* (*T. wilsoniana*). The dwarf, variable *T. humilis* group also does well here and makes excellent pot plants for the alpine-house. These are grown under many names: pink *T. pulchella*, bright red-purple *T. violacea* and salmon-pink *T. aucheriana*. The little mountain tulips of the *T. clusiana* group also need a hot dry rest to ripen their bulbs. *T. clusiana* itself is white with crimson outside and a purple centre; *T. stellata* is similar with a yellow centre; *T. c. chrysantha* is wholly yellow. *T. aitchisonii* and *T. a. cashmeriana* are other races sometimes available.

Zephyranthes (Amaryllidaceae)
Only the white, autumn-flowering *Z. candida* is hardy in the south of England, but this genus is well-known to gardeners in the warmer parts of North America, and those who garden in such climates where winters are almost frost-free or can offer protection can consider species like white *Z. atamasco*, yellow *Z. citrina* and pink *Z. grandiflora* and *Z. rosea*. These all have goblet-shaped flowers and grow about eight-inches (20 cm) high in sunny well-drained places. *Habranthus* are closely related but hold their flowers at an angle. Yellow *H. andersonii* and bright pink *H. robustus* grow about the same height and need similar conditions.

Grasses

Grasses are receiving ever more attention as decorative plants in modern gardens and this increasing appreciation is more than justified. They look particularly well in informal rock gardens, where their green and grey tufts give welcome relief to the eye, among all the stronger colours of the flowering plants. In seasons when blossom is scarce, their elegant stems lend a diffuse, natural air to the garden. Species are available for every position though most are sun-lovers.

Those who appreciate dwarf alpines will take pleasure in grey, downy *Alopecurus lanatus*, a grass from Turkey only about three inches (5–10 cm) high. This is so well-behaved that it can be grown on tufa or in troughs.

Among larger alpine grasses, *Poa alpina vivipara* is attractive, with its panicles bent under the weight of the young plantlets which dangle from their tips.

Carex montana, a mountain sedge, may be planted beside *Erica herbacea*, which it complements with its small, brownish-yellow spikelets. *Carex baldensis* is another pretty sedge with small, white clusters on stems eight to twelve inches (20–30 cm) high. This may be the only grassy plant which is pollinated not by the wind but by insects. *Carex firma*, a cushion-forming sedge, goes well with *Dryas*, *Aster alpinus* and edelweiss. It comes from the rocks and screes of the Alps and in the rock garden it will form a dark-green carpet. Those who like variegated grasses should obtain the variety 'Variegata', with yellowish-white leaves, striped with green. *Carex buchananii*, *C. petriei* and other sedges from New Zealand have quite a different habit and the uninitiated will think their rust-brown or bronze clumps quite dead, but planted next to silver-foliage (of *Raoulia australis* for example) they too have their own charm. Winter is the best time for these sedges, when their stems remain standing in magical feathery shapes, upright plumes and low, curled tufts.

Perhaps the most important of all grasses are the blue-grey species, which are particularly effective in creating an impression of dryness. *Festuca glacialis* is a small fescue from the Pyrenees, with pale blue-green foliage. The garden forms of *F. glauca*, *F. ovina* and *F. vallesiaca* have dense clumps in striking blue shades. *Koeleria glauca* is a duller blue. Stateliest and most prized is *Helictotrichon sempervirens* 'Glauca', the blue oat, with tidy bluish-grey tufts and flower stems over three feet (1 metre) high, which droop gracefully in the variety 'Pendula'. This decorative grass can be used in many positions, such as between flagstones on terraces or in heath gardens. It will also lend tone to gardens which echo the dunes, steppes and desert. *Corynephorus canescens*, a grey sand-loving grass and the feathery *Stipa pennata*, *S. capillata* and *S. barbata*, large, plumed grasses with long, waving, silver awns, are also useful for such arrangements.

If bright green cushions are wanted, *Festuca gautieri* (*scoparia*) from the Pyrenees is useful in sun or half-shade, even in quite arid ground.

Various species of *Luzula* are available for shady areas. These include the pretty, evergreen *L. sylvatica*, its fresh-green variety 'Tauernpass' and the yellow-edged form 'Marginata'. *L. pilosa* 'Greenfinch' is only eight inches (20 cm) high. *L. nivea* is particularly lovely, with its whitish heads and will withstand more sun. The Japanese sedge, *Carex morrowii* and its form 'Aurea Variegata' ('Evergold') with cream-edged leaves are also worthwhile. *Carex grayi* is a broad-leafed species from North America with delightful, star-shaped seed-capsules. Finest of all is the North American *C. fraseri*, with broad dark-green leaves and pure white flowers. This last needs a lime-free soil consisting of damp humus.

Grasses also look well beside water. The variegated varieties are more in keeping with formal water gardens where *Arrhenatherum elatius bulbosum* 'Variegatum', a white-striped grass and *Carex riparia* 'Variegata', a white-variegated sedge, look well in moist soil. In boggy patches of the peat-bed, you can plant *Juncus castaneus* alongside *Primula* and *Parnassia*. Here it will produce delightful, reddish-brown flower-heads, bringing some of the magic of the wild into the garden. The brilliant golden-green of *Carex elata* (*stricta*) 'Aurea' also looks well with candelabra Primulas and it is quite happy in limy soils, provided it is moist. The outstanding dwarf golden-leaved grass is *Milium effusum* 'Aureum', which will sow itself in shady places, blending with other woodlanders. One of the choicest grasses available is *Hakonechloa macra*, from moist shady cliffs in Japan. It has graceful bamboo-like tufts, and its gold and bronze variegated form 'Aureola' is especially striking. For more open sunny areas, the forms of *Molinia caerulea* are among the neatest, dwarf, tufted grasses. The variegated form looks well beside paving and the green-leaved selections such as 'Heidebraut' and 'Moorhexe' blend with heaths and heathers, as they do in nature in the northern moorlands.

Ferns

Ferns should always find a place in the rock garden, with their finely-cut, graceful fronds. They are available for every type of position, including sunny places. The best known of the sun-loving ferns is *Asplenium ruta-muraria*, with crisp, grey-green fronds, found growing on countless European walls both in town and country. Much prettier is *Ceterach officinarum*, with small, scaly brown, feathery fronds. It likes warmth and lime and is happy in narrow crevices. *Pellaea atropurpurea*, a slender rock-fern with pinnate fronds and wiry stems, from North America, is another lime-loving plant which grows in humus. *Asplenium septentrionale*, a small fern with narrow, fan-shaped fronds, and *Cheilanthes* (*Notholaena*) *marantae* are lime-haters. This last comes from southern Europe and needs shelter, lime-free soil and protection in winter. All these are unusual among ferns in being sun-lovers for a dry position. If they become too dry their fronds shrivel, but they wake as soon as the atmosphere and soil are moist again.

For rocks and walls in shady positions, the following are some of the best-loved European ferns: *Asplenium trichomanes*, with blackish-brown stems, and *A. viride*, with green-veined fronds. *Cystopteris fragilis* is taller and more vigorous and likes to thrust its pinnate fronds out from behind overhanging stones in walls, whilst its American cousin, *C. bulbifera*, prefers to grow in the earth, where it can spread freely. This species has striking, slender, bright-green fronds and brown stems. *Polypodium vulgare* will only thrive in acid soil, in a half-shady position. This is an evergreen fern, crested varieties of which are available. These have a quite different appearance from the type species. The best of the larger ferns for shady walls is *Phyllitis scolopendrium* (*Scolopendrium vulgare*). It grows particularly on chalk, where it will sow itself, unfurling its long and lovely fronds in moist ground. A whole range of forms of this fern exist, some with forked fronds, some with broad crests or wavy edges to their fronds.

The Club Mosses, *Selaginella helvetica* and *S. underwoodii* are not true ferns, but are included here because they have the same habit and needs as the shade-loving ferns. They are useful in rocky niches.

All sorts of woodland ferns can be used in larger gardens, on shady slopes. The stately *Matteuccia struthiopteris* is an example, but it can become a nuisance by spreading too far. For smaller gardens some of the really pretty small ferns are recommended, such as *Polystichum setiferum* 'Plumosum Densum' or *P. setiferum* 'Proliferum'. *Adiantum pedatum*, the Maidenhair Fern from North America is another lovely species. Its palmate, bright-green fronds are quite as elegant as those of its tropical relatives. There are very compact forms from high-altitude and Arctic localities, which have overlapping fronds only eight inches (20 cm) high. The garden plant is *A. p.* 'Imbricatum' (grown as *minus*, *aleuticum* and *compactum*). *Adiantum venustum* from the Himalayas is also a charming light-green. *Osmunda regalis* 'Gracilis' is a diminutive edition of the splendid Royal Fern. With *Onoclea sensibilis* it is a fine sight in spring, with its young, delicate, glassy shoots, and throughout the summer. Both these do best in moist, peaty soil. *Blechnum spicant* is a pretty fern with sleek, dark-green fronds, but will only grow in acid humus. Its small relative *Blechnum penna-marina* is much easier to grow; it comes from Australia and New Zealand. It prefers broad, shady crevices in rocks. Nor should we forget the lime-hating *Thelypteris phegopteris* with its spreading, triangular, simple, pinnate fronds, *Gymnocarpium dryopteris* with its clear-green carpets of fronds, or *G. robertianum*, a lime-lover which is lovely on account of its dainty, blue-green shoots alone.

Dwarf Shrubs

Shrubs must be planted with consideration and care. If they are destined to be planted in the rock garden, one should never be tempted into buying small shrubs in pots or containers, no matter how beautiful they may be, without finding out precisely what sort of size and shape they will grow into. When they are planted out and released from the restriction of their pots, they will often change from dwarfs to giants without warning. The following selection of species and varieties is intended to make the job of choosing suitable shrubs easier.

Acer, Maple (Aceraceae) **p. 153**
Only the slow-growing Japanese maples need concern us. In their native habitat and in moist, temperate climates they grow up to thirty feet (8 m) high, but they grow slowly and it may be many years before they reach six feet in height and grow too large for their surroundings. Do select and plant with caution, however, for this reason. There are many varieties of *Acer palmatum*, most of which have been cultivated in Japan for centuries. Some of the best for formal, decorative effects are 'Atropurpureum', with vivid, red shoots and wide lobes; the narrow-fingered 'Linearilobum Atropurpureum', red-leaved with finely divided foliage; 'Dissectum Atropurpureum' and the dark-red 'Dissectum Garnet'. In informal gardens, the lovely 'Dissectum', with its fresh-green, feathery leaves which turn red and yellow in autumn, may also be used. Japanese maples are particularly effective in spring, with their delicately tinted new growth and, in autumn, in their breathtaking, vivid autumn colours. The light shade they provide is good for *Anemonopsis*, *Epimedium*, *Mertensia virginica*, *Hylomecon*, *Jeffersonia* and many other attractive plants. Maples may be planted beside water or in shaded positions. They dislike lime and their delicate foliage is easily burnt in hot, dry or windy positions, so a sheltered site should be chosen.

Amorpha (Leguminosae)
A. nana (*A. microphylla*) is a dwarf from North America only one foot eight inches high (50 cm), of modest beauty. It will tolerate very dry conditions, however, and in summer bears purple spires dotted with golden stamens. It is in place in succulent gardens.

Andromeda, Bog Rosemary (Ericaceae)
A. polifolia is a moorland plant found all round the north of the northern hemisphere. It needs to be continually moist and requires acid, peaty soil. Nodding, pink bells appear on its twelve inch (30 cm) evergreen bushes from May until July. The variety 'Leucantha' has white flowers and the dwarf Japanese varieties such as the small, bushy 'Compacta' and 'Minima' are especially worthy of note.

Anthyllis (Leguminosae)
Mediterranean *A. hermanniae* is a useful plant for rock garden beds and troughs, where its congested mounds are covered with yellow flowers in June. It looks well with small carpets of *Antennaria* and *Raoulia*. *A. h. aspalathi* from Crete is a very slow-growing race, only reaching one foot high (30 cm) after many years.

Arcterica see **Pieris**

Arctostaphylos, Bearberry, Manzanita (Ericaceae)
A. uva-ursi is a pretty, Arctic plant with a

circumpolar distribution. Its pink flowers appear only rarely but it is worth growing for its flat, trailing, evergreen branches. It is good ground-cover for the peat bed and looks attractive creeping over and hanging down from rocky slabs. There are many other species in western North America, where they are one of the constituents of the chaparral. Most of these are too large or too tender for gardeners in colder climates, but prostrate plants like *A. nevadensis*, *A. pumila* and *A. nummularia* can be enjoyed in acid soils in sunny places.

Artemisia see page 76

Asteranthera and **Mitraria**
(Gesneriaceae)
Carmine-red *A. ovata* and scarlet *M. coccinea* are creeping plants from forests in the high-rainfall areas of Chile. Where summers are wet and winters mild, they will cover shady rocks with their rooting stems and evergreen leaves. Where the climate is less favourable they can be grown in humus-rich soil in moist shade in the alpine-house.

Azalea see **Rhododendron**   **p. 35**

Berberis, Barberry (Berberidaceae)
There are a number of slow-growing evergreen barberries: *B. buxifolia* 'Nana', with compact dark green bushes; *B. × stenophylla* 'Irwinii', with golden-yellow flowers; coral-red and yellow *B. × stenophylla* 'Corallina Compacta', only one foot (30 cm) tall; and orange-yellow *B. darwinii* 'Compacta', with black berries. In climates with severe, cold dry winters, these need some protection.

Of the deciduous species of Berberis, *B. thunbergii* has compact varieties, 'Kobold' with green foliage and 'Atropurpurea Nana' and 'Baggatelle' with red foliage. In spring these have profuse, bright-yellow flowers and in autumn coral-red berries and vivid yellow and red colours.

Betula, Dwarf Birch (Betulaceae)
B. nana is an Arctic shrub of quiet beauty with round, toothed leaves and spreading branches. It seldom grows more than eighteen inches (45 cm) high and needs moist acid soil. Plants suitable to put alongside it in the peat bed are *Andromeda polifolia*, *Linnaea borealis* and the Arctic Ericaceae.

Bruckenthalia (Ericaceae)
B. spiculifolia is a little heath about six inches (10–20 cm) high from the mountains of south-eastern Europe. It looks at its best with dwarf rhododendrons and bears dense cylindrical spires of pink flowers in June–July. It needs a peaty soil and a sunny position.

Bryanthus (Ericaceae)
B. gmelinii is a prostrate evergreen shrub from north-east Asia. It is related to *Phyllodoce* and has rose-pink flowers, but it is very shy-flowering even when grown in ideal conditions in the peat bed.

Calluna, Ling, Heather (Ericaceae)
The various garden forms of heather, *C. vulgaris*, require an absolutely lime-free soil. They look best in a heath garden, which forms a good adjunct to the rock garden. The following are recommended: 'Serlei', white and late; 'Alba Plena', double white; 'County Wicklow', dwarf, double pink; 'H. E. Beale' and 'J. H. Hamilton', double salmon-pinks; and among the turfy sorts: 'Mullion', dark-pink; 'Alportii', vigorous red; 'Gold Haze' and 'Robert Chapman', yellow leaves in summer, copper-coloured in winter. The compact, dense, cushion-forming 'Foxii Nana' looks like a dwarf conifer and is especially good for lime-free stone-troughs. Similar tightly compacted forms from the island of St Kilda are being used to breed dwarf hybrids in Scotland.

Caragana (Ericaceae)

C. jubata is a striking plant from east Siberia and west China. Its sparsely branched shoots grow up to three feet (1 metre) high, and in winter its thick, brown hairy covering gives it a most exotic and unusual appearance. In combination with *Yucca*, *Opuntia*, *Acaena* and *Helictotrichon sempervirens*, it can be used in dry-climate gardens. *C. arborescens* 'Nana' and the slender-branched, wider spreading *C. pygmaea* are also outstanding accent plants in such places. These plants are used to extremely low temperatures but also need hot summers to ripen their wood and produce their white or yellow pea-flowers.

Carmichaelia (Leguminosae)

C. enysii from the South Island of New Zealand and *C. orbiculata* from North Island are strange, slow-growing shrubs forming dense, compact thickets, about six inches (15 cm) high, of interlacing, flattened, dull-green branches which do the work of leaves. Many small white flowers densely veined with violet appear among the stems but these are inconspicuous unless the plant is raised near eye-level. These are suitable for sunny troughs or the alpine-house.

Caryopteris (Verbenaceae)

These are very worthwhile plants with late, long-lasting violet-blue flowers, complimenting the grey-green of their foliage. The prettiest are *C.* × *clandonensis* 'Heavenly Blue', a small, loosely built bush sixteen inches to two feet (40–60 cm) tall, and 'Kew Blue' with dark blue flowers. *C. incana* from China and Japan is taller and stiffer in appearance. They need winter protection in very cold areas.

Cassandra see **Chamaedaphne**

Cassiope (Ericaceae)

These evergreens grow only a few inches high (3–5 cm) with dark-green, scaly branches and white flowers which resemble lily-of-the-valley. They are plants for the peat bed or trough, if made of acid rock, and will only thrive in a cool, damp atmosphere. They also prefer a cold, dry winter, and gardeners interested in these and other Arctic or alpine ericaceous plants can grow them in a peat bed which can be covered with a plastic or glass light in winter. Among the more adaptable species are *C. lycopodioides*, a very dwarf mat from Japan to Alaska; the vigorous *C. mertensiana gracilis* from Montana and Oregon; and *C. tetragona saximontana* from north-west Canada. The up-right, Himalayan species, *C. fastigiata*, *C. selaginoides* and *C. wardii*, are not so easy in areas with hot summers but some of their hybrids are more vigorous. 'Muirhead' and 'Edinburgh' are outstanding. The two tiny moss-like Arctic species (*Harrimanella*), *C. stelleriana* and *C. hypnoides*, are the most difficult.

Ceanothus, California Lilac (Rhamnaceae)

These magnificent shrubs, whose distribution is centred on California, are not for gardeners in very cold climates. In most of Britain they will be damaged about once every ten years so are worth planting, as they are mostly fast-growing.

With bold planting, wonderful effects of colour can be achieved in the rock garden. (1) Golden-yellow *Alyssum saxatile* is edged with the violet of *Aubrieta*, and the whole composition is crowned with the red leaves of *Acer palmatum* 'Dissectum Garnet'. *Arabis* and rock phlox provide the white shades. (2) *Cytisus hirsutus demissus* is a creeping broom from southern Europe. (3) *Daphne blagayana* is a prostrate evergreen shrub.

153

Strangely, it is not to the mountains that we must look for many of the low-growing plants but to the coasts, where they have been beaten into a prostrate habit by the Pacific gales. Leathery, spiny leaved *C. gloriosus*, *C. thyrsiflorus repens* and *C. griseus horizontalis* are such coastal mat-forming plants. 'Blue Mound' is a garden variety of similar habit. These all cover themselves with flowers in varying shades of blue in early summer. While under a foot (30 cm) in height they can grow to ten feet (3 m) across, so need space. All will enjoy the hottest, driest site available. The prostrate alpine species, *C. prostratus* and *C. pumilus*, seem less willing to adapt to cultivation.

Ceratostigma (Plumbaginaceae)
C. plumbaginoides is a shrub which ought to have a place in every garden. It likes a dry, sunny position, forming thick carpets eight inches (20 cm) high of broad leaves, which turn reddish in autumn, when it is adorned with azure-blue flowers. *Potentilla nepalensis*, *Colchicum speciosum*, *Berberis thunbergii*, and *Cotoneaster horizontalis* look well alongside it.

Chamaecytisus see Cytisus

Chamaedaphne, Leather-leaf (Ericaceae)
Chamaedaphne (*Andromeda*, *Cassandra*) *calyculata* 'Nana' is a charming dwarf form of the type species only one foot (30 cm) high. Its broad bushes bear white bells in spring on their evergreen, horizontal branches. It is a lime-hater, best suited to the peat garden.

Cistus, Halimium and **Halimiocistus**, Rock Rose (Cistaceae)
Comments under *Ceanothus* apply equally to these shrubs which contribute to the Mediterranean maquis just as *Ceanothus* does in the Californian chaparral. They need hot, dry sites, are unsuitable for continental winters and may occasionally be damaged even in southern England. Few *Cistus* are dwarf enough for the rock garden: white *C. clusii*, crimson-blotched *C. × lusitanicus* 'Decumbens', pale pink *C. parviflorus* and its hybrid *C. × skanbergii*, brilliant cerise *C. × pulverulentus* ('Sunset'). These all grow about two feet (60 cm) but the finest and most compact, though not the hardiest, is *C. palhinhae* from Portugal with dark, sticky foliage and immense white flowers. The bigeneric hybrids with *Halimium*, × *Halimiocistus*, are all smaller. *H.* 'Ingwersenii', *H. revolii* and the very hardy *H. sahucii* are all white. *H. wintonensis* is very striking with white flowers marked with maroon round the golden centre. *Halimium* itself comes closer to *Helianthemum*. White *H. umbellatum*, yellow *H. commutatum* and yellow, crimson blotched *H. lasianthum formosum* are the dwarfest, all just over one foot (30 cm).

Clematis, Virgin's Bower (Ranunculaceae)
C. alpina is an elegant climber whose nodding blue flowers look as lovely in our gardens as in their native Alpine woods. *C. macropetala* from China is similar, with multiple bright blue petals, giving the effect of a double flower. Dull violet *C. koreana* and American *C. verticillaris* are similar but less easy plants. Charming colour effects can be obtained by allowing all these to clamber over *Rhododendron ambiguum* or *R. concinnum*. *C. texensis* has scarlet, pitcher-shaped flowers and looks best at the foot of a sunny, sheltered dry-stone wall.

Although these are normally climbing plants, several clamber over rocks at high altitudes; such are golden *C. chrysantha paucidentata* from Afghanistan and the distinctive, woolly, grey-leaved, cream-flowered *C. phlebantha* from dry areas in Nepal. The North American *C. douglasii* is another dry climate plant, usually grown in the race *C. d. scottii* with both silver-blue and pink forms, seen to advantage when trailing at the edge of a raised bed in full sun. This is herbaceous, as is the east European *C. integri-*

folia, a slightly larger plant with nodding violet-blue flowers for similar positions.

Coprosma (Rubiaceae)
C. petriei from New Zealand forms flat mats of foliage with bluish to wine-coloured fruits. *C. brunnea* is not so neat but has translucent blue fruits. Others have red or orange berries, but in all cases these will only appear if several plants are present, as male and female flowers are usually on different plants. All need cool moist summers.

Cornus, Dogwood (Cornaceae)
C. hessei forms a gnarled bush up to twenty inches (50 cm) tall with deeply veined, dark green leaves turning violet in autumn. It is an excellent trough-garden plant without any particular fads. The two small spreading dogwoods (*Chamaepericlymenum*), *C. canadensis* and *C. suecica*, are only two to six inches (5–15 cm) high; the former is the more useful. It is a lover of acid humus and will form thick colonies if planted in the peat bed. It has white star-like flowers in June and clusters of red berries in autumn.

Corokia, Wire-netting Bush
(Saxifragaceae)
C. cotoneaster is a strange and striking plant from New Zealand. With tangled, brownish-white twigs, hardly any leaves, small, yellow flowers and orange berries, it looks like a miniature tree from another world. It will only show off its character properly if planted in isolation or with carpets of *Muehlenbeckia axillaris*. It needs some protection in winter and is only suitable for mild climates.

Cotoneaster (Rosaceae)
Many cotoneasters are creeping plants effective in combination with stone. They are easy plants, decorative when crowning dry-stone walls or tumbling over them. The white or pink flowers, which are very attractive to bees, are followed by profuse red berries. Of the evergreen species the best are:

congestus: prostrate, bright-red berries

conspicuus 'Decorus': wide and spreading up to three feet (90 cm) high. If blackbirds leave the orange-red berries, they will still be there when the white flowers appear in May.

dammeri (*humifusus*): excellent, very vigorous, ground cover; *dammeri radicans* is even hardier and has darker, shinier leaves; *dammeri* 'Skogholm' is a particularly vigorous plant, useful for providing long-term ground-cover for large areas; *dammeri* 'Coral Beauty' is lower than 'Skogholm', wide-branching in habit, with very profuse scarlet berries; *dammeri* 'Streibs Findling' is slower in growth than the type, and especially suitable for rock gardens.

microphyllus cochleatus: prostrate, umbrella-like habit.

salicifolius: 'Perkeo' grows in mounds, with pendant branches; 'Parkteppich' ('Park Carpet') is a flatter ground-cover variety.

Deciduous species:

adpressus: prostrate, arching branches, leaves have wavy edges and turn scarlet in autumn;

adpressus 'Little Gem' forms thick cushions, with small leaves.

horizontalis: very well known species, with branching, fish-bone-shaped stems; very useful varieties are 'Coral', with profuse, large fruits, and 'Saxatilis', slow-growing, prostrate.

Cyathodes (Epacridaceae)
C. colensoi, *C. empetrifolia* and a few other species are heath-like New Zealand shrubs for lime-free peaty soils which are moist in summer. They have bluish-grey foliage and small clusters of white flowers. The white or red berries are seldom set in gardens.

Cytisus and **Chamaecytisus**, Broom
(Leguminosae)   **pp. 47, 153**
The following prostrate species grow only eight to twelve inches (20–30 cm) high and make a wonderful show in sunny well-drained places with their profuse golden flowers in May–June: *C. ardoini*, *C.* × *beanii*, *C. decumbens* and *C. hirsutus demissus* (*Chamaecytisus polytrichus*). The pale yellow, long-stemmed *C.* × *kewensis* is somewhat taller. *C.* (*Chamaecytisus*) *purpureus* has purple-pink flowers on dark green thickets eighteen inches (50 cm) high. *C.* × *praecox* has slender, arching branches and profuse, pale yellow flowers. It is suitable for larger gardens or as a background in the rock garden, along with its varieties 'Allgold' and 'Goldspeer' in intense, deep yellow, and 'Hollandia', two-toned purple and pink. Its striking clouds of blossom go well with aubrieta and lilac-blue phlox.

Daboecia, St Dabeoc's Heath (Ericaceae)
D. cantabrica is an evergreen, but not completely hardy, peat-loving shrub from western Europe. It has purple or white flowers from summer to autumn and should be planted in acid soil in the heath garden. *D. c.* 'Praegerae' is very low-growing and dense, with profuse, pink clusters of flowers. *D.* 'William Buchanan' is an outstanding Scottish hybrid between this and *D. azorica*. It is compact with luminous, carmine-pink bells.

Daphne, Garland Flower, Mezereon
(Thymelaeaceae)   **p. 153**
D. mezereum, with scented purple or white flowers, looks well in early spring with mountain pines, hellebores and hepatica around the rock garden. *D.* × *burkwoodii* 'Somerset' is a spreading three foot (1 metre) hybrid between *D. caucasica* and *D. cneorum*, with pale pink flowers in late spring, beautiful when underplanted with bright blue scillas. *D. cneorum* 'Eximia' is a real jewel, growing a foot high (30 cm), which turns into a scented cushion of deep-pink flowers in spring.

D. petraea from the Italian Alps is a small cliff plant and only feels at home in narrow crevices. It flowers best when grafted on to *D. mezereum* and is easier to manage in the alpine-house or in a trough. When its mound of close, stocky branches is covered with large, pink flowers in May, it is unparalleled among alpine plants. *D. jasminea*, another cliff plant, from southern Greece, is a less spectacular, though no less desirable, alpine-house plant, forming mounds of branches clothed with narrow greyish leaves and with clusters of starry white, purplish-backed flowers in June. *D. arbuscula* from Czechoslovakia, is another rock-dweller. It likes a sunny position, and in spring its compact dark-leaved bushes are covered with lilac-pink clusters. *D. blagayana* from east European woods prefers a slightly shady position and produces creamy white, sweet-scented flowers in March. Later in spring comes *D. sericea*, about three feet (1 m) high with rose-coloured flowers. This is not such a good garden plant as its south Italian race, the twelve inch (30 cm), deep rose-pink *D. collina*, and its taller hybrid *D.* × *napolitana*. These are all evergreen. *D. striata*, from the central European mountains, is a very difficult and unsatisfactory plant in the garden.

Among the east Asian species *D. tangutica* and its slow-growing compact race, *D. retusa*, are outstanding among the evergreen ones. These grow from one to four feet (30–120 cm) with clusters of sweet-scented, white flowers with purple exteriors in late spring. Tall *D. bholua* has similar flowers and has a compact variety, 'Sheopuri'. *D. giraldii* is deciduous and the best of the yellow-flowered ones, with clusters of fragrant flowers in late spring, followed by red berries.

Dorycnium (Leguminosae)
D. hirsutum, with heads of pink-flushed, white flowers and grey, hairy leaves, grows to about

eighteen inches (50 cm) and is the best of these summer-flowering Mediterranean plants, which grow easily in any poor, well-drained soil in a hot, sunny place.

Dryas, Mountain Avens (Rosaceae)
D. octopetala is a characteristic plant of the Arctic and the Alps. It will thrive in full sun and spread its dense mats over stones. Unfortunately its showy, white flowers last only a short time in May but its feathery-grey seed-heads are attractive in summer. *D. drummondii* from North America has small, nodding, yellow flowers and darker leaves. The hybrid, *D. × suendermannii* is more vigorous than either of these, and has creamy flowers. Dryas must be planted from pots to establish well and, if left alone when rooted, will prove easy, long-lived and rewarding.

Empetrum, Crowberry (Empetraceae)
E. nigrum is a heath-like evergreen shrub, up to one foot (30 cm) high, from moorlands all round the northern hemisphere. It forms mats in acid sandy or peaty soils, but the small purplish flowers and black or purple berries are not very generously produced.

Ephedra (Ephedraceae)
These strange plants resemble the horse-tail or broom, and are for the enthusiast. *E. gerardiana* and *E. gerardiana sikkimensis*, both from the Himalayas, are hardy and easy. The best species is the dwarf *E. minima* from Tibet, only four inches (10 cm) high, and with red fruits.

Epigaea (Ericaceae)
These are difficult and challenging evergreen creeping-plants for moist, acid humus in deep, sheltered shade. *E. repens*, from eastern North America, Japanese *E. asiatica* and their hybrid 'Aurora' all have clusters of tubular pink flowers in late spring. *E. (Orphanidesia) gaultherioides*, from moist, mountain forests to the

south-east of the Black Sea, has larger, more open flowers.

Erica, Heath (Ericaceae)   p. 19
The loveliest and most worthwhile species is the winter and early spring-flowering *E. herbacea* (*carnea*), which grows wild in the Alps with mountain pines and rhododendrons. Its great asset is that it does not dislike lime, so that it can be planted in any soil which is free-draining and rich in humus. The more open its position, the more profusely it will bloom. It is a good food-plant for bees. Of the numerous garden varieties, the earliest is rose pink 'Winter Beauty'; 'Springwood Pink' and 'Springwood White' and the deep ruby-pink 'Myretoun Ruby' are vigorous growers. 'Vivelli' has bronze leaves and deep carmine flowers. The best varieties of its taller, long-flowering hybrid, *E. × darleyensis*, are rose-pink 'Arthur Johnson' and white 'Silberschmelze'. All the other heaths must have a lime-free soil. *E. cinerea*, the Bell Heather, is summer-flowering. There are many named varieties: compact white 'Alba Minor' and glowing pink 'C. D. Eason' are well proven ones; newer 'White Dale', 'Pink Ice', 'Purple Beauty' and purple 'Cindy' with bronze foliage appear promising. Taller *E. vagans* flowers a little later in summer. White 'Lyonesse', cerise-pink 'Mrs D. F. Maxwell' and clear pink 'St Keverne' are the best varieties. *E. vagans* is not completely hardy in severe climates. The lovely summer-flowering *E. tetralix* should be planted in a moist part of the peat bed. White 'Alba Mollis' and crimson 'Con Underwood' are not only two of the most reliable varieties but have beautiful silvery-grey foliage.

Erinacea (Leguminosae)
E. anthyllis (*pungens*) is an eight inch (10–30 cm) rounded, prickly shrub. It likes to be as dry as possible and is happy between limestone rocks, only feeling perfectly at home if it can bake in the sun, as it does in its native Spain and North

Africa. It has unusual lilac-blue flowers in early summer.

Eriogonum, Buckwheat (Polygonaceae)
This is a large genus of half-shrubby plants from western North America. All demand plenty of sun and little water. *E. umbellatum* with yellow heads and *E. racemosum* with grey leaves and reddish-white flowers can be planted on a dry slope along with other dry climate plants. The higher-altitude species need alpine-house treatment in wet climates. There, the compact, woolly white mats of *E. caespitosum*, *E. ovalifolium* and *E. o. nivale* can be tried. There are many more worthwhile species but these are seldom obtainable and seldom easy to grow.

Euonymus, Spindle-tree (Celastraceae)
The many varieties of creeping, prostrate *E. fortunei radicans* are rather vigorous for the rock garden itself but are all excellent ground-cover plants for beds beside formal stonework, steps and paving. *E. f.* 'Kewensis' ('Minimus') is the smallest with tiny dull green leaves. Apart from the older creamy-white variegated 'Silver Queen' and 'Variegatus' (usually pink-tinged in winter) there are many other selections, such as 'Emerald Gold', gold-edged and copper-tinted in winter, 'Golden Prince' with golden young growth, and 'Sheridan Gold' with leaves suffused with yellow. These and many others have been selected in North America, where they have proved tolerant and useful evergreens even in such a difficult gardening climate as that of the north-eastern USA. These are all juvenile forms and never bear flowers or fruits, but *E. nanus* (*rosmarinifolius* of gardens) is a slender, spreading shrub, which bears the fleshy, pink four-lobed fruits, opening to show the orange seeds, typical of this genus. *E. alatus* 'Compactus' is a slow, dense-growing variety, noted for its fine, rose and red autumn colour, which seldom exceeds three feet (1 m).

Euryops (Compositae)   p. 69
E. acraeus (sometimes listed as *E. evansii*), eight inches (20 cm) high from the Drakensberg Mountains in Lesotho, has silvery-white leaves, on dense, round bushes, adorned in early summer with yellow flowers. It needs a sunny sheltered position in neutral, free-draining soil and dislikes wetness in winter.

Forsythia (Oleaceae)
The Korean *F. ovata saxatilis* and the newer, compact varieties *F. × intermedia* 'Minigold' and *F. ovata* 'Tetragold' quite rapidly reach three feet (1 m) in English gardens. As the prostrate 'Arnold Dwarf' seldom flowers, the only one of these popular, early-flowering shrubs for the rock gardener is *F. viridissima* 'Bronxensis'. This forms a congested one-foot high (30 cm) mass of twiggy branches with yellow flowers in spring, like all the others. It is best in a sunny place to ripen its wood and form flower-buds well.

Fuchsia (Onagraceae)
The many hybrids of *F. magellanica* are barely hardy in most British gardens, where even the hardiest ones are cut back to the base by the frosts of severe winters. In addition, their flowers are so different to the majority of hardy plants that they look uncomfortably exotic beside the northern rock garden plants. Nearer the house, on terraces and near paving, the dwarfer hybrids are very beautiful and long-flowering in summer, whether tight-growing ones like 'Tom Thumb' or 'Pumila', only eight inches high (20 cm), or the vigorous, wide-spreading, procumbent ones, like 'Corallina'. All these have the red and purple flowers of *F. magellanica*, but there are other colour combinations.

Those who garden in climates where winters are almost frost-free will find some of the wild species with very different flowers worth investigating for the rock garden. *F. microphylla* and *F. thymifolia*, both from high altitudes in Mexico, are much confused in British gardens, where most of the plants may belong to the hybrid between them, *F.* × *bacillaris. F.* × *b.* 'Cottinghamii' has especially brilliant red flowers. The plant grown in California as *F. cinnabarina* is a similar colour. The others, found under many names, are usually pink and all form relatively compact, small-leaved shrubs with many small, tubular flowers. *F. procumbens* from New Zealand is completely prostrate, forming mats of wiry stems, with small yellow, purple and green flowers with projecting blue anthers, followed by magenta fruits.

Gaultheria see **Vaccinium**

Gaylussacia see **Vaccinium**

Genista, Broom (Leguminosae)
There are many dwarf brooms suitable for the rock garden: *G. lydia* has slender, arching branches smothered with golden-yellow flowers in June; *G. radiata*, with dense, rounded mounds; *G.* (*Echinospartum*) *horrida*, a tight, spiny cushion resembling a giant grey hedgehog; *G. pilosa* 'Procumbens' with graceful prostrate branches; *G. hispanica*, a dense dull-green, prickly latticework, covered in summer with golden flowers; *G.* (*Chamaespartium*) *sagittalis*, a flat, creeping broom, with a dwarf French race *G. delphinensis*; *G. pulchella* (*villarsii*), very small, with gnarled twigs which cling to the ground; the double *G. tinctoria* 'Plena' grows only about six inches (15 cm) tall; *G. sylvestris* (*dalmatica*) forms neat, spiny hummocks about the same height. All these have yellow flowers and all are sun lovers, needing light, dry soil. They look their best in an informal arrangement, close to blue *Linum*, *Veronica*, Lavender, Junipers, and Mountain Pines.

Halimium and × **Halimiocistus** see **Cistus**

Harrimanella see **Cassiope**

Hebe, Parahebe and **Pygmaea**
(Scrophulariaceae)
These shrubby Veronicas are possibly New Zealand's most significant contribution to gardens in areas where winters are not too severe. They grow well in any well-drained soil in sun and will thrive in exposed situations, provided that winter temperatures do not drop too low. They are successful in most of southern and western Britain but in the occasional hard winter losses can be heavy. All are evergreen and flower from late spring to autumn, usually with white flowers. It is the diversity and colour of their foliage which is their main attraction, and this is evident in the following species which are all under or about eighteen inches (50 cm) high.

Among the very dwarf species from alpine screes *H. haastii* and *H. epacridea* have distinct columns of stiff, overlapping leaves. In *H. tetrasticha* they are compressed into scale-like, angular rows. This is one of the dwarfest of these 'whipcord' Hebes, most of which have their leaves arranged in more cylindrical columns, forming erect shrubs in the mountain grasslands. Conifer-like *H. propinqua* and the larger *H. cupressoides*, which has a very dwarf branch-sport 'Boughton Dome', are grey-green. *H. hectoris* and *H. lycopodioides* are golden green. *H. ochracea* (*armstrongii* of gardens), of which 'James Stirling' is a compact variety, is bronze. Conifer-like *H. loganioides* has white flowers, which appear more freely than in the other whipcords in gardens, and it may be a natural hybrid of one of them. Several species form low, wide, rounded shrubs and of these *H. vernicosa* and *H. canterburiensis* have highly polished green leaves. *H. buchananii* is dwarfer with small, rounded leathery leaves and has an extremely small variety *H. b.* 'Minor'. This last species is closely related to *H. pinguifolia*, which provides one of the best and most adaptable dwarf blue-grey leaved plants in its variety 'Pagei'. Other good blue-grey Hebes are *H. recurva*, *H. albicans*, *H. carnosula* and the very compact alpine *H. gibbsii*. These are all white-flowered, but prostrate *H. pimeleoides* has spikes of lavender-blue flowers over its blue-grey leaves. Its very small form *H. p.* 'Minor' is like a tiny thyme and is suitable for troughs. While the beautiful *H. hulkeana* grows too large for most rock gardens, the species closely allied to it are dwarf rock plants, with sprays of similar pinkish-mauve or white flowers and toothed leathery foliage. These are *H. lavaudiana* (*H.* 'Fairfieldii' of gardens may be a hybrid of this) and *H. raoulii*, from hot, arid rock crevices. *H. macrantha* from wet areas also has fine flowers in pure white and individually the largest of the genus.

Of the many hybrids, pale lavender 'Bowles' Hybrid' ('Eversley Seedling') and purplish-grey leaved 'E. B. Anderson' ('Caledonia') are dwarf enough for the rock garden. Eight-inch (20 cm) 'Carl Teschner' is outstanding with bright violet flowers and black stems, developed a stage further in its seedling 'Colwall' with bright red young growth.

All of the closely related genus *Parahebe* are ideal for the rock garden. These are less woody and closer to *Veronica*, mostly growing in damper gravelly places or shady crevices. Their flowers vary from white through pale blue and pale lavender to pink, often delicately veined. *P. catarractae* is the tallest of these at one foot (30 cm). *P. lyallii*, *P. decora* and others are very compact, mat-forming plants. Australian *P. perfoliata* is prostrate but too widespreading for small rock-gardens.

Though still closely related to *Hebe*, the high alpine *Pygmaea pulvinaris* is utterly different to all these, forming rounded cushions of grey-green velvet. The white stemless flowers reveal its relationship to *Veronica* but these are seldom produced in British gardens, where it is a challenging plant.

Hedera, Ivy (Araliaceae)

Of the many garden forms of ivy, *H. helix*, there are two compact, congested dwarfs, 'Conglomerata' and 'Conglomerata Erecta', which seem to have been expressly created for rock gardens and for miniature gardens in troughs, bowls and window-boxes. Many other small-leaved varieties can be used beside steps or paving for ground cover.

Helianthemum, Sun Rose (Cistaceae)

No dry-stone wall or rock bed should be without these semi-shrubby, dwarf summer flowers, mostly hybrids of *H. nummularium*, which vary in colour from white to dark-red, passing through yellow, brown and orange. Their only disadvantages are that they are not always completely hardy and that their flowers are all too quickly over. It is advisable to cut them back hard after flowering. The single varieties are charming but the flowers last only half a day in hot weather. The double varieties ('Jubilee', 'Mrs C. W. Earle', 'Cerise Queen' and 'Rubin') last much longer. The following singles may be recommended: carmine 'Ben Hope', 'Golden Queen', 'Wisley Pink', 'Sterntaler', golden yellow, and 'Wisley Primrose', bright yellow. These are sun-loving plants which like full exposure and will not stand moisture. In very cold climates they must be protected in winter with a layer of pine branches. *H. oelandicum alpestre* forms dense green carpets and *H. lunulatum* has small, neat cushions. These charming hardy yellow wild species should not be overlooked amongst all the hybrids.

Helichrysum see page 102

Hertia (Compositae)

H. (*Othonnopsis*) *cheirifolia* is a twenty inch (50 cm) succulent shrub from North Africa with grey-green, fleshy spatulate leaves and yellow heads in summer. Under well-drained conditions it is hardy and can be planted with yuccas and other succulents on a dry slope.

Hypericum (Guttiferae)   p. 77

These include many excellent yellow-flowered rock-garden plants for summer and autumn. Among the clump-forming species, *H. cerastoides* (*rhodoppeum*) and *H. olympicum* (*polyphyllum* of gardens), which has a lovely sulphur-yellow variety 'Citrinum', are outstanding and very hardy. The choice American *H. buckleyi* from North Carolina and Georgia has a similar, tufted habit. The thyme-like, mat-forming species are not so hardy in severe winters. Two of the best of these are Himalayan *H. reptans* and *H. trichocaulon* from Crete. Tiny *H. cuneatum* with scarlet buds is such a fragile plant that it is best in the alpine-house, where tender, grey-leaved *H. aegypticum* with flowers like a yellow flax, should also be grown. Of those with an evergreen, heath-like habit, *H. coris* is the hardiest. Upright *H. empetrifolium* from Greece and its prostrate Cretan variety *oliganthum* (*prostratum* of gardens), as well as the difficult *H. ericoides* from Spain and North Africa, are best protected in winter. These are all under one foot (30 cm) high and enjoy sunny, well-drained places.

Iberis, Candytuft (Cruciferae)   p. 43

These evergreen shrubs look like snow-drifts when in flower and are most useful plants in the rock garden. The more vigorous varieties of *I. sempervirens* such as 'Snowflake' are suitable for dry-stone walls. In smaller rock beds compact 'Little Gem' and low-growing *I. sempervirens garrexiana* are more appropriate. Prostrate, diminutive *I. saxatilis* is ideal for trough gardens.

Ilex, Holly (Aquifoliaceae)

There are several varieties of the slow-growing tiny-leaved, Japanese *I. crenata*, which are most unlike the more familiar hollies and are ideal for the rock garden. Yellow-foliaged 'Golden Gem', 'Stokes' and 'Helleri' from the USA all form dense, low, evergreen mounds. *I. c.* 'Mariesii' is the dwarfest of all, only growing a fraction of an inch annually and ideal for troughs.

Jasminum, Jasmine (Oleaceae)

J. parkeri from northern India forms evergreen bushes only eight inches (20 cm) high with yellow flowers in June. It is a dwarf for dry, sunny positions, where its wood can ripen, and it should be protected in winter or kept in the alpine-house.

Kalmia (Ericaceae)

The two foot (60 cm) rose-red *K. angustifolia* or the dainty one foot (30 cm) rose-purple *K. polifolia* and its dwarf alpine variety *microphylla* are shrubs for cool, moist, lime-free soil. They are widespread in North America and are among the loveliest late spring-flowering shrubs for the moister parts of the peat bed.

Kalmiopsis (Ericaceae)

K. leachiana from a few localities in Oregon is an extremely choice dwarf shrub about eight inches (20 cm) high, with upright clusters of open, rosy bells in spring. It is often grown in the alpine-house but is happier outside in a sunnier part of the peat bed or even better in a raised bed with other small Ericaceae, needing protection from winter wet. It has been crossed with *Phyllodoce* to produce the more vigorous × *Phylliopsis hillieri*.

Lavandula, Lavender (Labiatae)

Lavender can be planted in sunny, well-drained places beside steps and paving for its scent and lilac-blue summer flowers. The best garden lavenders are the vigorous 'Hidcote Giant', the low, early-flowering 'Munstead' and 'Hidcote', very dwarf white 'Nana Alba' and 'Hidcote Pink'. The species are more tender but woolly *L. lanata* and *L. stoechas* and *L. pedunculata* with violet bracts are worth trying in hot, dry sites.

Ledum, Labrador Tea (Ericaceae)
North American *L. groenlandicum* 'Compactum', an excellent lime-hating plant for damp parts of the peat bed, has white flowers and narrow, aromatic, evergreen leaves on bushes, recalling a rhododendron. Narrower-leaved *L. palustre* has a dwarf form *decumbens* but is not such a worthwhile species.

Leiophyllum, Sand Myrtle (Ericaceae)
L. buxifolium has glossy, rounded evergreen leaves on neat, dense bushes seldom more than two feet (60 cm) high, with profuse pink buds and white flowers in May and June. *L. b. prostratum* is usually dwarfer. This species comes from the eastern USA and looks delightful in a sunny or slightly shaded bed in sandy, lime-free soil.

Leptospermum (Myrtaceae)
Tasmanian *L. humifusum* (*L. scoparium prostratum* of gardens) is a completely prostrate but wide-spreading evergreen sheeted with white flowers in early summer. It is surprisingly hardy, especially if snow-cover protects it from cold winds. *L. scoparium* 'Nicholsii Nanum' is only suitable for the alpine-house. The true plant slowly forms a dense, bronze-leaved bush, eight inches (20 cm) high covered in June with bright crimson, dark-eyed flowers.

Leucopogon (Epacridaceae)
L. (*Cyathodes*) *fraseri* is a spreading mat-forming shrub a few inches (3–5 cm) high from the mountain heathlands of Tasmania, south-east Australia and New Zealand. Its tubular, white flowers are followed by translucent orange fruits. It needs a peaty, lime-free soil.

Leucothoe (Ericaceae)
There are a few members of this genus of lime-hating shrubs for half-shade, dwarf enough for the peat bed. The beautiful neat Californian *L. davisiae* and arching, zigzag-stemmed *L.*

fontanesiana 'Nana', from the south-eastern USA, grow compactly to about two feet (60 cm) but only Japanese *L. keiskei* is truly dwarf and under one foot (30 cm). It has bright red young growth, maturing to leathery foliage which turns crimson in winter. All have drooping clusters of white, lily-of-the-valley flowers and all these three are evergreen.

Linnaea (Caprifoliaceae)
L. borealis, a slender creeping plant from the Arctic and northern coniferous woods, must have lime-free, humus-rich soil in a shady, cool position. It can be planted in a peat bed to thread its way between dwarf rhododendrons and produce its delicate, nodding, pink twin-flowers in early summer. The American race, *L. borealis americana*, is usually the easiest.

Lithodora see page 107

Loiseleuria, Mountain Azalea (Ericaceae)
L. procumbens is a creeping, small-leaved shrub from the wind-swept mountain tops and the Arctic tundra. It is not very free with its small, pink bells and requires lime-free peaty soil, a cool, airy position and constant even moisture. Such conditions are easiest to achieve in a trough with other small plants such as *Cassiope* or the dwarfest willows.

Luetkea (Rosaceae)
L. pectinata is a small, tufted evergreen shrub with spikes of white flowers, from western North America. While it is closely related to *Spiraea*, when out of flower, its spreading mats of glossy divided leaves look more like those of a mossy saxifrage and it needs the same conditions as these in cool, moist crevices.

Luzuriaga see **Philesia**

Menziesia (Ericaceae)
M. ciliicalyx is a deciduous shrub from Japan,

about two feet (60 cm) high, with yellowish, purple-rimmed bells in May. *M. c. purpurea* is purplish-pink and not to be confused with the much taller species *M. purpurea*. They need a lime-free, peaty soil and look well with dwarf rhododendrons and autumn gentians. The other species are taller.

Mitraria see **Asteranthera**

Moltkia (Boraginaceae)   p. 93
M. petraea bears clusters of tubular, nodding flowers of a gorgeous pure blue in summer. Anyone who has been lucky enough to see this growing high in the mountains of the Balkans will always want to have it in his garden. *M. suffruticosa* (*M. graminifolia*), with narrow, dark-green leaves, has glossy, bluish-violet flowers in June. The hybrid between these, *M. × intermedia*, also has profuse, blue flowers. They all grow about eighteen inches (50 cm) high and need a dry position in full sun between stones or in gravelly soil.

Muehlenbeckia (Polygonaceae)
M. axillaris from New Zealand and Tasmania grows only a few inches (5-10 cm) high, spreading wide mats of thin, wiry stems with tiny, round, olive-green leaves which turn rust-brown in autumn. It needs a square yard (metre) of ground to achieve its full effect.

Myrtus (Myrtaceae)
Evergreen, mat-forming *M. nummularia* comes from the southernmost tip of South America, around the Straits of Magellan. It has dark, rounded leaves, tiny white flowers and pink berries in autumn. It prefers a moist, gritty, peaty soil and makes a fine pan-plant in the alpine-house.

Nandina (Berberidaceae)
The dwarf forms of the bamboo-like Chinese *N. domestica* are not very suitable for general garden use in most of Britain and even less so in more severe climates. They need a rich, moist soil and a warm sheltered position and their attractive berries are seldom seen. They are excellent plants in New Zealand and similar warmer climates, however. 'Pygmaea', purple-tinged 'Nana Purpurea', gold-leaved 'Woods Dwarf' and 'Burdens Dwarf', both becoming red-tinted in winter, are all elegant, clump-forming plants about two feet (60 cm) high.

Ononis, Rest Harrow (Leguminosae)
O. fruticosa and *O. rotundifolia* are two-foot (60 cm) lime-loving shrubs from southern Europe. In summer they have pink pea-like flowers. The semi-shrubby *O. natrix* has yellow flowers striped with red. These are recommended for the wild garden amongst linum, lavender, grey-leaved herbaceous plants and grasses.

Orphanidesia see **Epigaea**

Othonnopsis see **Hertia**

Ozothamnus see **Helichrysum**

Pachistima (Celastraceae)
North America is the home of *P. canbyi* and *P. myrtifolia* (*myrsinites*), both evergreen, prostrate shrubs with insignificant flowers. They thrive in sandy peat in half-shade but have no special value, apart from being another two pleasant dwarf evergreens for the peat bed or lime-free garden.

Pachysandra (Buxaceae)
P. terminalis is an indestructible evergreen from Japan. Its dark green leaves form tight, eight-inch high (20 cm) carpets and the variety 'Green Carpet' is especially recommended as ground cover for dry, shady positions or unfavourable places. *P. procumbens* from North America, with dull green leaves, is not quite so hardy but grows vigorously in more sheltered sites.

Parahebe see **Hebe**

Pentachondra (Epacridaceae)
P. pumila is a tiny, mat-forming, heath-like evergreen with bronze-tinted leaves from the moorlands of Tasmania, south-east Australia and New Zealand. It has small, white, tubular flowers and bright red berries. It must have a lime-free, peaty soil.

Pernettya see **Vaccinium**

Petrophytum (Rosaceae)
P. caespitosum (*Spiraea caespitosa*) from south-western North America clings closely to the rocks with its dense, flat, matted foliage. Its yellowish-white spires on four inch (10 cm) upright stems are pretty but their colour is not particularly striking. In spite of this, it is an attractive plant and a long-lived one, useful in dry-stone walls or on raised beds in the full sun. *P. cinerascens* is similar, but *P. hendersonii*, which grows only in the Olympic Mts of Washington, has larger, broader leaves and stockier spikes of creamy-white.

Philesia and **Luzuriaga** (Philesiaceae)
These are creeping, evergreen, leathery-leaved plants from the shade of wet forests in high rainfall areas of Chile. They need a high humidity throughout the year with cool summers and mild winters but are more damaged by drying winds than by extremes of temperature. Those unable to provide the sheltered shade and moist lime-free soil they need, can grow them beneath the alpine-house staging with hardy Gesneriaceae. *P. magellanica* has pendant, fleshy flowers of deep rose-pink and can grow from six inches (15 cm) to over three feet (1 m) in ideal conditions. *L. radicans* is less spectacular but dwarfer with white flowers and orange berries.

× **Phylliopsis** see **Kalmiopsis**

Phyllodoce (Ericaceae)
These are all six-inch (15 cm) heath-like shrubs with dense, evergreen leaves, suitable for cool, moist peaty conditions. Purplish pink *P. empetriformis* and *P. breweri* and yellowish *P. glanduliflora* come from western North America. The natural hybrid *P. × intermedia* is usually the best garden plant of these. White *P. aleutica* and *P. nipponica* come from north-east Asia. Bluish-purple *P. caerulea* from Arctic regions is the most difficult to grow in climates with hot summers.

× **Phyllothamnus** see **Rhodothamnus**

Pieris (Ericaceae)
Almost all these magnificent evergreens are too large for the rock garden. A dwarf, slow-growing and shy-flowering curiosity is *P. japonica* 'Pygmaea'. *P. taiwanensis* 'Crispa' with milk-white bunches of bell-shaped flowers in spring and attractive coppery shoots makes an excellent plant for the peat bed while still young and it grows slowly. *P. nana* (*Arcterica nana*) from north Japan and Kamtchatka, however, is a true dwarf, a tiny shrub with white flowers in spring and essential for the peat bed.

Pimelea, New Zealand Daphne (Thymelaeaceae)
P. prostrata (including *P. coarctata* of gardens) is the only member of this genus generally grown in European gardens. It is a prostrate, mat-forming shrub from New Zealand with neat, rounded, greyish leaves and clusters of numerous small, tubular, white flowers. The flowers on female plants are less effective but are followed by tiny, pearly, rice-like berries. It likes a cool root-run in gravelly soil.

Polygala, Milkwort (Polygalaceae)
It is a great pity that *P. chamaebuxus*, a lovely evergreen shrub from the European mountains, which grows hardly four inches (10 cm) high

and has glossy, leathery leaves and white and yellow flowers in early spring, is not always easy to cultivate. *P. chamaebuxus grandiflora* has purple-red, winged flowers. The easiest is the narrow-leaved, pink-flowering *P. vayredae* from the Spanish Pyrenees. All like gravelly humus, in a cool, moist position or the peat bed.

Potentilla, Cinquefoil (Rosaceae)
The many hybrids and garden varieties, usually found in catalogues under *P. fruticosa*, are useful, easy shrubs which flower for a long period in summer. The dwarfer ones grow well in any reasonably good, well-drained soil in sun and look in place in the rock garden or heath-garden. In bright buttercup-yellow there are 'Gold Drop', 'Klondike', 'Farreri Prostrata', 'Gold-digger', 'Goldfinger' and 'Beesii' ('Nana Argentea') which also has silvery leaves. 'Elizabeth' and 'Longacre' are paler, softer yellows. 'Daydawn' and 'Royal Flush' are pinkish shades. 'Sunset' and 'Red Ace' are coppery-orange and derived from the somewhat paler, low-growing 'Tangerine'. 'Tilford Cream' is a free-flowering white and 'Manchu' (*mandshurica* of gardens) is a dense, creeping variety only about one foot (30 cm) high with sparser white flowers over silky grey foliage.

Prunus (Rosaceae)
P. fruticosa 'Pendula', the Ground Cherry, covers its spreading branches in spring with white blossoms. Its dark-red fruits are concealed beneath glossy green leaves, which colour attractively in autumn. *P. pumila depressa* from eastern North America is a broad, flat shrub, just over one foot (50 cm) high, but six feet (2 m) across, with brilliant red autumn colour. Both these are excellent on large rock garden slopes and make a wonderful show in combination with blue *Ruta graveolens*. Pink *P. tenella*, the Dwarf Almond, covers whole limestone hills in parts of the Balkans. It looks lovely in the early part of the year next to *Iberis* and

Phlox subulata on dry-stone walls. There is a white variety and deep carmine-pink ones, of which 'Fire Hill' is outstanding. *P. prostrata* grows on dry mountain ranges from the west Mediterranean to the Himalayas. It is the slowest-growing and most compact species, varying in its flowers from white to pink, and in its habit, which is not always prostrate away from the compressing snow-cover and grazing animals of its native mountains.

Ptilotrichum (Cruciferae)
These are shrubby Alyssums from the Mediterranean mountains. *P. spinosum* is an intricately branched, spiny shrub about one foot (30 cm) high with grey leaves and white or pink flowers. It is very hardy and long-lived in a hot, dry place and is the only easy species for the rock garden. White-flowered, grey-leaved *P. reverchonii*, *P. pyrenaicum* and others usually require alpine-house cultivation.

Putoria (Rubiaceae)
P. calabrica, from gravelly places and crevices around the Mediterranean, is best grown in the alpine-house. It forms wide mats of pointed leaves and has clusters of pink, daphne-like flowers.

Pygmaea see Hebe

Rhamnus, Buckthorn (Rhamnaceae)
R. pumilus from limestone cliffs is a deciduous shrub which clings closely to rocks, with gnarled interlacing branches and round, dark-green leaves. It should be planted as a young plant in a deep crevice, where it will give a lifetime of pleasure.

Rhododendron (Ericaceae) p. 35
This is the most important genus of shrubs for gardeners on lime-free soils. There are many dwarfs among the eight hundred or so species. These are divided into related groups, of which

the most significant for the rock gardener is the Lapponica Subsection, dwarf alpines from the high moorlands of western China and south-east Tibet. Most are some shade between purple-red and purple blue and form dense, compact bushes with small, aromatic leaves, slowly reaching about three feet (1 m). Of these some of the best garden plants are *R. russatum*, *R. polycladum* (*scintillans*), *R. hippophaeoides*, *R. intricatum* and *R. fastigiatum*, which is much confused in gardens with the very dwarf *R. impeditum*. The two yellow-flowered ones, *R. rupicola chryseum* and *R. flavidum*, make a pleasant contrast to these. *R. orthocladum* 'Microleucum' is pure white. These are happy in quite open situations. The related Saluenensia Subsection from the same part of Asia prefers more shade and includes *R. saluenense* with its dwarfer race, purple-crimson *R. chameunum*; *R. calostrotum*, especially in its deep rose variety 'Gigha'; creeping, mound-forming crimson-purple *R. keleticum* and its even tighter prostrate race *R. radicans*, which is the tiniest of the genus. Its rivals for this title are the small Burmese members of the Uniflora Subsection, rose-purple *R. imperator* and *R. patulum*, which can be susceptible to frost in spring, and pink *R. pumilum*, from the eastern Himalayas. Close to the last is the temperamental, yellow *R. ludlowii* from Tibet, but the best garden plant from these is suckering *R. pemakoense* with profuse purple-pink bells. Equally floriferous and even more compact are bright yellow *R. hanceanum* 'Nanum' (Triflora Section) and the variable *R. campylogynum* (Campylogyna Subsection). *R. c. myrtilloides* is the dwarfest race, with flowers from crimson to pink. Even more variable is the adaptable pink *R. racemosum* (Scabrifolia Subsection) of which it is worth seeking a good form, such as the bright pink 'Forrest's Dwarf'. Another outstanding dwarf form of a variable species is *R. keiskei* 'Yaku Fairy' (*cordifolia*), prostrate with yellow flowers.

The Pogonantha Section (Anthopogon Series) is a distinct group with narrow aromatic leaves and flowers in daphne-like heads. The following all come from the east Himalayas and west China and grow from one to two feet (30–60 cm) high: *R. trichostomum*, rose or white; *R. sargentianum* 'Whitebait', creamy-white and more free-flowering than the pale yellow type; attractive, compact, pink *R. anthopogon* can take a long time to flower; *R. cephalanthum* is pink and the finest of this series for the small peat bed. The Boothia Subsection is slightly tender but contains several slow-growing plants, of which *R. leucaspis*, milky-white with chocolate anthers is an excellent alpine-house plant, as is the early-flowering pink or white *R. moupinense*. The very small, creeping, yellow, deciduous *R. lowndesii* (Lepidota Subsection) and its pink natural hybrid 'Pipit' are also usually grown here to protect them from excess moisture, but they are difficult plants. *R. (Therorhodion) camtschaticum* from north Japan to Alaska is an isolated species with rose flowers, usually less than one foot (30 cm). It is also deciduous, suckering and resentful of wet conditions and hot summers.

All mentioned so far have been Asian, but the European species are also mountain plants, sadly not always very free with their rose-pink to rose-red flowers in gardens. *R. ferrugineum* and *R. hirsutum* can slowly reach four feet (1.2 m) but *R. myrtifolium* (*kotschyi*) is never more than half this height. All the evergreen rhododendrons have excellent foliage but Chinese *R. lepidostylum* is unique in its mounds of hairy, silver-blue leaves. The new growth of compact Japanese *R. yakushimanum* is covered in white felt and is equally striking. With its large white flowers from pink buds, this species is rightly regarded as one of the most perfect of the genus and has been much used for hybridizing, but it is the original plant 'Koichiro Wada', which the rock-gardener should obtain. Several other species have bronze new growth, and pink *R. williamsianum* is outstanding, though it can eventually reach five feet (1.5 m) and more across. It is very slow-growing, however, as are several compact Chinese members of the wet climate Neriiflora Subsection, with their fleshy, waxen flowers, such as *R. dichroanthum*, *R. aperantum* and *R. chamaethomsonii*. These all have many colour forms and the last merges into one of the most striking of all dwarf species, prostrate *R. forrestii*, with its huge, scarlet flowers. These are not very freely produced, unless it is grown in well-drained, acid humus in a climate with cool, wet summers, but they have attracted many hybridists who have used this species to produce a large number of compact plants with brilliant red flowers. Among the best of these are 'Elizabeth', 'Little Ben' 'Carmen', 'Jenny' and 'Elisabeth Hobbie'.

At this point it should be stressed that hybridists have not necessarily considered the rock gardener and that many of the more compact hybrids can eventually reach ten feet (3 m) tall and as much in diameter. Bearing this in mind, the following are a few of the finest dwarfer hybrids. In violet-blue: 'Blue Bird', 'Blue Diamond', 'St Breward' and 'Sapphire'; magenta-pink 'Pink Drift', pale pink 'Cilpinense' and 'Seta'; in yellow, 'Chink' and two very dwarf hybrids, 'Chikor' and 'Curlew'; white 'Ptarmigan', 'Bric-a-Brac', and the hardy 'Dora Amateis' and 'Eider'.

The dwarf hybrid Japanese azaleas are rather overpowering for the rock garden or peat bed, with their solid masses of brilliant colour. Where the selection of the wild species is limited, in climates with hot summers such as central Europe or north-eastern USA, to such tolerant species as *R. racemosum*, *R. keiskei*, *R. hippophaeoides* and *R. yakushimanum*, then these dwarf azaleas become important plants. It is best to select from hybrids which have been bred for the area in which one lives, such as the several hundred named Glenn Dale and Gable hybrids in America. The Kurume hybrids are the most popular in Britain, needing full sun in the north and light shade in the south. None of the deciduous azaleas is dwarf enough for the rock garden, but of the wild semi-evergreen species there is the alpine race of *R. kaempferi*, *R. kiusianum*, about two feet (60 cm) with white or rose flowers, and the exceptional, prostrate forms of *R. nakaharai* 'Mt Seven Stars', and 'Mariko' from Taiwan. This last flowers after all the others, in July, needs full sun to ripen its wood and is quite stunning with its brick-red flowers on ground-hugging mats. It is debatable whether *R. tsusiophyllum* (*Tsusiophyllum tanakae*) from Japan should be included in *Rhododendron* but it is a charming, very slow-growing, twiggy shrub, eventually reaching one foot (30 cm), with tiny white bells in early summer, for similar acid, peaty soils.

Rhodothamnus (Ericaceae)   p. 35
R. chamaecistus is a slow-growing alpine shrub, about eight inches (20 cm) high. In May it bears disproportionately large, pink, bowl-shaped flowers. It likes a cool position in gritty peat. Its intergeneric hybrid with *Phyllodoce*, × *Phyllothamnus erectus*, is a delightful dwarf shrub where summers are cool and moist.

Ribes, Currant (Saxifragaceae)
R. alpinum 'Pumilum', a dense three-foot high (1 m) shrub with fresh-green young foliage, is useful as a background plant or for low hedges. *R. henryi* and *R. laurifolium* are dwarf evergreen species from China with drooping clusters of yellowish-green flowers in early spring.

Rosa, Rose (Rosaceae)
Difficult and temperamental *R. persica* (*R. berberifolia*, *Hulthemia persica*) can be attempted in a gravelly, sandy soil, in a dry, very sunny position. It is a common plant of the steppes in Iran, Afghanistan and central Asia. Its eight-inch (20 cm) suckering shoots carry round, toothed blue-green leaves and yellow flowers with a deep scarlet basal blotch. This is a

truly special plant for the enthusiast. The double pink *Rosa chinensis* 'Minima' looks best planted in bowls, troughs or terraced beds. There are many named hybrids of these miniature roses, but to the eye of the alpine-plant enthusiast they look alien and misplaced alongside the wild, mountain plants.

Rubus (Rosaceae)

R. arcticus, only about six inches (10–20 cm) high, with pink flowers in early summer, is more or less herbaceous and needs a lime-free soil. In the peat bed it makes a green carpet of foliage in summer. *R. calycinoides* from Taiwan has creeping, rooting shoots covered with round-lobed, wrinkly, dark green leaves, forming a flat evergreen ground-cover between dwarf rhododendrons or in other moist, peaty places. The other creeping ground-cover species are too vigorous for most rock gardens.

Salix, Willow (Salicaceae)

In the high mountains, the alpine willows form clumps between rhododendrons and scrub or neatly cover the rocks. *S. waldsteiniana* (*arbuscula* group) grows eighteen inches (50 cm) high, and looks very pretty in spring with its yellow-green catkins among *Erica herbacea* and rhododendrons. *S. hastata* 'Wehrhahnii', a spreading, dark-barked shrub with snow-white, woolly catkins, is one of the best as a young plant but eventually reaches five feet (1.5 m). The male form of *S. apoda* also has striking catkins of silver fur with orange-yellow anthers. It is widespreading but prostrate. In *S. alpina* (*S. myrsinites jacquinii*) the little catkins are ruby-pink. This is a slender, prostrate mound-forming species with attractive polished foliage, which is also a feature of several other carpet-forming willows, such as American *S. uva-ursi*, Japanese *S. yezoalpina* and European *S. retusa*. *S. repens* 'Voorthuizen' has grey-green leaves with silky undersides.

The woolly white shoots and yellow spring catkins of Arctic *S. lanata* are also lovely. This can slowly reach about three feet (1 m) but its variety 'Stuartii' always remains a small, gnarled shrub. In troughs, the very dwarf willows, *S. herbacea*, *S. reticulata* and *S. serpyllifolia* will form dense, interlacing mats. The very slow-growing *S.* × *boydii* from Scotland eventually forms a gnarled miniature tree with downy grey leaves.

Santolina, Lavender Cotton (Compositae)

These aromatic evergreen shrubs from the west Mediterranean grow two feet (60 cm) high and require plenty of sun. They dislike wet conditions and look best on dry-stone walls or between paving with *Alyssum*, *Sedum*, and *Sempervivum*. Most forms of *S. chamaecyparissus* are too large and vigorous for the smaller rock garden. *S. c. squarrosa* is the dwarfest race, and the most compact variety cultivated is *corsica* or *nana* of gardens, with dense mounds of finely divided, woolly white foliage. *S. elegans* from the Spanish Sierra Nevada is woolly, grey and only eight inches (20 cm) high.

Sarcococca (Buxaceae)

Evergreen *S. humilis* is an eighteen-inch (50 cm) shrub bearing small, white, scented flowers in spring and black berries in autumn. It needs a humus-rich soil and shade, where its suckering clumps of dark green, pointed leaves make an attractive background for small, herbaceous plants such as *Astilbe simplicifolia* hybrids and *Polygonum tenuicaule*.

Sorbus, Rowan (Rosaceae)

Chinese *S. reducta* is a dwarf, suckering shrub sending up erect stems to between one and two feet (30–60 cm). It has dark, glossy green pinnate leaves, which colour well to bronze and red in autumn, and white berries which turn to pink. It looks particularly well in the heath garden with prostrate Junipers and heathers.

Spiraea (Rosaceae)

S. japonica 'Bullata' is a compact, twelve inch (30 cm) dwarf from Japan with stiff stems, wrinkled, dark green leaves and crimson-pink heads. Its unusual habit suits formal beds and terraces. *S. japonica* 'Alpina' forms a dense mound up to two feet (60 cm) high covered for weeks on end during summer with rose-pink flower-heads. It has striking autumn colours as well. *S. j.* 'Little Princess' is of similar, mounded habit with deeper pink flowers. *S. decumbens* from the limestone screes of the south-eastern Alps is a small shrub which would happily occupy more space than one can allow it. It has rounded white flower-heads in spring and can be planted in dry-stone walls.

Syringa, Lilac (Oleaceae)

S. meyeri 'Palibin' (*S. palibiniana*) is a slow-growing plant from North China which flowers while it is still young, forming a rounded bush with panicles of violet-purple in early summer. *S. microphylla* is of similar compact habit with paler lilac-pink flowers. Both can reach over three feet (1 m) high and twice as much in diameter when mature. *S. afghanica* has a slightly dwarfer, more upright habit. It is one of the very few cut-leaved lilacs with pinnate foliage on dark stems and lilac-pink flowers in late spring. It needs a hot position to ripen its wood and make it flower well.

Teucrium, Germander (Labiatae)

T. chamaedrys is a twelve inch (30 cm) creeping shrub with glossy, aromatic, evergreen leaves and purple flowers. It looks at home in the heath garden or planted in dry-stone walls. *T. polium* is grey-leaved and cream-flowered. It forms low mounds of stems a few inches high and enjoys a hot, dry position. *T. subspinosum* from Mallorca is a small compact shrub, about six inches (15 cm) high, with sharp spines, grey-green leaves and pink flowers. It is suitable for the alpine-house or a trough. The very dwarf *T. aroanium*

is a limestone crevice plant from southern Greece needing similar treatment. It forms mats of grey foliage with comparatively large, veined lilac-pink flowers, almost stemless, upon them.

Therorhodion see Rhododendron

Thymus see page 130

Tsusiophyllum see Rhododendron

Vaccinium, Gaultheria, Gaylussacia and Pernettya (Ericaceae)

These are all outwardly similar inter-related shrubs, distinguished botanically mainly on the structure of their fruits, which for the gardener are all attractive berries. Most have white or pink-tinged, urn-shaped, lily-of-the-valley flowers and most are evergreen. Above all, they are all lime-haters for cool, moist, acid, sandy or peaty soils, making them ideal shrubs for the peat bed. Among the several hundred species, mainly centred on the mountains of South America and south-east Asia but distributed throughout the great ranges and moorlands of the world, are numerous dwarf plants for the rock gardener.

The prostrate American *V. macrocarpon* and European *V. oxycoccos* are the red-berried Cranberries. The European Bilberry, *V. myrtillus*, and the taller American Blueberries *V. corymbosum* and *V. angustifolium* are deciduous, thicket-forming shrubs up to about two feet (60 cm), worth growing for their vivid autumn colours as well as their edible blue-black fruits. The much dwarfer North American Blueberries, *V. caespitosum* and evergreen *V. myrsinites*, grow only six inches (15 cm) high. The spreading Cowberry, *V. vitis-idaea*, with rounded glossy leaves and red berries, has an excellent garden variety 'Koralle' and a very dwarf race, *minus*, from Arctic Asia and America. The smallest of the Huckleberries, *Gaylussacia brachycera*, superficially resembles this but has blue fruits. The other Huckleberries from the eastern United States are deciduous and grow too tall for small peat beds, except possibly for G. dumosa which has open pure-white bells and black fruits. Among the Asian Vacciniums, V. delavayi and red-flowered V. moupinense from China both form dense, neat clumps of rounded, glossy foliage with copper-tinged new growth and occasionally dark purple berries. Creeping V. praestans from north-east Asia is deciduous with good autumn colour and large, glossy red fruits. Compact V. nummularia with polished leaves and hairy stems sometimes has its new growth damaged by late frosts and is given the protection of the alpine-house, where it makes a splendid plant with clusters of pink-flushed flowers followed by black berries. The only South American species generally cultivated, V. floribundum (mortinia) from Ecuador, is also usually given some protection, though it appears hardy throughout most of Britain. It is an evergreen with striking red new growth.

In the genus Gaultheria, G. adenothrix from Japan makes a beautiful alpine-house plant with mats of dull, leathery leaves, pure-white flowers held in hairy, crimson calyces and red fruits. Two six-inch (15 cm) Himalayan species with wiry, creeping underground shoots forming mats are also slightly tender in severe climates. These are G. nummularioides with rounded leaves and blue-black fruits and G. trichophylla with narrow, pointed foliage and china-blue berries. The most striking blue-berried species, G. hookeri (veitchiana) and G. tetramera, grow too large for the small peat bed. Chinese G. cuneata, Japanese G. miqueliana and G. itoana from Taiwan are similar, spreading, dense, twelve inch (30 cm), clump-forming evergreens with conspicuous white berries. The related dwarfer G. pyroloides (pyrolifolia) from the Himalayas has blue-black fruits. It forms low mats of foliage in the same way as the better-known creeping Partridge Berry, G. procum-

bens, from eastern North America. This has pink flowers and red fruits, more showy in the selected variety 'Darthuizer'. G. humifusa from western North America is a much more compact, choicer, red-berried plant only four inches (10 cm) high. Its slightly larger, close relative G. ovatifolia is a less satisfactory garden plant. The New Zealand species are also not very easily grown or free-fruiting in the northern hemisphere. Of these, white or scarlet-berried G. depressa and G. antipoda and G. rupestris with dry fruits are the ones usually tried. No South American species is well known in gardens though the tender, hairy, Brazilian G. eriophylla (willisiana) is sometimes grown as an alpine-house plant by specialists.

The closely related and mainly South American genus Pernettya is, however, highly valued by gardeners. The best known species, P. mucronata, with fruits in every shade from pure-white through pink and red to dark purple, forms dense thickets over three feet (1 m) high and is best grown as a feature plant in the heather garden. 'Bell's Seedling' with deep red fruits is one of the best, free-fruiting named varieties. The group of species around P. prostrata grow from Mexico to the southernmost tip of South America, where two very dwarf races occur. P. leucocarpa grows about six inches high (15 cm) and P. pumila is even dwarfer, both forming mats of glossy leathery leaves with white berries. Further north many races occur with fruits from white to blue-purple and varying in habit and hardiness according to their habitat. P. pentlandii, P. buxifolia and P. ciliata are related plants all distinct enough for the gardener. Tasmanian P. tasmanica forms flat, evergreen mats of tiny leaves with large fruits, usually red in the cultivated forms. Related P. nana from New Zealand is a much less satisfactory garden plant.

Viburnum, Guelder Rose (Caprifoliaceae)
There is a dwarf variety of the Guelder Rose, V.

opulus 'Nanum', which forms a very dense bush about eighteen inches (50 cm) high. It was originally propagated from a witch's broom and flowers should not be expected. *V. opulus* 'Compactum' grows three feet (1 m) high, but has profuse flowers and red fruit.

V. *farreri* (*fragrans*) 'Nanum' is a dense, suckering, early-flowering shrub from China which grows to about three feet (1 m) high. Its fragrant, pinkish-white flowers appear in winter, before its leaves, and look pretty in front of dwarf conifers and surrounded by early bulbs. *V. plicatum* 'Semperflorens Nanum' ('Watanabe') eventually reaches about the same height. It never produces a great show of flower but is seldom without a few lacy heads edged with large sterile white flowers from late spring to autumn. It is a choice plant with good foliage, which usually colours to wine-red shades in autumn.

Vinca, Periwinkle (Apocynaceae)

Evergreen *V. minor* in its selected forms 'La Grave' or 'Bowles Variety' is a delight if allowed to spread its carpets of deep blue flowers beneath a forsythia. *V. major*, a larger-leaved, larger-flowered, more rampant plant, can only be used in shade among tall shrubs. Even *V. minor* can become too strong-growing and difficult to eradicate in choice beds or the small rock garden. When used in the right place there are few more worthwhile ground-covers. Apart from the blue ones, there are double and variegated varieties. *V. m.* 'Atropurpurea' is a rich plum-purple and 'Gertrude Jekyll' is the best white.

Yucca, Adam's Needle (Agavaceae)

Similar broad-leaved *Y. filamentosa* and *Y. flaccida* ('Ivory' is the best variety), narrow-leaved *Y. glauca* and the hybrid *Y. × karlsruhensis* are all hardy and striking desert plants. They need surroundings suited to their distinctive character, among gravel and boulders.

Dwarf conifers

Dwarf conifers may be used to create backgrounds and accent points and should find a place in every rock garden. They enliven seasons when flowers are scarce with their many different shapes and their evergreen foliage in varied shades. In the long winter months they look especially attractive when their branches are covered with hoar-frost or snow. There are dwarf forms of nearly all the conifers and the selection is increasing every year, as is the circle of enthusiasts.

Abies, Silver Fir (Pinaceae)

A. balsamea hudsonia is a high-alpine, dwarf race of the Balsam Fir from the White Mountains of New Hampshire, USA, with a broad habit and dense branchlets clothed in dark green needles. Both it and *A. balsamea* 'Nana', which grows in a spherical shape, are slow-growing and worthwhile.

A. *koreana* fruits while it is still a young plant, bearing small, violet-purple, cylindrical cones but it is only suitable for larger rock gardens, as after about ten years it will have reached a man's height. 'Compact Dwarf' and 'Pikkolo' are slow-growing dwarf forms but do not bear cones. *A. procera* 'Glauca Prostrata' is a picturesque, irregular, prostrate form of this blue-grey species from north-west America. It is a lovely tree but needs acid soil.

Cedrus (Pinaceae)

There are a few dwarf varieties of the huge Cedar of Lebanon: *C. libani* 'Nana' is a dense conical bush, while 'Comte de Dijon' is similar but even slower-growing: after a lifetime, it may reach three feet (1 m). *C. l.* 'Sargentii' is a slow-growing, weeping form, widespreading, so has possibilities in the larger rock garden.

Chamaecyparis, False Cypress
(Cupressaceae)

There is a whole range of different dwarf varieties of the well-known *C. lawsoniana* from Oregon and California: blue-green, broadly conical 'Forsteckensis'; compact, blue-green, 'Minima Glauca'; the dense, green spheres of 'Nana' and the spreading green 'Tamariscifolia'. *C. lawsoniana* 'Fletcheri' has feathery, blue-grey branches which grow into thick columns, eventually over fifteen feet (5 m) high. The dwarf forms of the Hinoki Cypress, *C. obtusa*, are exceptionally lovely and popular. These include 'Compacta', a densely branching conical form; 'Nana', a very low, slow-growing plant forming a flat-topped dome; 'Nana Gracilis', a small, conical tree with glossy, dark green, fan-shaped sprays packed tightly together, and 'Pygmaea', the daintiest of all, with tiers of bronze-green fanning out over the ground. The Japanese use this species to produce the famous bonsai miniature trees by means of special techniques of cultivation. Hundred-year-old specimens are often only between one foot six and two feet six inches (40–80 cm) high. There are also a few varieties of *C. pisifera* which answer our requirements. These are 'Filifera Nana', with green, fan-shaped, hanging branchlets, and 'Filifera Nana Aurea', smaller and burnished with gold. The attractive variety 'Boulevard' forms tufted, conical blue-grey bushes, which become rounded with age.

All these are particularly suitable for formal gardens, beds in paving and terraces near the house. They generally look rather out of place in natural-looking gardens.

Cryptomeria japonica, Japanese Cedar
(Taxodiaceae)

A few dwarf forms of this stately tree, often planted in groves around Japanese temples, have reached us from Japan: 'Bandai-Sugi' with irregular, mossy, bluish-green shoots; 'Jindai-Sugi' with fresh-green, fine needles, and a dense, flat-topped habit; the neat, hardy 'Globosa' and lastly the stiff, globular 'Vilmoriniana', fresh green in summer and reddish-purple in winter.

These trees need protection from winter sun and biting winds, so that they are best suited to temperate areas.

Juniperus, Juniper (Cupressaceae)

There is a dwarf form of the tall Common Juniper, *Juniperus communis*, called 'Compressa', which is quite extraordinarily slow-growing. Its small, blue-grey columns are well suited to stone troughs or the smallest rock garden. The many prostrate junipers are quite different in appearance. They are picturesque additions to the informal garden; examples are the flat, bright-green *J. communis* 'Hornibrookii' and the golden-yellow and bronze-coloured *J. communis* 'Depressa Aurea'. The alpine juniper, *J. communis nana* is also useful, together with 'Repanda', with grey-green, coarse needles. This flat habit is shared by *J. horizontalis* from North America. This plant creeps along the ground, forming wide carpets. Some of its proven varieties are 'Glauca', blue-green; 'Douglasii', brighter, steel-blue; and 'Plumosa', feathery brown-grey. All these are lovely ground-cover, especially when they trail over blocks of stone. There are many more selections, especially from North America, becoming available each year. Some of these will settle down and prove their worth as reliable garden plants. Among the most notable to date are bluish-silver 'Hughes'; bright green 'Mint Julep' and 'Emerald Spreader'; blue-green 'Turquoise Spreader'; grey 'Bar Harbor'; 'Gold Coast' and 'Old Gold'.

J. sabina, the spreading Savin is very useful in its prostrate, slow-growing form 'Cupressifolia'. *J. s. tamariscifolia* is also attractive, though it grows twenty inches (50 cm) high. *J. chinensis* is taller and more vigorous, with characteristic upright branches; it has a well known, low, angular variety 'Pfitzeriana', a strong-growing plant only suitable for large gardens. The bluish-green *J. chinensis sargentii* from northern Japan is somewhat slower in growth. *J. chinensis* 'Plumosa' is different again, having bowed branches with short side growths, and it has a golden-brown form 'Plumosa Aurea'. This last looks quite lovely in winter when it is covered with snow or hoar-frost. *J. chinensis* 'Blaauw' is a useful dwarf variety introduced from Japanese gardens.

J. squamata 'Meyeri' from China has a more or less erect, open growth, and *J. squamata wilsonii* has bright, grey-green foliage forming a broad pyramid. Both grow a few yards (metres) high in old age, but 'Blue Carpet' and 'Blue Star' are pretty, blue-grey dwarfs. There are dwarf varieties of the Virginian juniper, *J. virginiana*, too, such as the round, bushy 'Globosa' ('Nana Compacta') and 'Kobold'. 'Silver Spreader' is a grey, low-spreading variety suitable for ground-cover.

Microbiota decussata (Cupressaceae)

This is a newly introduced species from south-east Siberia. It resembles a *Thuja*, with prostrate, densely branched shoots that are green in summer and bronze-coloured in winter. It is extremely hardy and vigorous and so ideal for ground-cover in large, exposed areas.

Microcachrys (Podocarpaceae)

M. tetragona is a small, prostrate, evergreen shrub from Tasmania. The branches are slender and clothed with rectangular, scaly brownish-green leaves. It has terminal red-brown, ovoid cones. It is of no great beauty but will be appreciated by lovers of strange or unusual plants, who will find a place for it in the trough garden or alpine-house.

Picea, Spruce (Pinaceae)

Everyone is familiar with the spruce as a woodland tree, but it is less generally appreciated that there is a whole range of mutations. There are some hundred different aberrant forms of the Norway Spruce, *Picea abies* (*P. excelsa*), including many dwarf varieties, of which the following are among the most important: 'Ohlendorffii', 'Clanbrassiliana', 'Echiniformis', 'Little Gem', 'Maxwellii', 'Pumila', 'Pygmaea' and 'Remontii'. All of these form dense, slow-growing dome-shaped or widely tapering bushes. The following have a flat-topped spreading habit: 'Nidiformis', 'Procumbens', 'Tabuliformis', 'Gregoryana' and 'Repens'. The weeping form 'Inversa' is useful in large gardens.

P. glauca 'Conica' should only be planted where there is space for it to grow, in the course of time, higher than a man. There is a slow-growing mutation of this tree, which is a true dwarf, called 'Laurin'. Its fine-needled shoots grow less than half an inch (scarcely 1 cm) in a year, so that twelve-year-old specimens are only some eight inches (20 cm) high. This is a choice dwarf tree for troughs, growing as it does in the shape of a pyramid. *P. g.* 'Echiniformis' is also slow-growing. It grows outwards rather than upwards, and has blue-green needles. Also mound-shaped is *P. g.* 'Alberta Globe', another choice branch-sport from 'Conica'.

P. mariana 'Nana' is a fine dwarf form of the American Black Spruce, which forms cushions or globular bushes with its grey-green needles.

P. omorika 'Nana' is a dense, bushy variety of the slender Siberian Spruce. *P. pungens* 'Glauca Globosa' is a cushion-forming dwarf, whilst 'Glauca Procumbens' is a very decorative spreading form of the Blue Spruce, suitable for large rock gardens. It has broad, deep blue-grey needles on low, pendulous, sometimes prostrate, branches.

Pinus, Pine (Pinaceae)

The most important of the mountain pines is *P. mugo* (*P. montana*), especially its compact variety *pumilio* in its forms 'Hesse', 'Mops',

'Gnom' and gold-tinged 'Ophir'. Other useful dwarf pines are: *P. leucodermis* 'Schmidtii', *P. sylvestris* 'Beuvronensis', *P. densiflora* 'Umbraculifera', *P. nigra* 'Helga', *P. strobus* 'Nana' and *P. sylvestris* 'Viridis Compacta'. *P. pumila*, the creeping pine from east Asia, and *P. cembra* differ from all the other pines in disliking limy soil.

Podocarpus (Podocarpaceae)
There are two alpine species of these southern hemisphere conifers, which eventually form prostrate carpets a yard or more (1–2 m) across. *P. alpinus* binds together the steep, stony slopes of the Tasmanian and south-east Australian mountains, while *P. nivalis* does likewise in New Zealand. Both have narrow, leathery, yew-like foliage of a dark green, or bronze-tinged in *P. n.* 'Aureus'.

Pseudotsuga, Douglas Fir (Pinaceae)
A very useful, blue-green spreading dwarf form is *P. menziesii* 'Fletcheri', which would be worth growing for its aromatic needles alone. *P. menziesii* 'Nana' is a slow-growing, short-needled, bluish-green conical fir.

Taxus, Yew (Taxaceae)
T. baccata 'Prostrata' and 'Repandens' have wide-spreading, prostrate branches and are the prettiest yews for large rock gardens. For smaller areas, the dwarf form of the Japanese yew, *T. cuspidata* 'Nana', is more suitable. All are good in shady positions.

Thuja, Arbor-vitae (Cupressaceae)
T. occidentalis 'Globosa', 'Recurva Nana' and 'Umbraculifera' are all more or less rounded in shape, and are best in formal gardens. 'Rheingold' forms dense, broad, conical bushes, and grows about six feet (2 m) high in time. There are also dwarf forms of the Chinese *T. orientalis*: yellowish green 'Aurea Nana' and 'Rosedalis', yellow in spring and purplish in winter. These form dense, rounded bushes. *T. plicata*, the Red Cedar of western North America, has several slow-growing dwarf varieties also, with similar but more conical shapes: bronze-gold 'Rogersii', coppery-gold 'Stoneham Gold', and cream and gold-tipped 'Cuprea'.

Thujopsis (Cupressaceae)
T. dolobrata 'Nana' is a compact, flat-topped dwarf form of this pretty, bushy Japanese conifer, which gives continual pleasure with the silvery pattern on the undersides of its flat, scaly needles.

Tsuga, Hemlock Spruce (Pinaceae)
There are several extremely pretty dwarf forms of *Tsuga canadensis*, an elegant North American conifer which likes acid, humus-rich soil: 'Bennet', 'Jeddeloh', 'Minima' and 'Nana'. Many are so slow-growing and tiny, like 'Minuta', that they are ideal for trough gardens. 'Pendula' is also very decorative, with branches tumbling down in cascades forming green 'waterfalls' on the outcrops of large rock-gardens. Similar in habit is 'Cole', growing flat to the ground and forming a fresh-green carpet.

Propagation

Rock garden plants are propagated in so many ways, depending upon whether they are herbaceous, bulbous or shrubby plants, and have so many different requirements, that it will only be possible to provide a broad outline of the most important points here. Readers who wish to investigate the matter further are recommended to consult specialist literature.

Herbaceous plants

Seed

The most important method of propagation for many rock garden plants is by sowing seed. The method closest to nature would be to sow the seeds as soon as possible after they have been harvested. This is not always possible nor is it often necessary and, with only a few exceptions, all seeds can be sown between December and January. Use well-drained gritty soil and clean pots. The seeds are sown on a level surface, covered with a little grit, and the pots are then plunged in sand in a frame outdoors, where they will be safe from mice. Germination will begin under glass in early spring, as soon as the weather turns mild and sunny. The time before germination varies very considerably, with the Cruciferae the shortest, often in two weeks, and the Ranunculaceae the longest, often in the following year. The seedlings are pricked out into pans or potted into small pots, as soon as possible, and kept in the cold-frame under glass, shaded from the sun. When the young plants have been established and thoroughly hardened off, the tougher species can be planted out in the garden, whilst those plants which are more sensitive to being transplanted can be grown on in larger pots.

The chief plants to be propagated by seed are the following (* germinate best when the seeds are sown directly after being harvested):

Adonis*	Leontopodium
Allium	Lewisia*
Androsace*	Lilium
Anemone narcissiflora	Linum
Aquilegia	Meconopsis
Asphodeline	Meum
Astragalus	Morina
Athamantha	Oenothera
Callianthemum*	Onosma
Carlina	Penstemon
Corydalis*	Plantago nivalis
Cyananthus	Polemonium
Cyclamen*	Primula*
Dodecatheon	Pulsatilla*
Draba	Ramonda
Fritillaria	Roscoea
Gentiana	Saxifraga grisebachii,
Glaucidium*	longifolia
Haberlea	Silene
Helleborus*	Tunica
Incarvillea	Verbascum
Jeffersonia*	Viola

Cuttings

Herbaceous plants which produce seeds very infrequently, garden forms which do not come true from seed, and those which do not naturally lend themselves to division easily or successfully, are generally propagated by cuttings.

The cuttings are inserted in pots filled with coarse sand with a little peat mixed in, and placed in a covered cold-frame. Nurserymen propagate their plants in large numbers and place the cuttings directly into prepared frames. The amateur can content himself with pots, which he should half fill so that the cuttings can be covered with a sheet of glass. The pots are then put in a cool window or in a half-shaded place in the open air. It is extremely important to press the sand firmly down, and to press in the cuttings so that they are firmly held. The cuttings will usually take well if they are kept reasonably moist, but not wet, shaded from the sun and ventilated carefully when necessary. Rooting hormone should be used on plants which are difficult to root.

Some plants root best if cuttings are taken in early summer, while others are more successful if taken in autumn.

Early summer cuttings

The best time is generally after the plants have flowered and before the young shoots have hardened.

Achillea
Aethionema 'Warley Rose'
Alyssum saxatile
Anchusa
Androsace lanuginosa
Arabis albida
Azorella trifurcata
Campanula carpatica
Dianthus caesius and *plumarius* varieties
Gypsophila repens 'Rosy Veil'
Heuchera
Lithodora diffusa 'Heavenly Blue'

Oenothera missouriensis
Penstemon (mainly the semi-shrubby species)
Phlox
Saponaria
Satureja
Trachelium rumelianum (also by seed)
Tunica saxifraga 'Plena'
Veronica
Zauschneria californica

Autumn cuttings

Insert the cuttings in October–November and place the pots in a cold-frame, covering it against winter frosts. In frost-free weather, they can be gently ventilated. They should be shaded as necessary in spring. Rooting often takes place during the winter, otherwise in the early part of the year.

Acantholimon (cuttings should be pulled off, very hard to root)
Achillea
Arenaria tetraquetra
Armeria juniperifolia and × *suendermannii*
Artemisia
Campanula portenschlagiana
Convolvulus boissieri
Douglasia
Eriogonum
Erodium
Geranium argenteum
Globularia nana
Helichrysum
Lithodora oleifolia
Marrubium
Pterocephalus parnassii
Saxifraga
Scabiosa graminifolia

Root cuttings

A few small herbaceous plants can be propagated in late autumn or winter by means of root cuttings. The roots are cut into sections one or two inches (4–6 cm) long and laid in a sand and peat mixture about an inch deep (2 cm), watered and placed in a cold greenhouse or frame over the winter. Shoots will appear in the early part of the year.

Acanthus perringii
Anemone hupehensis hybrids
Brunnera macrophylla
Carduncellus
Crepis incana
Echioides longiflorum
Eryngium
Geranium
Limonium
Morisia
Phlox
Primula denticulata, sieboldii
Verbascum

Leaf cuttings

Haberlea, Ramonda and other Gesneriaceae, like the tropical members of this family (Saintpaulia), can be propagated by leaf cuttings. Full-grown leaves are pulled off down to the base of their stalks in summer, inserted in pots filled with sand and peat, and then put in a shady position in the glass-house, where they will root slowly but surely, and then send up shoots. Many species of Sedum can also be propagated by leaf-cuttings. Cardamine pratensis 'Flore Pleno' and various ferns (varieties of Polystichum setiferum) form new plants on the leaves or fronds. If these are weighed down with stones, so that they lie flat on the ground, the young plants will form in the axils of the leaves.

Division

The easiest method of propagation, especially for the inexperienced gardener, is division. Many plants which form cushions, mats or clumps can easily be increased by simply pulling them apart. It is, of course, essential to make sure that the plants naturally have many rooted shoots or rhizomes and that the whole plant does not come from a single tap-root, as is the case with Acantholimon, Pulsatilla, Limonium and such like. The best time for division is in the early part of the year, either before flowering or after, or else in late summer. If the plants are divided late this must be done in good time for them to take firm root by the autumn, so that they are not pushed up by frost. In most cases, the division is planted at once in its position. Only with delicate and valuable plants, which are best propagated in spring, should the divided portion be potted and allowed to take root under glass.

Bulbs and corms

Many of the bulbous plants for the rock garden come from nurseries, where they are propagated from seed, offsets or from scales (in the case of lilies). If they are happy with their soil and position, many will propagate themselves in large numbers by seed or natural division. Where a colony of bulbs has become too thick, they should be dug up and divided, when they are dormant. For most of them, summer is the appropriate time, but crocus, snowdrops, cyclamen and Eranthis will stand being transplanted while they are in flower, if the operation is performed carefully and they are replanted at once. Many of the rarer bulbs can only be obtained if one is prepared to grow them from seeds—cyclamen can only be increased in this way. These should be sown by autumn and will germinate in early spring. Most species take between three and five years to reach flowering size.

Shrubs

Seed

The principal shrubs to be propagated from seed are the various species of berry plants, *Berberis* and *Cotoneaster*, though seedlings from named selections will not necessarily resemble the parents.

As soon as the fleshy part of the fruit has ripened, the seeds should be laid in damp sand, stored and sowed in the new year, either in pots under glass or, in the case of the majority, in beds in the open. The seeds of the genera mentioned above often lie dormant for a year but the pots must be kept weeded all summer, and stood in a shady place. In order to prevent liverwort becoming a nuisance, pots which still contain seeds can be covered during the summer months with a layer of sphagnum. The seeds of *Caryopteris*, *Clematis*, *Cytisus* and *Petrophytum* should be treated like the seeds of herbaceous plants.

The fine seeds of *Rhododendron* and the other Ericaceae should be sowed in pots of sandy peat and kept moist and shaded in the glass-house. Only those with patience should attempt the long business of propagating these shrubs.

Cuttings from deciduous shrubs

Where a plant identical to the parent is required, propagation must be by vegetative means and, in most cases, this is by rooting cuttings. Woody cuttings should be taken from late spring until summer, depending upon the species, and whether the shoots are ripe or not. Species which are very hard to root, such as evergreens, should be treated with rooting hormone. The cuttings are inserted in pots and treated like cuttings of herbaceous plants. Bottom-heat supplied by an electric soil-warming cable is a great help in rooting the more difficult subjects, such as *Daphne* and *Erinacea*.

Many dislike hot, humid conditions, provided by electric 'propagators' and mist-propagators, however. The following shrubs are best increased by cuttings.

Arctostaphylos
Berberis
Caryopteris
Corokia
Cotoneaster (half-ripe stems)
Cytisus
Daphne
Dryas
Erica
Erinacea (cuttings pulled off in late summer)
Genista
Helianthemum
Iberis
Lavandula (roots well from hardwood cuttings in winter)
Moltkia
Ononis fruticosa
Polygala chamaebuxus
Potentilla fruticosa
Rhododendron
Santolina
Spiraea
Viburnum

Cuttings from conifers

All the conifers grown in the rock garden must only be propagated vegetatively, since this is the only process which will guarantee preserving the characteristic dwarf habit.

Cuttings of conifers are taken either in early spring before they shoot or after the shoots have ripened around the start of August. They are best torn off in such a way that they retain a small heel of the parent plant. This heel of bark should either not be trimmed at all or only very lightly. The cuttings are treated with rooting hormone and then tightly packed in pots. It is a good idea to store these in a cold greenhouse over winter to make the cuttings root more quickly. Many forms of *Abies*, *Cedrus*, *Picea* and *Pinus* can only be satisfactorily increased by grafting.

Layers
In spring branches and shoots can be carefully slit, bent down and buried in the earth which is heaped up around them. The following shrubs can be made to root in this way, generally being ready to sever after a year.

Acantholimon
Acer palmatum
Arctostaphylos
Betula nana
Daphne arbuscula, cneorum, blagayana
Dryas
Rhododendron

Grafting
Grafting is justified in the case of *Daphne petraea*, since only grafted plants appear to have sufficient vigour and bloom profusely. The stock should be a two-year-old specimen of *Daphne mezereum* raised in a pot, and the scion should also be at least two-year-old wood. The methods of grafting used may be whip and tongue or cleft-grafting, after which the graft is tied with bast (raffia) and sealed with wax. The grafted plant is kept in the greenhouse until it has properly taken. The best time for grafting is January–March, just before the sap begins to rise.

Division
A few dwarf shrubs, especially the semi-shrubby sorts, can be increased by division. They are:

Ceratostigma plumbaginoides
Cornus canadensis
Eriogonum
Gaultheria procumbens, miqueliana
Linnaea
Muehlenbeckia axillaris
Pachysandra
Rhododendron camtschaticum
Spiraea decumbens
Vinca

Calendar of Flowers

Spring

White
Anemone nemorosa, sylvestris
Arabis
Crocus
Daphne mezereum 'Alba', blagayana
Erythronium revolutum
Galanthus
Helleborus niger
Iberis
Leucojum
Matricaria oreades
Narcissus triandrus
Ornithogalum
Phlox subulata 'Nivalis'
Pieris
Ranunculus calandrinioides
Saxifraga burseriana, marginata, trifurcata
Trillium grandiflorum

Yellow, orange
Adonis
Alyssum
Anemone ranunculoides
Berberis
Caltha palustris
Corydalis nobilis
Crocus
Cytisus
Doronicum
Draba
Echioides

Eranthis
Erysimum
Euphorbia
Geum
Iris danfordiae, reichenbachii
Narcissus
Papaver nudicaule
Potentilla aurea
Primula vulgaris
Saxifraga × apiculata, 'Geuderi', burseriana 'Lutea', 'Haagii', sancta
Trollius
Tulipa
Uvularia
Vitaliana
Waldsteinia

Pink, red, purple
Androsace
Arabis aubretioides, blepharophylla
Bellis perennis varieties
Bergenia
Bulbocodium vernum
Cyclamen coum
Daphne cneorum, mezereum
Dicentra
Dodecatheon
Erica herbacea (carnea)
Fritillaria meleagris
Helleborus hybrids
Paeonia
Phlox subulata varieties
Primula rosea, juliae and hybrids
Prunus
Rhododendron

Saxifraga – Kabschia and Dactyloides hybrids
Tulipa

Blue, violet
Anemone blanda, nemorosa blue varieties
Aubrieta hybrids
Brunnera
Chionodoxa
Crocus
Gentiana – acaulis and verna groups
Hepatica
Houstonia
Ipheion uniflorum
Iris histrioides and reticulata hybrids
Jeffersonia dubia
Mertensia
Muscari
Myosotis
Omphalodes
Phlox subulata 'G. F. Wilson'
Polemonium
Primula
Pulmonaria angustifolia
Pulsatilla
Puschkinia
Rhododendron
Scilla
Synthyris
Veronica armena
Vinca
Viola odorata

Early to high summer

White
Achillea
Anacyclus
Anemone narcissiflora
Anthericum
Arenaria
Cerastium
Chrysanthemum

Cistus
Dianthus noeanus, suendermannii
Dicentra formosa 'Alba'.
Dryas
Helichrysum
Leontopodium
Meum
Minuartia
Moehringia
Nierembergia
Paradisea
Petrophytum
Ptilotrichum spinosum
Satureja
Saxifraga (Euaizoonia Section)
Spiraea decumbens
Tiarella
Yucca

Yellow, orange
Achillea
Alchemilla
Allium flavum, moly
Alyssum argenteum
Andryala aghardii
Anthemis biebersteiniana, sancti-johannis
Anthyllis
Arnica
Asarina procumbens
Asphodeline
Astragalus alopecuroides
Buphthalmum speciossissum
Calceolaria
Chiastophyllum oppositifolium
Coreopsis verticillata
Coronilla cappadocica
Corydalis lutea, ochroleuca, cheilanthifolia
Crepis aurea
Eriophyllum lanatum
Euryops acraeus
Genista
Gentiana lutea
Helichrysum orientale, plicatum,
    thianshanicum

Hieracium
Hypericum
Inula
Lotus corniculatus 'Plena'
Mimulus cupreus
Oenothera
Onosma
Patrinia
Potentilla fruticosa, recta
Primula florindae
Roscoea cautleoides
Santolina
Scutellaria orientalis
Sedum floriferum, aizoon kamtschaticum and others
Solidago
Verbascum

Pink, red, purple

Acantholimon
Aethionema
Allium pulchellum
Anthyllis montana
Armeria
Asperula nitida, suberosa
Aster alpinus varieties
Astilbe simplicifolia hybrids
Bruckenthalia
Calandrinia umbellata
Centaurea bella, pulcherrima
Centranthus ruber
Convolvulus althaeoides, cantabrica
Delphinium nudicaule
Dianthus
Erica cinerea, tetralix and vagans
Erinus alpinus
Erodium
Geranium
Gladiolus
Gypsophila 'Rosy Veil'
Heuchera
Incarvillea
Lewisia
Lychnis

Micromeria
Morina longifolia
Phuopsis stylosa
Potentilla 'Gibsons Scarlet', nepalensis
Roscoea
Saponaria
Sedum spurium varieties
Silene keiskei, schafta
Spiraea japonica varieties
Thalictrum
Teucrium chamaedrys

Blue, violet

Adenophora
Allium caeruleum, cyaneum
Anchusa angustissima
Aquilegia
Aster
Campanula
Clematis alpina
Codonopsis
Cyananthus
Cynoglossum
Delphinium
Dracocephalum
Edraianthus
Erigeron varieties
Eryngium
Gentiana asclepiadea, septemfida
Globularia
Haberlea
Horminum
Iris lacustris
Jasione
Lavandula
Limonium
Linaria alpina
Linum
Lithodora
Meconopsis betonicifolia, grandis
Moltkia
Nepeta
Penstemon alpinus, hallii, menziesii

Phyteuma
Platycodon
Prunella × *webbiana*
Ramonda
Scabiosa graminifolia
Scutellaria baicalensis
Thalictrum
Trachelium
Tradescantia
Veronica
Viola cornuta, gracilis
Wulfenia

Autumn

White
Anaphalis
Carlina acaulis
Chrysanthemum arcticum, zawadskyi
Leontopodium
Parnassia
Satureja montana
Saxifraga fortunei

Yellow
Kirengeshoma palmata
Ononis natrix
Potentilla
Solidago
Sternbergia lutea

Red, pink, purple
Anemone hupehensis hybrids
Calandrinia umbellata
Calluna vulgaris varieties
Colchicum
Daboecia
Dianthus campestris
Origanum
Polygonum affine
Saponaria

Satureja montana
Sedum cauticolum, sieboldii, telephium
Tricyrtis
Zauschneria

Blue, violet
Aconitum
Aster hybrids
Caryopteris
Ceratostigma
Crocus Autumn flowering
Cyananthus
Gentiana
Parochetus communis

Nurseries and Garden Centres

Britain

Ballalheannagh Gardens, Glen Roy, Lonan, Isle of Man (esp. *Ericaceae*)

Bressingham Gardens, Diss, Norfolk IP22 2AB (esp. conifers)

Broadleigh Gardens, Barr House, Bishops Hull, Taunton, Somerset TA4 1AE (bulbs, esp. dwarf *Narcissus* hybrids)

Butterfields Nursery, Harvest Hill, Upper Bourne End, Bucks. SL8 5JJ (*Pleione* only)

P. J. & J. W. Christian, Pentre Nurseries, Minera, Wrexham, Clwyd (unusual bulbs)

Jack Drake, Inshriach Alpine Plant Nursery, Aviemore, Inverness-shire PH22 1QS (esp. Himalayan and New Zealand alpines, fresh seed list)

Edrom Nurseries, Coldingham, Eyemouth, Berwickshire TD14 5TZ (esp. *Primula* & *Gentiana*)

Joe Elliott, Broadwell Nursery, Moreton-in-Marsh, Glos.

Glendoick Gardens Ltd, Glendoick, Perth PH2 7NS (*Rhododendron* only)

Hartside Nursery Garden, Low Gill House, Alston, Cumbria CA9 3BL (esp. *Primula, Ericaceae*)

Holden Clough Nurseries, Holden, Bolton-by-Bowland, Clitheroe, Lancashire

Hydon Nurseries Ltd, Clock Barn Lane, Hydon Heath, Godalming, Surrey GU8 4AZ (shrubs esp. *Rhododendron*)

W. E. Th. Ingwerson Ltd, Birch Farm Nursery, Gravetye, East Grinstead, Sussex RH19 4LE

Reginald Kaye Ltd, Waithman Nurseries, Silverdale, Lancs. LA5 0TY (esp. *Saxifraga*)

Orpington Nurseries Ltd, Rocky Lane, Gatton Park, Reigate, Surrey (*Iris* only)

Paradise Nurseries, Paradise Fold, Pasture Lane, Bradford 7, Yorkshire

J. & E. Parker-Jervis, Martens Hall Farm, Longworth, Abingdon, Oxon. OX13 5EP (esp. *Galanthus* & *Colchicum*)

J. R. Ponton, Old Cottage Gardens, Legerwood, Earlston, Berwickshire

Potterton & Martin, The Cottage Nursery, Moortown Road, Nettleton, Caistor, Lincs. LN7 6HX

G. Reuthe, Ltd, Jackass Lane, Keston, Kent BR2 6AW (shrubs esp. *Rhododendron*)

Robinsons Gardens, Knockholt, Kent (esp. dwarf conifers)

Robinsons Hardy Plants, Crockenhill, Swanley, Kent

A. C. Smith, 127 Leaves Green Road, Keston, Kent BR2 6DG (*Sempervivum* only)

Barry Starling Ltd, Garden Cottage Nursery, Rolls Park, Chigwell, Essex (esp. *Ericaceae*)

Southcombe Gardens, Widecombe-in-the-Moor, Newton Abbot, Devon TQ13 7TU

Wansdyke Nursery, Hillworth, Devizes, Wilts. (esp. dwarf conifers)

Washfield Nursery, Hawkhurst, Kent

Waterperry Horticultural Centre, Wheatley, Oxford OX9 1JZ (esp. *Saxifraga*)

Germany

Joachim Carl, Alpengarten, 5730 Pforzheim-Würm

Heinz Hagemann, 3001 Krähenwinkel/Hanover

J. D. zu Jeddeloh, 2901 Jeddeloh 1/Oldenburg (dwarf shrubs)

Kayser and Seibert, 6101 Rossdorf b. Darmstadt

Heinz Klose, 3503 Lohfelden b. Kassel

Dr Hans Simon, 8722 Marktheidenfeld

F. Sundermann, Alpengarten, 8651 Lindau-Äschach

Holland

P. G. Zwijnenburg, Rijneveld 35, 2771 Boskop (dwarf shrubs esp. *Erica*)

Israel

D. Shahak, Tirat Tsvi, Doar Na, Emek Beit Shean, 10815 (*Oncocyclus* iris)

Japan

Kazuo Mori, 5–8 Matsushita-Cho, Nishinomiya-Shi, Hyogo-Ken, P.C. 662 (native plants)

New Zealand

J. le Compte, RD2, Ashburton

Parva Plants, P.O. Box 549, Tauranga

North America

Not all of the nurseries listed below have catalogues or supply plants by mail order.

Alpenflora Gardens, 17985 40th Ave, Surrey, B.C. V3S 4N8 Canada

Alpenglow Gardens, 13328 King George Highway, Surrey, B.C. V3T 2T6 Canada

Samuel F. Bridge, Jr, 437 North St, Greenwich, Conn. 06830

Charlotte's Alpine Gardens & Crafts, 508 East Frank, Darlington, Wisc. 53530

Colvin Gardens, R.R.2, Box 272, Nashville, Ind. 47448 (*Sempervivum*)

The Cummins Garden, 22 Robertsville Rd, Marlboro, N.J. 07746 (esp. dwarf *Rhododendron*)

Dilatush Nursery, 780 Route 130, Robbinsville, N.J. 08691

Far North Gardens, 15621 AR Auburndale, Livonia, Mich. 48154 (*Primula*; seeds)

Joseph T. Ferdula (rocks), 300 Litchfield St, Frankfort, N.Y. 13340

Robert Fincham, 425 North 5th St, Lehighton, Pa. 18235

Foxborough Nursery, 3611 Miller Rd, Street, Md. 21154 (conifers)

Greer Gardens, 1280 Goodpasture Island Rd, Eugene, Or. 97401 (*Rhododendron*, conifers, *Lewisia*, etc.)

Gull Harbor Nursery, 3944 Gull Harbor Rd, Olympia, Wash. 98506

Nature's Garden Nursery, Route 1, Box 488, Beaverton, Ore. 97005

Oakhill Gardens, 1960 Cherry Knoll Rd., Dallas, Ore. 97338 (*Sempervivum*)

Oliver Nurseries, 1159 Bronson Rd, Fairfield, Conn. 06430 (*Rhododendron* and other *Ericaceae*)

Orchid Gardens, 6700 Splithand Rd, Grand Rapids, Minn. 55744 (native plants)

Palette Gardens, 26 West Zion Hill Rd, Quakertown, Pa. 18951

Paw Paw Everlast Label Company (labels), Box 93-E, Paw Paw, Mich. 49069

Puskas Wildflower Nursery, Kent Hollow Rd, Route 1, Box KH-37A, Kent, Conn. 06757 (native plants)

Rakestraw's Perennial Gardens, 3094 South Term St, Burton, Mich. 48529

The Rock Garden, Litchfield, Maine 04350 (*Erica* and *Calluna*)

Rocknoll Nursery, 9210 U.S. 50, Hillsboro, Ohio 45133

David B. Sindt, 1331 West Cornelia, Chicago, Ill. 60657

Siskiyou Rare Plant Nursery, 2825 Cummings Rd, Medford, Ore. 97501

Joel W. Spingarn, 1535 Forest Ave, Baldwin, N.Y. 11510 (esp. conifers and Japanese maples)

Stonecrop Nurseries, Cold Spring, N.Y. 10516

Sally Walker, P.O. Box 50503, Tucson, Arizona 85703 (native seeds)

Watnong Nursery, Morris Plains, N.J. 07950 (esp. conifers, *Ericaceae*)

The Wild Garden, Box 487, Bothell, Wash. 98011

Woodland Rockery, 6210 Klam Rd, Otter Lake, Mich. 48464

South Africa (seeds of native plants)

Blombos Nursery, Moresonlaan 15, Durbanville, 7550–SA (bulbs & corms only)

Honingklip Nurseries, 13 Lady Anne Avenue, Newlands, Cape, 7700 (esp. *Proteaceae* and *Ericaceae*)

185

Specialist Societies

Australia

The Alpine Garden Society—Tasmania Group, 136 Nelson Road, Mt Nelson, 7007 Tasmania

The Alpine Garden Society—Victoria Group, Bella Vista, Olinda, Victoria 3788

Australian Rhododendron Society, Olinda, Victoria 3788

The Iris Society of Australia, Uralba Road, Uralba, Alstonville, New South Wales

Western Australian Iris Society, 11 Lindsay Street, Kalamunda, West Australia 6076

Britain

The Alpine Garden Society, Lye End Link, St Johns, Woking, Surrey GU21 1SW. (The Society has many local groups throughout England; there are assistant secretaries in USA, Canada, New Zealand and Switzerland.)

The British Iris Society, Species Group, Professor M. E. A. Bowley, Brook Orchard, Graffham, Petworth, Sussex

The Royal Horticultural Society, Vincent Square, London SW1P 2PE

The Scottish Rock Garden Club, Morea, Main Road, Balbeggie, Perth PH2 6EZ (several local groups throughout Scotland)

Canada

The Alpine Club of British Columbia, 590 East Kings Road, North Vancouver, B.C.

The Vancouver Island Rock and Alpine Garden Society, 5021 Prospect Lake Road, RR1, Royal Oak P.O., Sannion, B.C.

Denmark

The Alpine Garden Society (There are several local groups; for addresses, contact secretary in England)

France

Société des Amateurs de Jardins Alpins, 84 Rue de Grenelle, Paris VII

New Zealand

The Canterbury Alpine Garden Society, 157 Hackthorne Road, Christchurch, 2

New Zealand Rhododendron Association, Dr Yeates, Massey College, Palmerston North

USA

The American Iris Society, 6518 Beachy Avenue, Wichita, KS 67206

The American Primrose Society, Grout Hill, South Aiworth, NH 03607

The American Rhododendron Society, Route 2, Box 254, Aurora, Oregon 97002

The American Rock Garden Society, Box 185, Hales Corner, Wisconsin 53130

The Aril Society International, 29130 Triunfo Drive, Agoura, California 91301 (*Oncocyclus* and *Regelia* iris)

Further Reading

There is a large number of books concerned with rock gardens and alpine plants. It is possible to build up a considerable personal library on the subject. Of course, many of these books are out of print but most can be obtained through specialist book dealers, some of whom advertise in the journals of the rock gardening societies. If they are wanted for short-term reference only, almost all should be obtainable (in Britain, at any rate) by requesting them from local libraries. At present, however, quite a good number are in print and should be available through booksellers.

The standard reference work is usually considered to be Farrer's *The English Rock Garden* though it is very out of date. It is best read as a historical document, when the prejudiced and florid Edwardian verbosity of its author can be best enjoyed. Clay's *Present-day Rock Garden* was published in 1937 to supplement Farrer's work and cover the species omitted by Farrer. This is a superlatively researched work but attempts to cover so many species that it often degenerates into lists of names and most gardeners will find it tragically frustrating as a reference work. More up to date, though more compact, books concerned mainly with cultivated material, are Anna Griffiths' *Collins Guide to Alpines* and Ingwersen's *Manual of Alpine Plants*. Perhaps the finest source of information is a complete series of the *Bulletin of the Alpine Garden Society*. This is well indexed and dates from 1930, throughout which period a very high editorial standard has been main-tained. The other specialist societies' journals also contain a vast amount of information.

Books on traditional rock garden construct-ion are few. H. B. Symons-Jeune *Natural Rock Gardening* (1932) is still considered to be one of the soundest. L. Bacon's *Alpines* (1973) devotes quite a lot of space to this aspect also. Equally few are books which have been written with a view to their readability rather than for their reference value. Farrer's *In a Yorkshire Garden*, *My Rock Garden* and *Alpine and Bog Plants* are in the tradition continued by E. A. Bowles, whose *My Garden* trilogy contains many references to rock garden plants, Clarence Elliott's *Rock Garden Plants* (1935) and R. C. Elliott's *Alpine Gardening* (1963) are also eminently readable. The American L. Beebe Wilder's *The Rock Garden* (1933) and *Adventures with Hardy Bulbs* (1936) can also both be highly recommended as regards this aspect.

The bulb enthusiast is comparatively well supplied with reference material. B. Matthew's *Dwarf Bulbs* (1973) and E. B. Anderson's *Dwarf Bulbs for the Rock Garden* (1959) are two general reference works. Many of the standard garden-ers' monographs are now rather outdated as so much new material has been collected in south-west Asia over the past twenty years. Until superseded, E. A. Bowles *A Handbook of Crocus and Colchicum* (1924), C. Beck's *Fritillaries* (1953), A. D. Hall's *The Genus Tulipa* (1940), F. C. Stern's *Snowdrops and Snowflakes* (1956) — *Galanthus* and *Leucojum*, also M. J. Jefferson Brown's *Daffodils and Narcissi* (1969) and Alec

Gray's *Miniature Daffodils* (1955) will remain indispensable. A new botanical monograph on *Crocus* and a gardener's monograph on *Fritillaria* by the world authorities on these genera are anticipated in the near future.

Specialist works on particular genera of alpine plants are fewer. Currently in print is Mary Bartlett's *Gentians* (1975) but H. C. Crooks *Campanulas*, D. Wilkie's and G. H. Berry's works on gentians and K. C. Corsar's *Primulas in the Garden* (1948) are not so readily obtainable. The British Alpine Garden Society has done much to fill this gap by publishing gardeners guides to several genera such as *Androsace*, *Cyclamen*, *Dionysia*, Asiatic *Primula*, *Lewisia* and *Saxifraga*. These, while obviously varying in quality, are without exception useful, while some such as *Daphne* by C. D. Brickell and B. Matthew are superlative and likely to remain standard works. These publications are only obtainable from the AGS Distribution Manager, 278/280 Hoe Street, Walthamstow, London E17 9PL.

Dwarf shrubs are dealt with by R. E. Heath's *Shrubs for Rock Garden and Alpine House* (1954) and H. J. Welch's *Dwarf Conifers* (1968). Such standard works as *Hilliers Manual of Trees and Shrubs* and Bean's *Trees and Shrubs*, of course, include dwarf species as well as larger ones. There are quite a few books on the heaths and heathers and P. A. Cox's excellent *Dwarf Rhododendrons* is indispensable to rock gardeners on acid soils.

Most books on alpine-house cultivation are rather dated, but the Alpine Gardening Society's booklets *Alpines in Pots* and *Bulbs under Glass* are in print. Stuart Boothman's *The Alpine House* (1938), R. E. Heath's *Alpine Plants under Glass* (1951) and Gwendolyn Anley's *Alpine House Culture for Amateurs* (1938) are all well worth reading.

When the alpine enthusiast goes in search of alpine plants in their homes, a large suitcase would be necessary to carry all the books published on the central European alpine flowers. The most recently published *Collins Guide* by C. Grey-Wilson or A. J. Huxley's *Mountain Flowers in Europe* (1967) will be quite sufficient for the Alps, however. For Spain and Portugal, *Flowers of South-west Europe* by Polunin and Smythies is excellent. L. Bacon's *Mountain Flower Holidays* covers European travel on a regional basis. Gardeners outside Europe will generally find equivalent books exist for their areas. For instance, there are two excellent books on Alaskan wild flowers, field guides to New Zealand mountain flowers and Rocky Mountain wild flowers and a book on Australian alpines. For the less accessible mountain ranges of the world, however, the traveller will have to learn to use botanical floras for the areas in question. By that time, however, this book will have served its purpose.

Jim Archibald

Index to Latin plant names

Picture credits

Martin Haberer, pages 19(2), 133(2), 137(3); Fritz Kohlein, 77(3), 133(1); Fritz Kummert, 51(1); Dieter Schacht, 51(2), 55(3), 59(all), 65(2), 73(2), 81(3), 85(3,4,5), 89(2), 101(6), 125(1,2,3,4), 141(2), 145(4), 153(2,3); Wilhelm Schacht, 19(1,4,5,6), 23(1,2,3), 27, 35(1,2,3), 39(1,2), 43(all), 47(1,2,3), 51(3), 55(1,2), 65(3), 69(2,3), 73(1,3), 77(1,2,4,5,6), 81(2), 85(1,2,6), 89(1), 93(1,2), 97(1), 101(1,2,3,4), 117(1,2,3), 121(1,2,3), 129(1,2,3), 133(6), 145(1), 153(1); Hans Siebold, 69(1), 133(3,4,5); Sebastian Seidl, 19(3), 81(1), 93(3), 97(2,3), 101(5), 137(1,2), 141(1,3), 145(2,3,5,6); Gunther Ulmer, 65(1).